RELIGION

VS

REALITY

Go figure out what this Scripture means:
"I'm after mercy, not religion."
I'm here to invite outsiders, not to coddle insiders.
(Matt. 9:13,14TMB)

Other books by Gordon Dalbey

Healing the Masculine Soul

Sons of the Father:
Healing the Father-Wound in Men Today

Fight like a Man:
A New Manhood for a New Warfare

No Small Snakes:
A Journey into Spiritual Warfare

Broken by Religion, Healed by God:
*Restoring the Evangelical, Sacramental,
Pentecostal, Social Justice Church*

Do Pirates Wear Pajamas?
and Other Mysteries in the Adventure of Fathering

Gordon Dalbey may be reached
for resources and speaking engagements at
www.abbafather.com
Box 61042, Santa Barbara, CA 93160

RELIGION

VS

REALITY

FACING THE HOME FRONT IN SPIRITUAL WARFARE

BY

GORDON DALBEY

CivitasPress

Publishing inspiring and redemptive ideas.[sm]

ISBN # 978-0615924045

Published by Civitas Press, LLC

San Jose, CA,

www.civitaspress.com

CONTENTS

The enemy distracts from God's power
by impressing us with our own.

To deny the power of evil
is to forfeit the power to overcome it.

Religion is a surrogate father,
for those who feared Dad's judgment.

When we forget what the media distracts us from,
the media settles in as definition.

A woman-hating spirit follows religion,
whose shame is unmasked by feminine grace.

The cross reflects the hard truth of sin's consequences
mediated by the grace of sacrificial love.

Life-threatening reality strips the façade
from religious presumption.

Religious men kill Jesus,
now as then.

If you're real, God can make you right;
if you're right, the enemy will make you real.

Shame is overcome not by pride before others,
but by humility before God.

Spiritual warfare allows no spectators,
but only deluded deserters and persevering victors.

The antidote to materialism
is not frugal self-denial, but authentic spirituality.

God commands us to enjoy His blessings,
not to foster indulgence but to inspire reverence.

Religion is about what we do for God;
Jesus is about what God does for us.

Since Jesus, religion is obsolete.

> The enemy lulls us away from the battle with material comfort and distracts from God's power by impressing us with our own.

FOREWORD

> *They do not believe, because their minds have been kept in the dark by the evil god of this world. He keeps them from seeing the light shining on them, the light that comes from the Good News about the glory of Christ, who is the exact likeness of God.*
> (2 Corinth. 4:4)

"GOD STILL HAS A LOT MORE BOOKS He wants written...." the conference speaker declared, and paused. Leaning forward excitedly, I was then puzzled as he added, "He's just looking for someone willing to pay the price."

Some years later, on a dark stretch of freeway near home, I understood.

Shortly before the prequel to this book *No Small Snakes: A Journey into Spiritual Warfare* went to press, my then-teenaged son and I were enjoying the summer breeze on a late-night drive in our trusty old convertible. Just that morning, I had carefully folded the windshield sunscreen and stuffed it securely under the back of the driver's seat so it wouldn't blow away with the top down.

That night in the outside lane, as a pickup was about to pass us, we were startled by a loud POP! FWHOOSH! Suddenly, the sunscreen leapt out from behind us under the driver's seat and somehow flew up above us and foreword, unfolded, and fell spread-out across our faces. In a flash of blindness, we sideswiped the pickup and shot off the freeway. Slamming from 65 to zero in seconds, an explosive blast of impact left us stunned and wedged under a foot-thick tree branch just inches above the windshield.

Dazed and covered with dirt and leaves, we managed to pull ourselves out of the wreckage and debris. A patrolman arrived soon afterwards, to find my son and me standing and holding each other, dusty and trembling.

The grey-haired officer studied the crumpled remains of our beloved sports car wedged under the huge branch—low enough to have crushed through the windshield and cabin of any sedan. Finally, he shook his head in amazement and turned to my son.

"Do you go to church?" he asked.

Shaken, but alive and filled with grace, we both nodded.

PLANET AT WAR

This book, like its prequel, presumes that ours is a planet at war. What's more, the enemy of God quite deliberately attacks first and most fiercely those surrendered to Jesus, because we're the only ones capable of recognizing the kingdom of darkness and empowered to overcome it. Those who are not surrendered to Jesus dare not even see the battle, because they have no power to win it. Thereby opting out of the battle into denial, they bear no threat to the enemy (see 1 Corinth. 2:14).

Spiritual warfare, that is, allows no conscientious objectors, but only deluded deserters and persevering victors. To withdraw is neither honorable nor safe—but simply to capitulate to the enemy, whose objective is precisely to remove opposition from the battlefield.

The process in doing so is devious, and therefore, often unseen. Killing a Christian outright, for example, might suffice a short-term evil goal, but as a long-run strategy could be too graphic, draw too much attention, and—hopefully—risk counterattack from the people of God.

More often, the enemy simply lulls us away from the battle with material comfort and distracts from God's power by impressing us with our own, natural human abilities. Having turned us away from God, its most promising ploy is thereby to blind us to its presence and proceed with destruction unrecognized and unopposed. Hence, the arrogant hubris of our "modern/scientific" Western worldview, that to believe in demons is medieval foolishness.

This book invites you to press into the larger reality defined by God's rule over your life and over this world. You'll see here how the evil spirit portrayed in the bible is deliberately at work in this world—even your own—and how unto today the Holy Spirit who animated Jesus provides every weapon we need to recognize and overcome it.

You'll see how the basic strategies of spiritual warfare apply to the broad spectrum of evil in and about us today. From racism, psychic horror films, and terrorism to gender confusion, Halloween and state lotteries, **the topics here are designed to reveal the enemy among us and recruit you as a warrior in the advancing, overcoming Kingdom of God.**

This broader perspective requires you to eschew the world's neatly polarized worldview. What you read about here is neither liberal politically-correct ideology nor conservative religiously-correct morality.

It's war.

PEACE IS NOT QUIET

In fact, this world has been at war ever since the Genesis of humanity, when the Serpent seduced us into a false image of the Father and set us against God—and ultimately, therefore, against one another (see Gen. 3). In Jesus, God has revealed Himself clearly and powerfully, overcoming the Serpent's deception and this gap between Himself and humanity. What's more, He has poured out His Spirit on us with power to unite together against this, our true spiritual enemy.

From God's perspective, war in this fallen world is an eternal reality until Jesus returns to engineer His Final Victory. Meanwhile, peace is rooted in a faith that God is working out His purposes in, through, and among us—the more powerfully insofar as we willingly surrender to Him and cooperate in trust.

Contrary to our self-centered fantasies, that is, the peace God bears is not synonymous with quiet. Yes, before departing this world, Jesus declared his legacy of peace would remain among us. "Peace is what I leave with you," he proclaimed. But in the same breath he qualified that "It is my own peace that I give to you; I do not give it as the world does" (John 14:27).

Victory in spiritual warfare therefore begins with seeing that **peace is not the absence of conflict, but the presence of Jesus.** It's not about what we don't do, but rather, about what God is doing. "He is our peace," as Paul declares simply and emphatically (Ephes. 2:14). *Shalom*, the Hebrew word for peace, is not about external circumstances, but about internal centeredness—which allows you to receive God's Spirit, turn from worldly violence, and wield "not the world's weapons, but God's powerful weapons" unto His victory (2 Corinth. 10:4).

From this Kingdom view, **the problem is not that human beings fight wars, but that we have fought the wrong wars out of spiritual blindness.** For Christians, therefore, peacemaking is first not about laying down arms, but indeed, deliberately taking up God's arms and engaging our authentic spiritual enemy (see "Jesus Is Our Peace: The Alternative to Warmaking" in *Broken by Religion, Healed by God*).

Our rebellious sin-nature, however, yet continues to blind us to this reality (see "The Bible as War Story" in *No Small Snakes*).

In recent history, the Vietnam conflict spawned a vigorous anti-war movement as it crystallized a growing consensus that military war is senselessly destructive. Since wars have historically been conceived and fought by men, those movements implied that masculinity is inherently destructive and must therefore be reframed by feminine virtues such as sensitivity, tenderness, and restraint.

We tried hard. As hippies, we men marched for "Peace and Love," grew our hair long, and squelched our warrior calling with drugs, sex, and aimlessness. Ultimately, this mis-focused effort to become more like women hosted a man-hating principality, manifesting unto today in politically correct ideology and its gender confusion.

While we were busy protesting military war, the enemy of humanity was conquering us, rendering men passive in the face of his advance (see *Fight like a Man: A New Manhood for a New Warfare*). "For we are not fighting against human beings," as the Apostle Paul noted, "but against the wicked spiritual forces in the heavenly world, the rulers, authorities, and cosmic powers of this dark age" (Ephes. 6:12).

To recognize this eternal battle at hand requires a revised, if not wholly redeemed vision of war itself. Its beckoning poster image is no WWII finger-pointing Uncle Sam declaring, "I Want You," but rather, the mighty hand and outstretched arm of a Father urging, "Receive my Spirit" (John 20:21-22; see also Acts 1:4,8).

Today, the Father is accelerating His redeeming agenda, and the enemy is counterattacking furiously. From 9/11 and corporate greed to increasing addictions, divorce, and shame-based religion, the enemy is sabotaging Father God's kingdom and calling us out.

Creation itself demands a response (see Romans 8:19). We can no longer afford to indulge our comfortable fantasy of well-being and control. The battle today, both in our hearts and in the world, is simply too fierce, and the consequences of passively ignoring it too destructive.

Not to report the battle at hand is to censor the Father's hard-wrought victory on the cross. **In fact, to deny the power of evil is to forfeit the power to overcome it.** And so, I write herein to reveal not only our blindness, but indeed, the Great Physician who heals it.

Born in 1944, I no longer have energy to run from the truth. I can't afford to invest my dwindling natural strength in the fantasy of my own power. The God revealed in Jesus and present today in Holy Spirit is my only resource.

As increasingly, I'm discovering that He's more than enough. "You don't know that Jesus is all you need," as wisely said, "until Jesus is all you have."

It's not that I'm so righteously faithful. Aging is simply stripping from me all pretense of physical and even moral strength. In my life journey, getting older is forcing me to exchange my natural weakness for the supernatural strength to live as God intends—and provides.

HUMBLING PATH OF TRUST

In that process, I've learned to beware exhortations to "obey God" and instead, to welcome a heart to trust my Father. At my age, it's no longer about trying harder to be good, but instead, crying out for God to empower me when so often I can't be good (see Rom. 7:18ff).

The avenue of obedience proceeds upon what I do. Ultimately, it detours from the Father's heart and dead-ends into the judgmental, divisive Tree of the Knowledge of Good and Evil. Rather, my journey today is increasingly about discerning what God is doing and learning to cooperate with him on the more narrow, humbling path of surrender and trust—which promises free access to the Tree of Life. **In spiritual warfare, that is, you're only as bold before the enemy as you are humble before the Commander-in-Chief.** Out of that humility and that boldness, the momentous occasion before us today emerges.

Over two thousand years ago, Jesus came to upend the world's understanding of warfare. In recent history, that re-visioning process has quickened.

In the mid-20th century, the focus of warmaking shifted from the age-old national turf battles, as WWII, to boundary-less ideological conflict—in particular, communism vs. capitalism, as in Korea and Vietnam. Later, toward the end of that century, the fall of the Berlin Wall, expanding Chinese consumer economy, and growing demand for freedoms in Cuba signaled the passing of communism.

That vacuum beckoned yet another quantum shift in world war, namely, **the imperial claims of shame-based religion, heralded by the explicitly religious focus of 9/11.** In this new dispensation, on the Right, rigid dogma replaces national boundaries; on the Left, all-accepting New Age spirituality supplants universalist ideology.

THIRD OPTION

The decline of both petty nationalism and high-minded ideology prepared humanity at last for God's authentic, third option to resolve human conflict. It is Jesus—who came to promote neither his own nation nor some philosophical ideal, but rather, the Kingdom of God.

A kingdom is the territory in which the king rules. Lest the rule of God be confused with that of the world's authorities, the Cross demonstrated graphically that restoring God's kingdom in this present world is a costly enterprise, which requires not only ultimate sacrifice, but in fact, ultimate war.

Today, the enemy of God has seized upon the Western world's denial of spiritual evil and paraded himself as God's Third Option, righteously masked by religion so as to usurp the authentic saving work of Jesus. "Even Satan can disguise himself to look like an angel of light," as Paul warned the Church. "So it is no great thing if his servants disguise themselves to look like servants of righteousness" (2 Corinth. 11:14,15).

Thus, 9/11 marked a refocusing of world war today from nationalism to ideology to presumptive religion. Insofar as this process has re-defined warfare in such biblical terms, it has God's fingerprints on it.

The stage has been set for history to be revealed at last as "His story."

The US defeat in communist Vietnam revealed the ineffectiveness of mere firepower against ideology and thereby heralded the death of national war.   Significantly, in its sectarian religious zeal, 9/11 announced the death of ideological war.

May both rest in peace, that indeed, the true and timeless war in the spirit realm might be revealed and God's forces come at last to life—and to victory.

9/11 showcased the deadly consequences of assumed righteousness and thereby, not only the unholy alliance between death and religion, but the very death of religion itself. Its calculated murder of innocent thousands revealed at last the face of the Final Enemy, the ultimate divisive and destructive force which creation itself can neither abide nor survive.

It is religion.

"It is (God) who made us capable of serving the new covenant," as Paul declared, "which consists not of a written law but of the Spirit. The written law brings death, but the Spirit gives life" (2 Corinth. 3:6). In 9/11, the religious quest for human perfection, for right-ness before God, has been revealed as not only an illusion, but a deadly sham.

The bad news is, We can't do it. The Good News is, Jesus has done it. He's born our shame on the cross, washed it away with his blood, and flung wide the gates to the Father's heart.

Since Jesus, religion is obsolete.

In this present age, humanity is being forced, both dramatically and tragically, to face the truth: Human nature is fatally flawed. Only the centering truth and renewing grace of God in Jesus can draw humanity beyond the innate human shame of un-right-ness into the hope of redemption and fulfillment.

The post-9/11 question is not, How can Western culture defeat the despotic goals of radical Islam? but rather, **How can humanity overcome the crippling shame that fuels religion and thereby distracts us from God's living presence, calling, and power?**

Certainly not by retreating into Western secular ideologies, even in their finest, most humanitarian form. Muslim extremists scorn the cherished European ideal of social and political freedoms by murdering a Dutch journalist for his cartoon of Mohammed and by promoting "honor killings" of women who appear immodest.

"Europe has tried to fight religion with non-religion," as one commentator scoffed.

It doesn't work, but only mocks the emptiness of a secularized culture.

In fact, there must be a Third Option if humanity is to prevail.

That's what this book is about.

THE OLDEST WAR

The old wars, even as human sin-nature, will remain until Jesus returns. Meanwhile, **the focus of battle is shifting not to any new war, but at last, to the oldest war which underlies all human conflict— born in the spirit realm and fought ultimately in the human heart.** Those who refuse to face this reality have removed themselves from the battlefield today and thereby, have served the enemy of God and of humanity.

In this continuum of warfare, the question not only for today but for the future of civilization itself is this: If not nationalism, secular ideology, or religious conviction, what then follows as the legitimate impetus of battle to save and fulfill humanity? Indeed, if not another nation, ideology, or religion, who or what is our enemy?

Even as sheep bowed low to the grass cannot see the lurking lion, an ingrown culture addicted to its own comfort is easy prey to deception. The unyielding current of this fallen world's myopia is carrying us all toward a deadly waterfall, the warning roar of which is drowned out by thundering cultural voices of denial and preoccupied indulgence.

To do nothing is to be swept away. To withdraw from the spiritual realm which infuses life itself is simply not possible. Those blessed enough to be jarred alert, often through severe loss and pain, learn to train their ears toward a larger reality, elevate their vision, and face the battle at hand. In that process, these become the most promising recruits in God's overcoming forces.

"It is not the healthy who need a doctor, but the sick," Jesus charged his Pharisee inquisitors, who condemned him for eating with "tax collectors and 'sinners'":

> Go and figure out what this scripture means: "I'm after mercy, not religion." I'm here to invite outsiders, not to coddle insiders. (Matt. 9:13-14TMB)

If only the perpetrators of 9/11 had known this God!

Indeed, if only His Church today could embrace Him!

I pray this book will stir you not only to acknowledge the battle in the larger world, but to face it within yourself; not to surrender to the enemy's deceptions as a comfortably ensconced POW, but to surrender to Father God as an active, victorious combatant.

The Father of us all has set our destiny.

Jesus has blazed the trail.

Holy Spirit has empowered us to get there.

History awaits us.

> Our "modern scientific" worldview is not scientific enough. We decide what's true not by evidence, but by whatever reassures us that we're in control.

INTRODUCTION

OVERCOMING SPIRITUAL DENIAL

> *This is the crisis we're in: God-light streamed into the world, but men and women everywhere ran for the darkness. They went for the darkness because they were not really interested in pleasing God. Everyone who makes a practice of doing evil, **addicted to denial and illusion, hates God-light and won't come near it, fearing a painful exposure.** But anyone working and living in truth and reality welcomes God-light so the work can be seen for the God-work it is.* (John 3:19-21TMB)

WE DON'T LIKE real mysteries.

Sure, the TV detective shows can be thrillers. But the virtual film mysteries are just that: two-dimensional and thereby, unreal.

At the outset, a crime is committed and only the evil criminal knows "whodunit." Crime stirs the primal fear that we can't control evil, that universal law can be broken undetected and we'll suffer the consequences.

We thought our healthy choices and well-managed portfolios protected us! Could evil yet invade our lives, even unseen, as a nighttime burglary or unwitnessed murder?

As your heartbeat rises, the action is interrupted by a commercial for materialism and the saving power of humanly designed product: A sweaty jogger finds renewal in a sports drink; a worried homeowner gains security in a new insurance policy.

A subliminal contract is thereby offered: "Our product—our cars, our deodorant, our soda pop—will save you from the unsettling mystery. Stick with us—buy our product—and we'll tell you whodunit. **We'll save you from the mystery and reassure you that you're in control after all.**

"We know what you want and will provide it. We'll restore you to your comfort zone and bring your heart rate down."

When we engage life's mysteries on Hollywood's terms, we're in control again soon after the last commercial. By the end of the show, the criminal has been caught and our fear dispatched. The sponsor has fulfilled its part of the contract—and we're stirred to fulfill ours.

"Gee, an ice cold, refreshing soda would taste good right now!

"And Honey—I don't mean to sound critical, but you could use twice the power of the other leading deodorant."

SUPER-NATURAL MYSTERIES

Meanwhile, the authentic mysteries of life reflect a power beyond our natural ability to control, that is, of a *super*-natural dimension. In fact, they emanate at will from the realm of the spirit and therefore, bear a risk far greater than waiting thirty minutes in your easy chair to find out whodunit. From nightmares to death itself, life's real mysteries warn, "You don't know what's making things happen here—and even if you did, you couldn't control the outcome."

That's when drama turns from excitement to primal fear.

In shunning true mysteries, our modern technological mindset betrays itself. Often our problem in approaching the spirit realm is not that we're too reasoned and scientific, but precisely the opposite: **We're not scientific enough. We decide what's true not by evidence, but by whatever reassures us that we're in control.** We retreat thereby into materialism—not a lusting after money and things, but a dogged, if not desperate conviction that no reality exists beyond what our natural human senses can perceive, mind can understand, and technology can overcome.

The word "science," in fact, comes from the Latin verb *scire*, "to know." The scientist researches, therefore, in order to make known what has otherwise been hidden. In determining not to know something—because such knowledge would upset our prevailing, comfortable worldview—he or she by definition becomes no longer a *scien*-tist.

Fortunately for civilization, many scientists who faced resistance to their discovered truths have nevertheless persevered. Galileo, following on Copernicus, declared that the earth is not the center of our solar system—and was promptly excommunicated by the Church and threatened with death. Eventually, he capitulated to religion and renounced that scientific truth. Many at first resisted Einstein's theory of relativity when it shattered the more manageable conclusions of Newtonian physics.

REAL SCIENTIST

Some years ago, when investigating healing prayer, I visited my younger sister, a biochemist who was then researching a new procedure for blood-typing. "What would you say," I asked her, "if I told you I'd prayed for someone with a blood disease, and that person was healed?"

"I'm a scientist," she offered. "My research is designed to help people get well. If some procedure brings about good results, I want to know how and why, so I can replicate it." Matter-of-factly, she shrugged her shoulders. "Tell me more about your prayer."

Now *that's* a real scientist!

In order to engage the true mysteries of life beyond the natural, physical realm, we must begin with the selfsame openness to truth inherent to the classical "scientific method." **Even as the early Church condemned Galileo's scientifically demonstrated solar system, unto today our human fear of losing control amid powers greater than our own makes us balk at the truth.**

This conundrum becomes dramatic when we approach the very deepest and most consequential mystery of life, namely death.

What, indeed, is that life-force which can animate a flesh-and-blood human body for decades—even a common housefly for hours—and yet leave in a flash, never to return, in spite of our most accomplished human efforts? Amid this humbling reality, a graphic example of turning from truth in order to cover our fear is the popular documentation of near-death experiences.

All of these stories, we're led to believe, report literally glowing accounts of uplifting encounters with powers in "the afterlife." Always, it would seem, comes The Light, bright and warm, and often The Voice, gentle and comforting.

Delightful and reassuring as this may sound, it's simply not true.

Though rarely published—likely because they so convincingly upend our comfortable fantasies—many medical case histories report deathbed encounters with manifestly dark and destructive powers. In his book *Afterlife*, for example, Morton Kelsey laments the historical onset of our modern materialistic worldview and its determination to obscure evil. "As belief in the spiritual world began to fade," he notes, "the less attractive parts of it quite naturally disappeared first."[1]

HELL AND SCIENCE

Kelsey then points to the groundbreaking 1975 research in Dr. Raymond Moody's bestselling *Life after Life*, in which all accounts of the afterlife are portrayed as entirely positive. Largely eclipsed by the popularity of his pioneering first book, Moody's second book, *Reflections on Life after Life*, nevertheless dares to explore the discomforting question, in Kelsey's terms, "Is there perhaps another spiritual reality beyond life besides heaven, namely hell?"

Indeed, Moody discovered that, while post-operative patients themselves could recall only positive experiences, **attending surgeons reported many examples of persons who, during their period of clinical death, seemed clearly to be wrestling with a dark and negative reality.** "In his first book," as Kelsey notes,

> Moody seemed to give a totally pleasant view of everything he encountered in the near-death experience. But in his second book he tells of several persons who reported seeing

other people who had evidently died and were caught in a rather unfortunate state of being.

They seemed to be in a state similar to Sheol, a place of gray, dull, meaningless existence. They appeared bewildered.[2]

Similarly, Kelsey cites Dr. George Ritchie, who in his book *Return from Tomorrow*, describes encounters during his own near-death experience with "spirits who appear to be caught in their own desires and hates and fears."

Again, he notes Dr. Maurice Rawlings, who documents in *Beyond Death's Door* the "frightening experience" of a patient who "dropped dead" during a stress test and "apparently found himself tormented in hell":

The man had to be revived more than once, and each time, in spite of his physical suffering, he begged to be kept alive and saved from the hell he was experiencing. Yet two days later, when he was able to talk, the patient remembered almost everything that had happened *except his terrifying experience of hell.*[3] (italics mine)

This last statement suggests a staggering conclusion, namely, that **our compulsion to deny the negative dimension of spiritual reality is subconscious, if not innate—*a reflex so powerful as to overrule and discount even our direct experience of it.***

Real mysteries—that is, uncertainties which emanate from the super-natural realm—apparently trigger a neurological overload, something akin to shock or post traumatic stress in the human psyche. They're just too overwhelming to entertain in our natural, human capacity.

Thus, in the Bible, Jesus tells the story of a rich man who dies and goes to hell, and a poor man Lazarus who died and instead, "was carried by angels" to "Abraham's bosom." Tormented in hell, the dead rich man—ironically, awakened to the truth by death—begs Abraham to send Lazarus back to the world of the living to warn others that they must reckon with negative spiritual forces even after death.

"If someone were to rise from death and go to them," he pleads, "then they would turn from their sins" (Luke 16:30).

Abraham speaks to our modern age when he flatly refuses. God has already offered evidence enough, the Patriarch explains; those who refuse to believe the prophets and the saving God who prompted their message "will not be convinced even if someone were to rise from death" (Luke 16:31). Clearly, the text here foreshadows Jesus' crucifixion and resurrection—and subsequent rejection.

HISTORICAL DENIAL

In a more poignant, historical portrait of denial, Holocaust survivor Elie Wiesel tells the haunting story of the itinerant "Moshe the beadle" who frequented his hometown in pre-WWII Poland. [4] "Weak and shy," Moshe was among the first "undesirable aliens" to be sent to the Nazi death camps in 1942.

As Wiesel recalls,

> How many were deported at that time? A hundred, a thousand. Perhaps more, surely more. I remember: the entire community—men, women, and children—accompanied them to the station, bringing along sacks stuffed with food. Then the train pulled away. Destination unknown. Few came back. One who did was Moshe the beadle. He was unrecognizable; gone were his gentleness, his shyness. Impatient, irascible, he now wore the mysterious face of a messenger pursued by those whose message he carried. He who used to stutter whenever he had to say a single word, suddenly began to speak. He talked and talked, without pity for either his listeners or himself....
>
> He went from one synagogue to the next, from house to house, from store to store, from factory to factory, he spoke to passers-by in the street, farmers in the marketplace. He told and told again tales so heinous as to make your skin crawl. Accounts of his journey somewhere in Galicia, his escape, his experience of death.

And his family? Left behind. And his children? Left behind. And his friends? Left behind, over there, at the bottom of a mass grave. Shot, all of them. In broad daylight. He too had been shot, falling only a fraction of a second before it would have been too late. Protected by those who followed, he alone survived. Why?

So that he could come back to his town and tell the tale. And that is why he never stopped talking. **But his audiences, weary and naive, would not, could not believe. People said: Poor beadle, he has lost his mind.**

Finally he understood and fell silent. Only his burning eyes revealed the impotent rage inside him.

No one among Wiesel's townsfolk dared to believe this graphic first-hand report of the Nazi evil unleashed in their native Germany.

Granted, someone else's story is a dimension removed from your own experience, and thereby may lack credibility. Yet, in another book, Wiesel records his own arrival at a death camp later, and his disbelief as a boy standing right in front of the horror:[5]

I remember the midnight arrival at Birkenau. Shouts. Dogs barking. Families together for the last time, families about to be torn asunder. A young Jewish boy walks at his father's side in the convoy of men; they walk and they walk and night walks with them toward a place spewing with monstrous flames, flames devouring the sky.

Suddenly an inmate crosses the ranks and explains to the men what they are seeing, the truth of the night: the future, the absence of future; the key to the secret, the power of evil. As he speaks, the young boy touches his father's arm as though to reassure him, and whispers,

"This is impossible, isn't it? Don't listen to what he is telling us, he only wants to frighten us. What he says is impossible, unthinkable, it is all of another age, the Middle Ages, not the twentieth century, not modern history. The world, Father, the civilized world would not allow such things to happen."

TERRIFYING MYSTERY

Forced eventually to confess the awful reality before his very face, Wiesel must then confront the **terrifying mystery that mere human intellect and willpower is not only insufficient to dispel evil, but indeed, a suspect accomplice in it:**

And yet the civilized world did know, and remained silent. Where was man in all this? And culture, how did it reach this nadir? All those spiritual leaders, those thinkers, those philosophers enamored of truth, those moralists drunk with justice—how was one to reconcile their teachings with Josef Mengele, the great master of selections at Auschwitz?

I told myself that a grave and horrible error had been committed somewhere—only *I knew neither its nature nor its author.* (italics mine)

Certainly, compassion for the victim and justice for the perpetrator are essential responses to any offense. But we do not honor those who died nor insure the future safety of others by truncating the truth. In order to avoid its recurrence, the more heinous the crime, the more deliberate and diligent must be the forensic autopsy.

Toward that end, we must ask: How could one so deliberately Jewish precisely because of his suffering, not name the Evil One so clearly portrayed by his spiritual forebears in Hebrew Scriptures and so manifestly real before his very eyes in the Holocaust?

The near-death experiences, Jesus' story of Lazarus, and Wiesel's first-hand Holocaust account beg the vital question: Must we remain blinded by evil even as its deadly flames consume us? If not the testimony of medically certified reports, of Jesus in Scripture, of face-to-face encounter itself—whatever in Heaven's name will open our eyes to the reality of evil?

Indeed, **What human impulse, more exigent than any engendered even by in-your-face experience, causes us to deny such manifest, virulent reality?**

As I write these words, I sense how Moshe the Beadle must have felt.

DENIAL AND ADDICTION

The intensity of irrational response to spiritual evil—this unyielding blindness and overwhelming denial—suggests the term *addiction*. Anyone who has ever seen, or experienced in themselves the consuming draw of substance abuse or similarly compulsive behavior, can't help being struck by its power similarly to blind human vision, to seize and command human will.

The only more astonishing—and gripping—dimension of addiction is the capacity of addicts to deny the reality of their craving and its crippling effects. An Alcoholics Anonymous pamphlet title, *The Secret Everybody Knows*,[6] makes the point.

"How do you know when addicts are lying?" goes the old AA joke:

"When their lips are moving."

Like those who deny the reality of evil even as it destroys their lives, alcoholics can sacrifice home, family, finances, and every comfort, relationship, and security for a drink—and yet steadfastly resist when anyone says that they have a drinking problem. Tormented by inner shame, often from childhood emotional abuse, their most desperate—albeit self-defeating—efforts focus on proving a manifest lie, namely, "I'm OK and in control."

Typically, often in order to wrest control from whoever violated their childhood vulnerability, addicts deny their weakness and strive after accomplishments to appear self-sufficient and thereby no longer so dangerously vulnerable to another human being. In fact, **many addictive/compulsive behaviors are an effort to cover the**

shame of not measuring up—a common affliction in materialistic, production-oriented societies (see "Battling Addiction" in *Fight like a Man*).

Because our natural, human abilities are patently inept in the face of spiritual power, efforts to save ourselves from our deepest brokenness ultimately fail—which only increases the shame. Thus, another AA tract, *Alcoholism: A Merry-go-round Named Denial.*[7]

Hence, the common biblical association of evil with darkness (see 1 Pet 2:9).

Ultimately, we're left with two choices. We can allow shame to blackmail us into aborting our destiny via either performance burn-out, addictions, or suicide. Or at last, we can face the truth of our weakness and cry out for saving power beyond our natural human abilities.

Thus, the foundation of AA's 12 Step Program:[8]

Step I: We admitted that we were powerless over alcohol—that our lives had become unmanageable

Step 2: We came to believe that power greater than ourselves could restore us to sanity.

Step 3: We made a decision to turn our will and our lives over to God as we understood him.

TRUTH AND SHAME

Most often, we deny truth in order to avoid facing the shame which it stirs. That's why Jesus came not only as "the way, the truth and the life," but also to bear our shame on the cross, remove thereby its sting, and draw us cleansed and acceptable into the Father's heart (see John 14:6). In addictive denial, that is, the compulsive behavior, from alcoholism and pornography to overeating and religious performance, becomes **an idol, a deceptive ruse to supplant God and deliver us from shame—not by openly resolving it, as Jesus does, but by covering it up.**

Hence, spiritual denial and its accomplice religion.

The truth which most convincingly upends our pride and stirs our deepest shame is simply that we human beings are not God. Indeed, we're fallen creatures, hopelessly addicted to sin and its turning away from God toward our own inadequate, ultimately self-destructive power (see Rom. 7:18-25). We're literally hell-bent to deny that even the most college-degreed, securely portfolio-ed, daily-exercised, and well-armed ones among us are at the mercy of spiritual powers far greater than our own ability to control.

DIABOLIC CHARADE

In fact, the primordial Snake in the Garden of Eden birthed this diabolic charade by seducing Adam and Eve with precisely such shame and fear. "Did God really say, 'You must not eat from any tree in the garden?'" it scoffs.

When Eve explains that only the Tree of the Knowledge of Good and Evil is off limits, the Snake smirks: "God knows that when you eat of it, your eyes will be opened, and you will be like God, knowing good and evil" (Gen 2:1-5).

The shame of our ultimate inadequacy before God makes us afraid to confess our need for Him. But efforts to hide a truth—like the one fruit denied to Adam—only make the lie the more attractive, if only in baiting our curiosity and thereby commanding attention.

Hence, the popular fascination with darkness and evil. Ultimately, ironically, such denial of evil leads you in fact to embrace it. Those who lie to themselves about spiritual reality are more easily seduced by the Snake's "promise"—as in self-affirming, New Age spiritual practices, which imply that you can manipulate spiritual powers.

Access to Divine power and authority sounds great. **The enemy will feed you nine uplifting truths, however, in order to sucker you into the one lie that brings you down.**[9]

Since the Holocaust, the Atomic Bomb, and 9/11, any trust in an intrinsic human goodness—so cherished by liberal universalists—is simply no longer feasible. We look around us, if only at the mayhem on the evening news—and within us, if we dare—and confess, like Wiesel, that a grave and horrible error has been committed somewhere, only we know neither its nature nor its author!

Meanwhile, however, we dare not know its nature or its author, for to do so would expose our shameful deficiency, even our terrifying weakness before the overwhelming powers which enforce it. And so, we hide from the truth—if not with compulsive-addictive behaviors, then either behind moral exhortation on the Right or sophisticated rationalizations on the Left.

These two escape options characterize today's much-ballyhooed "culture wars," as in the conservative vs. liberal "split"—namely, the hardline, legalistic fundamentalists vs. the open, "free-thinking" universalists. It's Pharisees vs. Sadducees, Orthodox vs. Reform Jews, Sufi vs. Shi'ite Muslims, Theravadin vs. Mahayana Buddhists, and Baptists vs. Unitarians—unto Republicans vs. Democrats.

We may disagree over doctrine and practices, but such fundamentalists and universalists alike are bedfellows in their common denial of an active, present-day spiritual reality, and thereby, of deliberate, super-natural evil. Ironically, it's precisely these pundits of rationalism—ensconced in both the Left and the Right—who are in fact the most irrational and un-scientific, in their unwillingness to explore after spiritual truth.

Proudly, fearfully—in classic addictive denial—they teach us to stifle the deep cry of the human heart for palpable spiritual connection and lie to ourselves about ultimate reality. The sparks from their apparent conflict, in fact, serve as a smokescreen to hide this deadly farce.

Blinded by shame, the two polarities would blind us to God's presence by co-opting the debate. That is, **in denying evil as both present and active among and within us all, they deny us power to overcome it**.

FALSE SECURITY

How, then, do we in our Western "modern scientific" culture escape our addiction to rational naturalism and its concomitant materialism? Adrift in a spirit realm beyond our control, how can we trade the false security of our comfortably truncated worldview for the encompassing reality of God's mighty hand and outstretched arm?

Could it be that God wants so passionately for us to embrace His reality that He Himself initiates that process?

These stirrings led me to write *No Small Snakes*. My personal journey therein led to a host of larger questions about the scope of evil today.

That's what prompted this book.

Some of the chapters here are stories of my personal encounters with evil; others reflect the larger work of evil among us. All grow out of my bedrock faith that the God and Father of us all longs not only to "deliver us from the Evil One," as Jesus urged in The Lord's Prayer, but into our destiny as agents of His Kingdom rule "on earth as it is in heaven" (Matt. 6:10,13).

All proceed upon my experience that God has come in Jesus and released the power of His Spirit among us to do just that.

Toward this end, you and I are responsible to the best of our ability to humble ourselves before this God, to seek deliberately His healing and deliverance, and to allow Him **not only to search out and cleanse your life of evil spirits, but to re-occupy it with His Holy Spirit**. "Find out if there is any evil in me," as the warrior king David prayed, "and guide me in the everlasting way" (Ps. 139:24).

We're not slaves, variously subject to the will of Master Evil. We're sons and daughters of Almighty God, who renders evil as nothing but a "footstool" (Ps.110:1). As such, we're eligible to receive the "inheritance" of our Father's own Spirit (Galat. 4:7TMB), Who empowers us supernaturally to discern and carry out His agenda. In that process, Jesus declares that we will "do even greater things" than himself (John 14:12).

GREATEST MYSTERY

Amid such unfathomable promise, the greatest of mysteries remains: Why has the God of heaven and earth sacrificed His very Son to recruit fearful, comfort-seeking posers like us as warriors to restore His Kingdom on earth? Why has he given us undeserving runaways "every spiritual blessing in the heavenly world" (Ephes. 1:3), recruited us inveterate liars to bear His truth to the world, and us vengeful schemers to bear His grace?

How can it be that "long, long ago he decided to adopt us into his family through Jesus Christ" so that we who so deliberately dismiss His discerning eye and saving hand might "enter into the celebration of his lavish gift-giving by the hand of his beloved Son"? (Ephes. 1:5,6 TMB).

Indeed, why has he entrusted to divisive control freaks like us "*the mystery of his will according to his good pleasure, which he purposed in Christ*...to bring all things in heaven and on earth together under one head, even Christ" (Ephes. 1:9,10 NIV italics mine)?

What could we broken human beings ever do to earn such cosmic privilege?

To engage this, the most genuine and upending of mysteries, is to fall on your face in worship, confess your unworthiness, let go of your control, and release all shame to God. As we thereby become real before Him and each other, we're freed at last to make the choice and experience its consequences. We can either be humble before the mystery, or be humiliated by it; **that is, we can either rise in the Father's uplifting grace and be set free by His truth, or fall to the enemy's crushing shame and be shackled by his lies.**

Having tasted both, I recommend the humble pie. In fact, don't waste another minute. God is too good, life is too precious. Indeed, the battle at hand—now as always—is all too real. Fall on your knees before Father God, confess your brokenness and your lies which cover it. Seek His truth and trust His grace in Jesus. Cry out for His merciful hand to heal you and His Spirit to empower you for your appointed role in His Kingdom victory.

In sending Jesus, Father God has made His choice, and it's you.

I pray this book will stir you to make yours.

> **To uphold the Law, agents of religion kill Jesus, who came to set us free from it.**

1

CHRISTMAS AFTER 9/11

THE BIRTH OF JESUS,
THE DEATH OF RELIGION

> *But now God's way of putting people right with himself has been revealed. It has nothing to do with Law, even though the Law of Moses and the prophets gave their witness to it. God puts people right through their faith in Jesus Christ. He does this to all who believe in Christ, because there is no difference at all: everyone has sinned and is far away from God's saving presence. But by the free gift of God's grace all are put right with him through Christ Jesus, who sets them free.* (Romans 3:21-24)

ON SEPTEMBER 11, 2001, millions of astonished TV viewers watched the enemy of God strut across the world's stage in one of his most impressive performances. Suicide hijackers exploded airliners into two skyscrapers, people leapt 100 stories to their deaths, thousands were killed, a city of millions was literally seized with terror. In the end, the most powerful nation on earth was left shocked and immobilized.

As the enemy exited to stunned silence worldwide amid the blood and rubble, I could almost hear him turn to God and sneer, "Top that!"

How strange, how marvelous, how offensive to our natural human sensibilities, that God's response to evil is a baby born in a barn, far not only from the comfortable inn out front, but also from the large urban center of worldly power in Jerusalem—even as New York. It makes you wonder: Is God so out of touch with the world? Or does God know something about war and victory that the powers of the world do not?

Shortly after the attack, world champion middleweight boxer Anthony Mundine of Australia, a convert to Islam, was stripped of his title by the World Boxing Council for a public statement as profoundly revealing as it was offensive: "(Americans) call it an act of terrorism, but *if you can understand religion* and our way of life, it's not about terrorism. *It's about fighting for God's laws*, and Americans brought it upon themselves" (italics mine).[10]

TRUTH AND GRACE

Nowhere amid countless editorials and interviews with politicians, military experts, professors, and media pundits was portrayed so clearly the battle Jesus came to win—and in that profound sense, the essence of Christmas: "God gave the Law through Moses," as John declared, "but *grace and truth came through Jesus Christ*" (John 1:17TEV italics mine) **The "Joy to the World" which Christmas proclaims, is precisely that "He rules the world/With truth and grace"—not with religion and law.**

Our Father is truthful because He wants us to recognize and hold His course that fulfills His created purposes. He's graceful because we're unable in our own strength to do that.

Nor are we capable of bearing the shame from not measuring up to His calling. So He sent His son Jesus not to cover up our shame, as with religious performance standards, but indeed, to bear it for us on the cross, so His Spirit could empower us in His calling (see Romans 7:18-8:1).

Christmas is not about understanding religion. It's about knowing your Father.

Here's how to "understand religion": Don't trust your Father God. Grab your moral-achievements fig leaf and hide your shame from Him and other people. "Lay heavy burdens on others," as Jesus excoriated the Pharisees, but don't "lift a finger to help them" (Matt. 23:4). Righteously exhort others to measure up to God's standard, but don't ever let them know how far you yourself fall short. Don't cry out to Jesus, but instead, fabricate your own righteousness, pretend you're OK, and bear your shame by yourself.

Granted, you'll look good for awhile. Eventually, however, you'll crumble under its weight—from addiction to suicide.

Or you'll dump your shame onto others.

Thus, 9/11.

Biblical faith understands that "It is God who made us capable of serving the new covenant, which consists not of a written law, but of the Spirit. The written law brings death, but the Spirit gives life" (2 Corinth. 3:6). On 9/11, agents of God's enemy sacrificed over 3200 souls to the Law in a religious effort to cover their own shame and fortify their righteousness.

On Christmas, however, God offers humanity another way to deal with our inadequacy. He sends His son to be sacrificed to the Law, in order to uncover our shame, free us from its grip by His grace, and empower our destiny.

A desperation to cover your shame reflects a distrust in God, a belief that Jesus did not remove our shame on the cross and we have no recourse before a punishing, even vengeful Father God. This diabolic false image of God is often born in a child's heart before unforgiving parents. In any case, it fuels not only religious sectarianism—often found in Christian groups as well as in the Taliban and Al Queida— but also a host of other prejudices, from racism to sexism, all aimed at making me look good by denigrating others in comparison (see *Broken by Religion, Healed by God*).

RELIGION AND WOMEN

In a graphic example, this compulsion to save face leads men to fear and scorn women. Not only do women see through our male pretensions but—most frightening of all—**femininity bears grace, the God-ordained antidote to the Law's threat of shame**. **Religion thereby requires a woman-hating spirit**. Thus, the Taliban and their fellow religionists would literally efface women, hiding them behind a veil and excluding them from socially viable roles.

How a religious community treats women indicates most clearly how deeply it's bound by shame. Where religion rules, women are limited, ruled, and subjugated. That's why freedom for His daughters is an integral part of Father God's plan to overthrow it (see "Fathers and Daughters" in *Healing the Masculine Soul*).

Law is about obedience and punishment; grace is about trust and blessing. God's antidote to Law is Jesus, who embodies a balance of both "truth and grace" (John 1:17). Truth without grace—as in religiously correct morality—is the hallmark of the Law, which by itself soon becomes punitive and aggressive; grace without truth—as in politically correct "tolerance"—becomes naïve and passive.

Eventually, those who grasp either polarity so fear the other's reality that they revert to hostile extremism and lose credibility. When balanced by mutual respect, however, these two polarities convey **both truth that warns of dangerous consequences and grace that promises restoration**.

Most of us experience this reality as children before imperfect parents. A child's options when wounded by a parent are either rebellion or compliance. Later as an adult, you may flee the truth of your childhood wounds for the ever-open arms of unquestioning grace—and become unable to recognize destructive behavior, both in yourself and in others. Or you may become likewise judgmental, hiding from the vulnerability of grace behind the hard truth of law and morality—and lose any capacity for intimacy.

Universalists do not make good doctors; Pharisees—unto today—do not make good lovers.

Ultimately, like the terrorists, those bound by religion become anxious to fight not for freedom, but rather, for the binding judgment of

"God's Laws." They've never experienced loving parents who speak truth and set boundaries for their protection instead of for constrictive punishment (see "From Law to Love" in *Fight like a Man*).

Such men see grace as not only feminine, but shamefully unmanly and suppress their natural need for it. Thereby, they deny grace to others as to themselves. They grow up to fear grace and despise the women who bear it.

Enter Osama bin Laden, a lost little boy among 52 siblings before his distant and strictly religious father.

Religion is a surrogate father, embraced by those who have learned to fear Dad's judgment. In overcoming religion's seductive promise to cover your shame, healing the father-wound is the essential first step, the gateway to knowing God and opening to His presence and power (see *Sons of the Father: Healing the Father-Wound in Men Today*). In fact, it's why Jesus came: not to establish yet a new religion, but indeed, to bring an end to religion altogether by revealing the true Father of us all and blazing the trail to His heart.

With His Spirit among and within us, we don't need to fabricate relationship with God by pretending to perform correctly. We can trust His love and power, fall humbly at His feet, confess we can't perform, and receive His Spirit to do in and through us what we could never do for ourselves.

It's called grace.

Legalistic religion, however, is not about responding to internal needs, but rather, conforming to external demands. It rewards compliance and punishes dissent—thereby producing not sons and daughters, but slaves—who dare not cry out to the master for help.

Recognizing your internal needs can stir shame, which requires vulnerability and trust to overcome. In fact, this defines a child's longing. for a father. "For the Spirit that God has given you does not make you slaves and cause you to be afraid," as Paul countered; "instead, the Spirit makes you God's children, and by the Spirit's power we cry out to God, 'Father! My Father'!" (Rom. 8:15).

In contrast, Sharia/Islamic law court spokesman Sheik Abdallah Ali of Somalia has declared that Muslims "who do not pray five times a day should be put to death." In fact, "He who does not perform prayer will be considered as infidel and our Sharia law orders that person to be killed."[11]

What human being with a beating heart needs to be threatened and commanded to talk with a Father whose "love endures forever" (Ps. 118)? Clearly, those who do not truly know this Father.

Thus, the Taliban not only murders dissidents, but lauded its 9/11 perpetrators as "martyrs," promising them both monetary reward for their surviving families and "heavenly reward" in sex after death with many virgins. These are shame-bound boys, fearful of the vulnerability and honesty required for committed relationship with a real-life woman.

ARAB SCIENCE

It wasn't always this way in the Middle East. Amid relatively recent TV images of Afghani troops advancing on horseback, few realize that ancient Arab culture was justly famed for its achievements in science. Arabic numerals, the world's very number system today, freed mathematics from cumbersome Roman numerals and blew open the doorway for virtually all later scientific advance—including the computer with which I write this.

Algebra is an Arabic word. Chess is believed to have originated in Persia.

With the coming of Islam, however—in striking similarity to Galileo's excommunication from the Christian Church—scientific study was seen as a threat to the religious authorities. In the Arabic world, "The study which took the place of the discarded sciences was not, however, theology," as my seminary textbook on Islam notes. Rather, "the master science of the Muslim world was Law."[12] Thus, upon his capture after 9/11, Californian convert to Islam and Taliban soldier John Walker Lindh explained, "The Taliban are the only government that actually provides Islamic law."[13]

This devotion to Law, my text notes,[14] undergirds "the basis of all Muslim theology and ethics," namely, a belief that "God is the omnipotent master and man His creature who is ever in danger of incurring His wrath." The "characteristic sign of the Believer," therefore, is "an ever-present fear of God, and its opposite is 'heedlessness' or frivolity'."

And so Mohammed stressed not only "the final retribution of the Judgment," but also "the prospect of some awful calamity in the present life in punishment for their rejection of his warning."

Now, there's someone who "understands religion"!

There's 9/11.

The battle we face today is manifestly spiritual, and the ultimate victory belongs to Jesus. But as he declared, "How can Satan cast out Satan?" (Mark 3:23). No matter how evil our enemy or how truthful our doctrine, **as long as Christians ourselves remain trapped in the seductive grip of Law—striving to do it right when we've never trusted our Father enough to confess we can't—this all-too-familiar spirit of religion within us will sabotage our efforts to battle it in others.**

The Tree of the Knowledge of Good and Evil is the Law, manifested in performance religion. Based on a lie—namely, that we're capable of keeping that Law—it serves the father of Lies and usurps Jesus as savior. The Law promises righteousness and power, but generates only pride, separation from God and each other, and thereby, aborted destiny.

The Tree of Life, on the other hand, is Jesus. He offers truth, grace, and the Spirit of the very God who saves and empowers us for His purposes.

CHRISTIAN TERRORISTS

Under the New Covenant in Jesus, God's primary persona is revealed not in religion, as Judge, but in relationship, as Father. He knows we're incapable of keeping the law, so banks rather on trusting relationship to motivate and empower us to do so.

As Pastor Bill Johnson of Bethel Church in Redding, CA, notes,

> Many approach the teachings of Jesus as just another form of the Law. To most, He just brought a new set of rules. Grace is different from the Law in that the favor comes before the obedience. Under grace the commandments of the Lord come fully equipped with the ability

to perform them…to those who hear from the heart. Grace enables what it commands.[15]

Sadly, the spirit of religion at work in the terrorists has also blinded many Christian leaders to Father' God's heart for us as His children—even for themselves. Soon after 9/11, for example, Moral Majority leader Jerry Fallwell and 700 Club ministry founder Pat Robertson together condemned "all…who try to secularize America," and declared "I point the finger in their face and say you helped this happen."[16] In 2013, Congresswoman and former Presidential candidate Michelle Bachman declared similarly that "Our nation has seen judgment not once but twice on September 11"—including the 2012 attacks on the American embassy on that day in Benghazi, Lybia.[17]

These are people who understand religion well but, in spite of their image as esteemed Christian leaders, know little of Jesus—because they know little of a father's heart.

Certainly, God grieves a modern culture that scorns His protective boundaries. What father, however, would throw his children off a skyscraper and murder them in an embassy, no matter how severely they disobeyed him? Thankfully, no Christian parents today have been known to do this; yet news stories have noted Muslim parents who murdered their daughters for adopting Western dress and not obeying their Law.

This belief among many Christian leaders that the carnage of 9/11 was God's judging and punishing America for our ungodly morals is precisely the terrorists' theology. It squares entirely with the shame-bound Taliban and its proponent boxer Mundine. These so-called "Christian spokesmen" thereby aligned precisely, indeed scandalously, with the very perpetrators of the attack, even with the enemy of God.

It's one thing for Muslim extremists to defame Father God's character; quite another thing for prominent Christian leaders to do so.

Satan's primary stratagem is to perpetrate a false image of Father God. Thus, the Snake so cleverly misrepresented God as a jealous egotist (see Genesis 3:4). Jesus, however, portrayed the Father's character most authentically on the cross, as **the hard truth of sin's consequence mediated by the overwhelming grace of sacrificial love.** Far too many Christian leaders—like the Taliban—are enslaved by the former and ignorant of the latter.

The shameful truth, as the Apostle Paul declared in the chapter opening scripture, is that "there is no difference at all." We're all sinners. If the price for our sin were ours to pay, we'd all be dead, whether liberal or conservative, Christian or Muslim.

In framing as God's work the patently diabolic pre-meditated murder of over 3200 souls, Fallwell and Robertson exposed the demonic stronghold of religion in their hearts and in the larger Church today. In fact, it marked themselves as unholy collaborators with the enemy of God. Eventually, they retracted their statements in concession to public opinion—sadly, not because offended fellow-Christians demanded it, nor in humbly confessing their ungodly mindset or renouncing the demon of religion which animates it.

This essential lesson must not be overlooked or forgotten by those who would witness to the Father's truth and grace as revealed in Jesus—that is, those who would seek victory over this demonic principality of shame-based religion so graphically revealed on 9/11. It was, after all, the religious legalists who crucified Jesus, when even the atheist Roman leader Pontius Pilate washed his hands of the affair (see Matt. 27:22-26).

NO GRACE FOR DEMONS

The evil of 9/11 not only exposed many conservative church leaders as ungodly, but also many liberals as blindly un-equipped for the battle at hand. The reality of evil confounds high-minded universalists—whose grace is necessary, but far from sufficient in a world subject to powers of darkness.

Evil as manifested on 9/11 is neither to be tolerated nor accepted. You don't extend grace to a demon. With nothing but "tolerance" and "acceptance" in your arsenal, you give evil free rein and are quickly dispatched on the battlefield, leaving others at the enemy's mercy.

And so God's Story, from dirty manger and lowly shepherds to a woman's conceiving apart from her husband, proclaims that **Christmas is not about doing it right before others, but about being real before God.** When Jesus is born in your heart, that is, you can face the truth of who you are: broken and needy, like a child, weak and lost amid a world of darkness both within you and without.

What's more, you can trust your Father's grace. You can go to Him openly for mercy and saving power. You don't have to burn yourself out pretending you're OK, or hide your shame from not measuring up to His Law by killing others who don't.

You don't have to be a righteous law-keeper, simply because that's impossible. "I know that good does not live in me," as Paul confessed, "that is, in my human nature, because even though the desire to do good is in me, I am unable to do it" (Rom. 7:18). As you surrender to Jesus, you can trust God's promise, "I will give you a new heart and a new mind.... I will put my Spirit in you and will see to it that you will follow my laws and keep all the commands I have given you" (Ezek. 36:26,27).

As any destructive enemy, those who perpetrated 9/11 must be brought to justice and stopped from further destruction. The enemy revealed in this explicitly religious act, however, is no less than the Final Enemy assigned to pre-empt the saving work of Jesus, cut us off from the Father, and thereby destroy humanity.

We dare not imagine, therefore, that locking up or shooting any number of human beings, no matter how evil their deeds, will win this war. At best, it will bring the war home as God intends, that is, stem the violence long enough for us at last to confess our shared and fallen human nature, and cry out to Him to overcome it in and through us.

Our true, spiritual enemy is not only in our face, but in our hearts. We dare not focus only on human enemies in order to divert attention from our shame and the One who came to bear it.

We overcome this enemy only and precisely insofar as we appropriate the freedom Jesus died to give us, namely, to trust your Father's grace and get real before Him and each other. Freely, hopefully, you can cry out "I can't do it right!" like the Apostle Paul in Romans 7:18. You can fall at Jesus' feet and surrender to Him in all your shameful inadequacy and rebellion. You can let Him then take you restored and open before "the Father from whom all fatherhood in heaven and on earth receives its true name" (Ephes 3:21NIV footnote).

There, like an excited child on Christmas morning, you can at last receive the gifts you need to let Him do it right by the power of His Spirit working in you. Indeed, you can ask God's forgiveness for not receiving what Jesus died to give you, that is, for trying to hide the shame of your inadequacy instead of confessing it openly to Him.

ACHIEVING VS. RECEIVING

You can take authority over the demon of religion and the demon of shame which fuels it, and in the name of Jesus renounce and cast them out of yourself and into his hands. You can cry out at last for God's spirit of sonship/daughtership to replace them.

Moses came to tell us *what* to do, but Jesus came to show us *Who* does it. Hint: It's not you. (see Phil. 2:13; Rom. 12:1-2). Religion is about what we do for God, as another has said; Jesus is about what God has done for us (see 1 John 4:10).

God's gift to us at Christmas is therefore not about *achieving* but about *receiving;* not about mere standards of behavior, but heartfelt relationship with a Father who loves His children. In that love, He not only reveals protective boundaries in His law, but sacrifices His Son to enable us to receive His Spirit and thereby, empowers us to walk safely within those boundaries (see Ezek. 36:26ff.).

Jesus died not to ensure the Law's condemnation and destruction—as promoted by the oppressive religionists of 9/11 and their shame-based Christian counterparts today—but rather, to free us from it.

The principality of religion is hard at work today, distracting us from Father God's mighty hand and outstretched arm. But God is still the Initiator. The apparent enemy "offensive" among us is really a counter-offensive. That is, 9/11 and the current darkness in our world is a response to a prior, even more powerful move of God.

The intensity of the battle indicates the significance of the victory. The imperative which 9/11 bears Christians is to discern what God is doing in this world today and join Him.

We can begin by surrendering to Him and begging Him, like the ancient Psalmist,

> Examine me, O God, and know my mind;
> test me, and discover my thoughts. Find out
> if there is any evil in me and guide me in the
> everlasting way. (Ps. 139: 23,24)

Thus, when the deceptive, destructive powers of the world have overwhelmed and broken us open enough to confess at last we can't save ourselves, the Father pours His empowering Spirit into us. That's how He makes us into His sons and daughters (see Rom. 8:14-16),

animated no longer by our misguided natural desires, but rather, by His supernatural desire to fulfill our created destiny (see I Peter 1:23; John 1:13; John 3:6). Becoming a "real Jew"—that is, a true man or woman of God—is therefore "the work of God's Spirit, not of the written Law" (Rom 2:28-29).

It's a good thing. For decades I've tried, really hard, but just can't come up with enough discipline, talent, energy, and perseverance to overcome my thoughts and behaviors that separate me from God and sabotage my destiny. In fact, at my age, the main ability I'm improving in is not to resist sin, but to surrender to my Father and trust Him to overcome it in me.

The older I get, the more I know this is the true freedom human hearts long for—and the grace which God has given us in Jesus.

That's why I still get excited about Christmas.

It's an act that can't be topped.

> "Don't allow those young men fighting at the Dunkirk battlefront to do more than you do here praying in our sanctuary."

2

TERRORISM & SPIRITUAL WARFARE

LESSONS FROM THE BATTLE OF BRITAIN

> *Remember that there will be difficult times in the last days. People will...hold to the outward form of our religion, but reject its real power. Keep away from such people.* (2 Timothy 3:1,5)

> *The weapons we use in our fight are not the world's weapons but God's powerful weapons, which we use to destroy strongholds.* (2 Corinth. 10:4)

EARLY IN THE FALL OF 1940, as Nazi forces blazed across Europe and stood poised to invade England, pastor and former coal miner Rees Howells led students at the Bible College of Wales not only to hold fast, but to counter-attack. These persevering prayer warriors blazed a trail for us today, when murderous acts of explicitly religious terrorism have at last revealed the truth not only that we battle a spiritual enemy, but that the world's weapons—from atomic bombs to spy satellites—are not powerful enough to eliminate terrorism.

When the Nazis came to power in 1936, Howells' determined congregation in Wales began interceding tirelessly for God's victory. As Christians, they recognized their enemy—and it was neither the nation Germany nor the man Hitler. "In fighting Hitler," Howells declared early in 1940 after war broke out, "we have always said that we were not up against man, but the devil. Mussolini is a man, but Hitler is different. He can tell the day when this 'spirit' came into him."[18]

NEARSIGHTED WORLDVIEW

Similarly, the terrorists we face today act not as citizens of a nation state, but rather, as self-proclaimed martyrs of a transcendent religious faith, factions of which clearly encourage and celebrate their demonic deeds. This vital perspective on their deadly attacks cannot be gained until we renounce our arrogant, nearsighted materialistic worldview.

Only then can we recognize that ultimately our enemy is neither the terrorists nor their commanders—though pursue and overcome them we must—but rather, the spiritual powers that animate them. As the Apostle Paul implored Christians 2000 years ago, "For we are not fighting against human beings but against the wicked spiritual forces in the heavenly world, the rulers, authorities, and cosmic powers of this dark age" (Ephes. 6:12).

Significantly, this biblical Christian worldview implies neither denial of natural circumstance nor passivity, but is rooted in God's larger view of reality. "We are going up to battle," as Howells wisely declared in May of 1940, when Nazi forces had overrun France. "God gets at the enemy *visibly and invisibly, through the army and through us.*" (italics mine)

All British forces had been committed to Europe, which had now fallen to Hitler. Miraculously, as the College fasted and prayed day and night, the vast majority of Allied troops managed to escape

Hitler's advancing forces and retreat to Dunkirk, on the French English Channel shoreline—and waited for rescue the next day.

"God will not do a bit more through you than you have faith for," Howells exhorted his prayer warriors. "The victory last night was in seeing that no matter how near the enemy came, the Holy Ghost is stronger than he."

When the stranded British armed forces were powerless themselves either to fight back or to escape further, Howells stepped boldly into the gap. Early the next morning he exhorted his battalion of intercessors, **"You are more responsible for this victory today than those men on the battlefield. You must be dead to everything else but this fight."**

This proclamation came not from grandiose egotism, but a sober recognition of dire circumstance and the need for God's power to overcome it.

In their retreat, the British army yet remained perilously exposed, trapped between the waters behind them and the advancing enemy ahead—strangely reminiscent of the early Israelites pursued to the Red Sea by Pharaoh's chariots. In that season, Britain alone stood between demonic Nazism and world civilization—and now the total of its manpower lay at the enemy's mercy. America yet remained out of the war, distant and lost in denial—much as before the unprecedented 9/11 terrorist attacks on our own soil.

NEW DARK AGE

"If we fail," as Winston Churchill so eloquently warned, "then the whole world, *including the United States*…will sink into the abyss of a new Dark Age." (*italics mine*)

The immense significance of the task ahead was not lost on God's regiment in Wales. "The next 24 hours will be the crisis in this great battle," Howells declared. "They are ready to take our country at any moment. Even before lunch-time the history of the world may be changed. Such a thing as this has not happened to us before, and you do not know how much faith is needed. We are coming to the Lord this morning, and telling Him our eyes are upon Him today. Unless He intervenes, we are lost."

Significantly, these intrepid believers in rural England saw themselves not merely as spectators, nor even helpful bystanders or expendable encouragers, but as major players in the action—indeed, as God's agents in history-making itself. **In arguably the most significant exhortation ever imparted to spiritual warriors, Howells urged his battalion in Wales: "Don't allow those young men at the Front to do more than you do here."**

Even as they battled in the Spirit, Howells focused their ministry on God's perspective and connected it firmly to events at hand: "It is not you struggling, but God doing, and you coming to know what God is doing. Is it God who has drawn Hitler across that line with his 2500 armored cars? I want the Lord to discomfit this man and those armored cars."

At last, every available vessel in Britain—both private and military, from sailboat to steamer—raced across the Channel to the stranded soldiers at Dunkirk. To the world's astonishment and cheers, an estimated 330,000 soldiers were safely evacuated to England.

As biographer Norman Grubb notes of Howells' intercessors, "Was there anywhere else in the whole of Britain or America or elsewhere among God's people another such company, maybe a hundred strong, who were on their knees day by day, holding fast the victory by faith, while our soldiers across the water were retreating mile by mile, whole countries surrendering and the enemy within sight of their goal?"

Unwilling to risk the losses of an immediate amphibious invasion, Hitler thereupon set out first to break the British spirit by ruthlessly bombing the populace, both with aircraft and rockets. In this, the Battle of Britain, explosives rained on the country both day and night, striking homes, office buildings, and even the king's palace alike.

Amid the blazing fires and crumbling rubble, some 60,000 civilians were killed. Yet, as the spiritual warriors in Wales battled alongside British air, land, and sea forces, the nation held on.

ASSURANCE FROM GOD

Howells' journal of intercession during these perilous months rings with impact, including the assurance from God, "The enemy will not invade Christian England." Yet he had human doubts, which validate his faith with humble honesty:

> We have never walked this way before. The important thing is to find out where God is in this. When you are in danger every night, it takes you a long time to be sure that you are under God's protection. Can you say you are safe in the air raids? Has God told you? You may try to use the Word of God without having His power behind it. If God is going to deliver from this hell, there will have to be some power released. Unless you are sure of your own victory, you will never be able to pray for the deliverance of the country.
>
> **We have bound the devil over and over again...If you can believe that you have been delivered from hell, why can't you believe that you have been delivered from air raids?**

On September 8, 1940, the Government declared a National Day of Prayer, which prompted a breakthrough for the forces of God. At the Bible College of Wales, the day began with repentance. "*Our country has only the outward form of religion,*" Howells confessed in his journal, "neither cold nor hot, like the church at Laodicea. May God bring the nation back" (italics mine).

That afternoon, when he rose to speak at the College chapel, sirens wailed and Luftwaffe bombs blasted outside. Yet, even as he preached amid the enemy onslaught, a profound sense of release fell upon everyone. "What victory!...What joy! What praise!" he recalled. "How the Holy Ghost came down this morning in the communion service and told us of His victory!... We had never been in such victory before, carrying on exactly as if there was no war. How could we get victory for the world, unless we had first believed it for ourselves?"

Emboldened, on September 11 the College began to pray daily that "London would be defended and that the enemy would fail to break through," convinced that "unless God can get hold of this devil and bind him, no man is safe."

That very week, God honored these prayers dramatically. In his *War Memoirs*, Prime Minister Churchill noted September 15, 1940, as "the culminating date" in the Battle of Britain. Visiting the Royal Air Force Operations Room that afternoon, he stood stunned as wave after wave of Luftwaffe bombers and fighters poured over the Channel toward the vastly outnumbered British airmen.

"What other reserves have we?" he asked the Air Marshal anxiously.

"There are none," came the terse reply.

And then, after grave moments of silence, something very strange happened. "It appeared that the enemy was going home," Churchill recalled with surprise. "The shifting of the discs on the table showed a continuous eastward movement of German bombers and fighters. No new attack appeared. In another ten minutes, the action was ended."

The tension here suggests that of the prophet Elisha's servant who awoke in terror to see an entire regiment of the Syrian army surrounding their home. "We are doomed, sir! What shall we do?"

"Don't be afraid," Elisha asserted. "We have more on our side than they have on theirs!" (2 Kings 6: 18ff.). Whereupon God opens the servant's eyes to see the Syrian forces surrounded by "chariots of fire."

DIVINE INTERVENTION

Thus, Air Chief Marshal Lord Dowding, Commander-in-Chief of Fighter Command during the Battle of Britain, declared in his memoirs shortly after the war, "Even during the battle one realized from day to day how much external support was coming in. **At the end of the battle one had the sort of feeling that there had been some special Divine intervention to alter some sequence of events which would otherwise have occurred.**"

God was clearly at work, and the prayer warriors in Wales had done their job well in joining Him.

These faithful men and women demonstrated that in Jesus, God has offered us not only an open door to our destiny, but protection and power to fulfill it. As a good Father, He has respectfully given us free will to walk victoriously through that door with Him. But to mature us in faith and fit us for His larger Kingdom purposes, God has placed us in community—as families, nations, even citizens of this ever-shrinking planet—bound together for better or worse by His common destiny for us.

In a fallen world where deceptive powers of darkness and destruction lurk, even the passionately faithful will suffer—as Jesus, indeed *with* Jesus—precisely in order, as the ancient prophets, to bear that suffering to God as intercessors in behalf of the nation, and seek its redemption.

Whether the Prime Ministers and Presidents, Commanders and Air Marshals of this world see it or not—indeed, whether the very people saved see it or not—Almighty God is present among men and women who humbly confess they have turned away from Him and cry out for His saving power in Jesus. His deliverance may not come on our timetable nor to our desired scale. But He remains in charge, working out His purposes, regardless of whether we recognize it or not.

Thus, the question Jesus raised when anticipating His return to earth was not whether He would find churches, or even religion, but rather, "Will the Son of Man find faith on earth when he comes?" (Luke 18:8)

A century and a half before Hitler, Napoleon ran roughshod over Europe and boasted of his victories. When the Pope warned him to cease his destruction, the French emperor scoffed, "How many divisions does the Pope have?"

AGELESS ENEMY

Similarly, Christians condemn today's acts of terrorism. And God's ageless enemy at work in the terrorists sneers, "How many explosives and suicidal slaves do the Christians have?"

To this, we affirm clearly and boldly: "We have none. For 'the weapons we use in our fight are not the world's weapons' (2 Cor.

10:4)—which can intimidate and destroy, but cannot free human hearts from fear, overcome our proud separation from God, and draw us back into our created purpose as His sons and daughters. And so, instead, we wield the mighty super-natural weapons of God, poured out through Jesus in His Holy Spirit even now to reveal, to bind, and to destroy your strongholds!"

As the second twin tower in New York crumbled on 9/11, our secular political leaders at last recognized that we are at war. Christians, however, know that this battle did not explode suddenly on September 11, 2001. **Rather, it began long, long ago in the spirit realm and is waged on earth unto today in the hearts of men and women who long to see God's rule restored to earth**—even as to their personal lives and nations.

This is the battle Jesus came to win, and through his life, death, and resurrection God has poured out upon us the power to walk with Him in that victory. As surely as He turned Hitler's bombers away from Britain, the God who split the Red Sea and raised His Son from death can locate demonically inspired terrorists and deliver them into the hands of justice.

Even as the prophet Elijah saw supernaturally the enemy Syrian plans and warned Israel's army how to avoid attacks, Christians can join together as a battalion and pray for terrorist hideouts to be revealed and destroyed (see 2 Kings 6:8-23).

God has promised us His victory. Meanwhile, in this fallen world we suffer pain and loss. Yes, Christians know that someday Jesus will return to claim the earth wholly for the Father. Nevertheless, "we groan" as we await the fullness of God's promises to be revealed (Rom. 8:22).

Those who grieve faithfully will come to know **not only the Father's Spirit of comfort for His children, but also His Spirit of anger toward any who would harm them** (see 1 Samuel 11:1-6). Memorial flowers, flag-waving, and candle-lighting, that is, may be necessary to comfort the afflicted, but will not suffice to subdue the afflictor.

TIME FOR THE LION

When the lamb in us has wept faithfully the tears of God, it's time for the lion in us to roar His victory, like the WWII intercessors in Wales—that is, together to engage fiercely in deliberate spiritual warfare with the authority of Jesus and the power of His Spirit. Thus, we move from hospital to barracks and discover that the Great Physician who heals us is none other than the Commander in Chief who deploys us (see Joshua 5:13-15).

Destructive evil has performed flamboyantly before us on 9/11. As spectators, we watched helplessly and trembled. But what if the Great Playwright of human destiny would now use this drama to induct us into His story as actors, like God's praying platoon in Wales, with a definitive role in its outcome? The battle against evil in such terrorism is not finished because our capacity to grieve has waned and the 24-hour newscasts give way to commercials and ball games once again.

The Father is compassionate in the face of His children's short attention span; "He knows what we are made of" (Ps. 103:14). Still, our turning away from the battle has real and often destructive consequences. Must we allow the enemy enough rein to destroy us before we return to God and battle in the Spirit for His victory?

In this post-9/11 world, we face deliberately destructive acts sponsored by an enduring, avowedly religious community. No natural borders insure protection for any country. As Howells declared, unless God can get hold of this devil and bind him, none of us is safe.

This is war, and it has only begun. We dare not succumb to the seductive call to return to normal and "go shopping," as our leaders urged. This neither honors the victims nor reassures the survivors. Our comfortable norm has literally crumbled to a 10-story pile of dust. We can rebuild nice monuments on that spot and walk away feeling reassured—or allow God to use the awful pain of this cataclysm to recall us to His norm, lest in a complacent stupor we leave ourselves yet more vulnerable to future attacks.

Amid the rubble, we discovered among us a heart to feel and hands to aid. But as Howells' prayer warriors in the Battle of Britain, we must now discover among us the Spirit to discern and overcome the evil celebrity who has too long dominated the stage of world attention. **Let it not be said of Americans simply that we grieve and rebuild well, but that we battle fiercely and overcome faithfully, with every powerful weapon Jesus died to give us.**

Mere patriotism, even moral support, will not sustain our political or military leaders in the battle ahead. Today we must ask, as Howells' biographer, Is there anywhere in America or the whole of the world among God's people a committed battalion of intercessors willing to stand in the gap against demonic acts of terrorism?

TOO LATE TO HIDE

It's too late to hide either in lukewarm religion as tolerant cowards, or in incendiary morality as blind avengers. Like the early Pilgrim settlers who fled the then-repressive Church of England, American Christians seek not vengeance, but freedom for God to fulfill His created purposes in, among, and through us. At times, God's victory in this fallen world may require restraint, and at other times, armed conflict. But its fountainhead is a passionate and committed relationship with God in order to see His Kingdom of truth and grace restored to this broken world.

This relationship and its crown of victory is born in surrender—not to the enemy or to worldly circumstance, but to the saving God revealed in Jesus. Like the prophets of ancient Israel, the Apostle Paul in early Church, and the Wales intercessors, first we confess that as a nation we have fostered the outward form of religion, but not genuine relationship with the active, living God revealed in Jesus.

Because the consequences of our complacency are now unbearably painful, we cry. And cry we must, for indeed, this is the Spirit of a loving, grieving Father crying in and for us. Our tears restore relationship with Him, allowing Him access once again to our hearts.

Confronted thus with both the frightful limits of our own power and the limitless power of our Father, we beg God to receive us yet again and restore His covering. We renounce our natural vision, so hopelessly clouded by our human fears and desires.

We then ask God to fill us with His Spirit, so we might receive His super-natural vision in order, as Howell's prayer warriors, "to see what God is doing" and join Him, armed with His powerful weapons to destroy enemy strongholds in the spirit realm.

Is it too much to ask of the Body of Christ today that we claim our history unto ancient Israel as God's warriors in this besieged world? Can we not face honestly the battle at hand, lie humbly before the Father who has come in Jesus to win it, and rise boldly to wield His weapons after victory?

Our troops have been fighting and dying in the Middle East since the first Gulf War in 2002. Far too many are returning to the US emotionally and spiritually crippled, committing suicide at an alarming rate (see "Epilog," *Fight like a Man*). As Howell's urged his band of spiritual warriors, **we Christians today dare not allow politicians and soldiers to do more than we do together on our knees.**

What if, indeed, we are more responsible for God's victory than those now on the battlefield in the Middle East?

> Holy Spirit's supernatural word of knowledge can reveal the enemy's plans and draw people to know Jesus as Lord.

3

THE GIFT OF KNOWLEDGE

INTEL FROM THE COMMANDER-IN-CHIEF

> *The Spirit's presence is shown in some way in each person for the good of all. The Spirit gives one person a message full of wisdom, while to another person the same Spirit gives a message full of knowledge.* (1 Corinthians 12:7,8)

HOLY SPIRIT'S GIFT OF KNOWLEDGE confers the ability to access supernaturally information not otherwise available through natural means. This gift serves two major purposes.

Every gift of the Spirit is designed to build up the Body, by serving the "good of all"—not to build up the ego of the one who exercises it.

The gift of knowledge is therefore portrayed in the Bible as serving God's saving purposes for the larger community of believers.

Thus, the prophet Elisha intercedes in Israel's behalf during wartime:

> The king of Syria was at war with Israel. He consulted his officers and chose a place to set up his camp. But Elisha sent word to the king of Israel, warning him not to go near that place, because the Syrians were waiting in ambush there. So the king of Israel warned the men who lived in that place, and they were on guard. This happened several times.
>
> The Syrian king became greatly upset over this; he called in his officers and asked them, "Which one of you is on the side of the King of Israel?"
>
> One of them answered, "No one is, Your Majesty. The prophet Elisha tells the king of Israel what you say even in the privacy of your own room." (2 Kings 6:8-12).

Clearly, not even the Syrian king's officers know what he does in his own room—but all-knowing God has access even to such detailed, hidden information, and shares it with His prophet. First, therefore, **the spiritual gift of knowledge enables God's people to know the enemy's plans—to call the enemy out of darkness into the light, where all destructive purposes can be exposed and foiled.**

Natural human vision simply cannot perceive the supernatural stratagems of our spiritual enemy—who revels in darkness, where destruction can proceed unrecognized and thereby, unopposed. One ancient Greek word for Holy Spirit was *paraclete*, a military term. Greek soldiers went to battle in pairs, fighting back to back; your partner covering your blind side was called your *paraclete*.

BLIND SIDE COVERED

Similarly, Holy Spirit protects you in spiritual warfare by covering your blind side, that is, **by revealing activity in the spirit realm which your natural human eyes can't see.**

I once prayed for a man who felt confused and lost. *Lord*, I asked, *what do you want most for him now?* At once, an image came to mind of a red Irish setter hunting dog, nose pointed and body stiffened ahead pointing to prey. I shared that vision with the man and asked if it might mean anything to him.

Noting that he'd gone hunting several times, he replied simply that the dog "just senses things in the forest that you can't see, and goes ahead of you to find the game."

Uncertain, we prayed for more understanding, and it struck me that in the wilderness, the dog's sense of smell and sight far outstrips that of human beings. The dog thereby ministers, as it were, the gift of knowledge to the hunter in territory where he's otherwise incapable of knowing information via his own natural human powers. I therefore prayed and asked God to give this man the gift of knowledge, and thereby, enable him to see the life goal to which God was pointing him.

As we prayed further, Holy Spirit showed us an enemy spirit of confusion that had long hampered his spiritual vision. He cast out the confusion and claimed for himself instead God's spirit of "firmness, strength, and a sure foundation" (1 Peter 5:10).

"I've never felt at peace like this before," the man sighed eventually.

I then encouraged him to draw closer to his church fellowship in order to let Holy Spirit guide him in several important decisions by using the combined wisdom of trustworthy brothers, and to stand on the text:

> The peace that Christ gives is to guide you in the decisions you make; for it is to this peace that God has called you together in one body. (Coloss. 3:15)

WISDOM AS COMPLEMENT

The Spirit's gift of knowledge supernaturally reveals truth.

As its complement, **the gift of wisdom reveals how God would have you act on that truth.** If you receive a word of knowledge for someone but no word of wisdom about what to do with it, often that person knows him/herself what the knowledge means.

A woman with a clear gift for serving others once came to me overcome by fear and unable to step out in her calling. When we prayed, in my mind's eye I saw a picture of her standing in a dark tunnel, like a subway. Knowing the woman was born and raised in Los Angeles, I doubted she had ever been in a subway, but decided at least to share that vision with her.

"No, I've never been in a subway before," she said, musing over the vision. I shrugged my shoulders and was about to go on to another topic, when matter-of-factly she noted that ten years earlier she was driving to the Los Angeles airport and panicked when she entered the quarter-mile tunnel just before the airport exit. In fact, she had frozen in terror and stopped her car, causing a traffic jam, and paramedics had to be called to help her out of the tunnel. "I've always been afraid of tunnels!" she declared.

With that confirmation, I decided to pray further for wisdom: what fear did she associate with the tunnel? Soon a question popped into my mind: What is the very first tunnel a person goes through, which bears life-or-death urgency? Obviously, the birth canal.

"Did your mother ever tell you anything about any trouble, maybe, when you were being born?" I asked.

"Oh, yes," she exclaimed. "Mom always said, 'It was awful trying to get you out of me—we almost lost you!'"

I invited her to close her eyes, imagine herself as a newborn coming out of her mother, and ask Jesus to be with her in that moment. Soon, she was bent over in her chair, trembling and crying, coughing deeply.

"Call out for Jesus!" I urged.

"Je-Jesus!" she cried out. "I can't get out of the womb! I'm trapped and afraid I'll die! Come and save me!" I prayed fiercely for her in the Spirit with my prayer language, and after some moments of convulsion and crying out to Jesus, her body began to settle.

Eventually, she sat quietly, smiling and shaking her head in amazement. "Soon after I called out for Jesus, I saw Him come to me, and He just kind of pulled me up out of the womb and I was free!"

As we talked about this experience, the woman told me she had been diagnosed as agoraphobic by a psychiatrist. Together, we bound the spirit of agoraphobia and cast it out of her. Today, she ministers to a wide variety of persons in need and has little fear any more of "going out." Through the gift of knowledge, this woman was set free from the enemy's work to sabotage God's calling on her life.

The second major Scripture portraying the gift of knowledge unfolds as Jesus meets the Samaritan woman at the well for the first time:

> "Go and call your husband," Jesus told her, "and come back."
>
> "I don't have a husband," she answered.
>
> Jesus replied, "You are right when you say you don't have a husband. You have been married to five men, and the man you live with now is not really your husband. You have told me the truth."
>
> "I see you are a prophet, sir," the woman said (John 4:16-19).

As a Jew, the Samaritan woman knew her Bible well enough to recognize the supernatural knowledge which only a prophet, such as Elisha, might access. When Jesus then identifies Himself to her as the Messiah, she runs into town and calls everyone to come and meet Him:

> Many of the Samaritans in that town believed in Jesus because the woman had said, "He told me everything I have ever done." So when the Samaritans came to Him, they begged Him to stay with them, and he stayed there two days
>
> Many more believed because of his message, and they told the woman, "**We**

believe now, not because of what you said, but because we ourselves have heard Him, and we know that He really is the Savior of the world (John 4:39-42)."

KNOWLEDGE AND EVANGELISM

The gift of knowledge, that is, leads people to know Jesus as Lord—that is, to evangelize and draw people into the Body of Christ.

I once prayed with a woman who had been sexually molested as a girl and was therefore extremely distrustful of men. When I invited her to turn to Jesus for healing, she balked. "He won't do anything for me!" she scoffed.

I shared several scriptures on God's steadfast love, and then urged her to give Him a chance to show how much He cares for her. Folding her arms, she dug in and flatly refused. In desperation, I prayed aloud, "Lord, I can't find any opening in (her) heart to you, but you know her better than I do. I give up. Show her in whatever way you want, how much you love her."

Jane sat resolutely quiet, head bowed over her folded arms, and I could only wait hopefully—if uneasily—in silence.

To my surprise, a strange picture soon came to my mind, of a girl and a man in a Ferris wheel bench. I waited, prayed again, and the picture remained. Finally, I decided I had nothing to lose by sharing it. When I told Jane about it, however, she remained silent and angry behind her folded arms—and then suddenly, sat bolt upright.

"How did you know that?" she demanded.

Startled, I drew back. "Know…what?"

"About the time when my father took me to the amusement park and I got so afraid when he insisted I go on the Ferris wheel with him!"

"Well, I …uh, that is, of course I didn't know that at all. Apparently, Holy Spirit just showed it to me."

Disarmed, and now more intrigued than angry, she loosed her arms and sat back. "You mean God knows about even those small things that hurt me years ago?"

I nodded. "Maybe it wasn't such a small thing, for a little girl to be so afraid of her father and unable to trust him to respect her feelings."

I hesitated, then decided the door was ajar enough to proceed. "Would you be willing to give the Lord a chance to heal that fear in you, even back then?"

Amazed, the woman agreed.

In prayer, she invited Jesus to be with her and her father in the Ferris wheel seat. There, she was able to tell her father out loud about her fear of heights and the pain she felt when he scoffed at that. In the prayer, he apologized for his thoughtlessness, she forgave him for not respecting her feelings, and the two embraced. Drying her tears moments later, the woman sighed. "I guess…Jesus really does know me…and care about me after all!"

Soon I was able to re-read the related scriptures, and this time she listened intently. We cast out a spirit of unbelief and she later welcomed Jesus fully into her life.

The ultimate word of knowledge is that Jesus loves you and is present in Holy Spirit to save you from your sin nature that separates you from Father God.

Thus, the Spirit's gift of knowledge leads to salvation. As Paul declared, "No one can confess 'Jesus is Lord,' unless he is guided by the Holy Spirit" (1 Cor. 12:3b).

SHORT-CIRCUITED GIFT

While the gift of knowledge can serve God in these two powerful ways, nevertheless it can be short-circuited.

First, the believer may be tempted to discount and so ignore it. Often, that is, the word of knowledge may seem strange and even bizarre; why risk sharing it and looking foolish? But certainly, if the word were purely natural and evident, it wouldn't require supernatural gifting in order to come forth; we would see it readily with our human faculties and not need God's help.

Paul therefore introduces the gifts of the Spirit to the Corinthian church by declaring gently, "I would not have you ignorant" of them (1 Cor. 12:1). He then urges Timothy proactively to

> keep alive the gift that God gave you when I laid my hands on you. For the Spirit that God has given us does not make us timid; instead, his Spirit fills us with power, love, and self-control (2 Tim. 1:6-7).

Again, he says, "Set your hearts on spiritual gifts (1 Cor 14:1)."

We must be willing, therefore, to risk looking foolish in order not to risk muffling the transforming word of God among us. At the same time, I always offer the words and visions that come to me with an open door for the person to reject it, as, "Here's what I sense—does it mean anything to you?" I then trust God either to confirm it as His own, or to discard it graciously.

Often, the person may not immediately see the meaning—only to discover later that indeed, as with my Ferris wheel vision, the word was on target. No need to push for confirmation; leave that to Holy Spirit for His timing. **It's not about confirming your giftedness, but about giving God room to work according to His will**.

"OK, Lord," you can pray out loud, "we don't get any sense right now that this word is from you. I leave it in your hands. Keep going, show us what more we need to see here."

Significantly, in the previous 1 Corinthians 14:1 passage, the Apostle urges believers to "set your hearts on" such gifts as knowledge but to "strive for" such a *fruit* of the Spirit as love. Another translation reads "eagerly desire" the gifts, and "Make love your aim" (RSV). The gifts, that is, seem to bear upon an external focus and attitude of receptiveness; the fruit, upon our human will and determination.

Thus, when your thoughts and actions are not consonant with the fruit, the Spirit is not at work in you. That lack stirs you to "earnestly desire" the gifts and more of the Spirit who provides them.

The intent here would seem to be: "Be willing to wait, and let God bestow the gifts of the Spirit. Once He's done that, then set out to cooperate with Him and use them to foster fruit." When praying with another, therefore, I always invite Holy Spirit to come, and then await any word of knowledge. When I sense a word or vision, I work with the other person to understand what it means and follow through on it for the healing intended.

If nothing comes to mind, don't panic. Holy Spirit is at work whether you sense anything or not.

TEMPTATION TO FORCE

Without that trust in God, you may be tempted to force a word of knowledge, in an effort to gain its fruit or intended benefit. Often, when I pray for others and ask Holy Spirit to give us a word of knowledge, they close their eyes and knit their brows, to "try and think of something." I gently encourage the person instead simply to "just watch and wait," to let go and allow the Lord to bring anything to mind, as I pray in the Spirit.

When the Resurrected Lord appeared to the disciples prior to Pentecost, therefore, he commanded them, "Do not leave Jerusalem, but wait for the gift I told you about, the gift my Father promised" (Acts 1:4).

He did not say, "Charge out and conjure up words and images out of your own imagination and experience." Rather, he said essentially, "Wait for my Holy Spirit—and go out only after He has come." **If no word of knowledge emerges when you pray, don't worry. God still wants to heal and will work in other ways**.

I once prayed for a woman of Spanish-speaking heritage and saw a picture in my mind of a full moon. Without asking Holy Spirit for wisdom, I leapt ahead, sharing my picture and telling her that the sun represented God, shining on her like the moon, and she was to reflect God's light to the world even as the moon reflects the sun.

When I managed to pause in self-satisfaction, however, she graciously and matter-of-factly noted that her mother's surname was Luna, meaning 'moon' in Spanish, and her father's surname was also Luna. "My brothers and sisters and I were all called 'full moons' by our relatives."

Humbled, I tossed aside all my wonderfully misguided interpretations and asked the Father to give us His wisdom. Soon, in fact, we uncovered a spirit of incest in her heritage and cast it out.

Forcing a spiritual gift is like killing the marvelous goose in order to seize more golden eggs: it's worse than getting nothing. Indeed, doing so beckons a spirit of despair—as a distrust in the Lord's caring presence and power—and thereby, invites the enemy. **The person who is desperate for a word of knowledge and unwilling to trust Holy Spirit to speak in His time and way, often will hear from an enemy spirit of divination**.

Demons prey upon distrust. (see "Seeking God's Will, Trusting His Love" in *Sons of the Father*).

Furthermore, the word of knowledge can be useless, even dangerous, by itself apart from the word of wisdom. If the enemy cannot foil God's work by blocking His word of knowledge, he may urge you to rush ahead with that knowledge without consulting the Lord for wisdom in how He wants you to use it.

PASTORAL SENSITIVITY

Years ago, shortly after I received the baptism of the Spirit, a fellow pastor invited me to minister with him at a special Sunday afternoon healing prayer group. At one point, a distraught woman stood uneasily and came forward. As we stood beside her and laid hands on her shoulder, immediately an image came to my mind of her kneeling in the middle of a living room with a mob of shouting children jumping on her.

I was about to blurt out a blow-by-blow account of what Holy Spirit was showing me, when suddenly I heard my pastor-friend speak aloud in a gentle voice: "Being a mother can be a hard job sometimes." He then proceeded with pastoral sensitivity to minister words of reassurance and encouragement to the distraught woman before us, and she left us with a smile.

Clearly, both of us had received the same supernatural word of knowledge. Unlike me, however, he had immediately submitted that word to God for wisdom as how best to use it. Thus, he was able more wisely to minister the word of knowledge in a spirit of gentleness and compassion, which allowed the woman to receive it.

When someone comes to me saying, "The Lord has shown me" this or "God has told me" that," I always respond, "Let's pray and ask Him a) to confirm that word, and if He does, b) for wisdom on what He wants us to do with that knowledge."

A word of knowledge can be confirmed by others in the Body. That is, when a word is offered, "others are to judge" what is said (1 Cor. 14:29). A humble sense that in this present age we "see through a glass darkly" at best, keeps you from leaping ahead beyond Holy Spirit's leading (1 Cor. 13:12).

Once, in a small group, one member asked us to pray about a "deep frustration" he was experiencing with a loved one. After praying, we waited for the Spirit. "This sounds strange," one member said eventually, "but I see a big human eye, with something like a tree in the middle of it...?"

Puzzled, we prayed for wisdom: "Lord, if this is a word of knowledge from you, show us what it means."

At once, I remembered the scriptural warning to remove the "log in your own eye" before judging others. "Could it be," I asked the man, "that you yourself might need to confess and be cleansed of something, before we can deal with faults in the person who wounded you?"

Sighing, the man poured out several thoughtless and insensitive things he had himself done to the other, and prayed for forgiveness. We all urged him to go and ask the other's forgiveness first, and we would be praying for him. One member of the Body thereby brought the word of knowledge, another the wisdom, and the whole Body affirmed the scriptural path to healing.

Finally, remember that, even as the ancient prophets spoke both promise and warning, **a word genuinely from God "brings help, encouragement, and comfort."** (1 Corinth. 14:3).

I once mentioned at a conference that my father, then 82, had suffered a heart attack. Afterward, a man came to me and said, "I was praying for you and the Lord told me that your father is going to die from this."

I waited, but the man said no more. "Thank you for coming to me," I said, "but if that's all you heard, I don't receive it as a word from God, because I don't hear any 'help, encouragement and comfort' in it." My father lived another 11 years and died at 93 from skin cancer.

Ultimately, therefore, the gift of knowledge must be kept in proper perspective. It is no more—and no less—than a tool for bringing God's children closer to Him through Jesus and for thwarting any plans of the enemy to prevent that. Two thousand years ago, the Apostle Paul set the standard for us even today, praying that the people of God might "know the love of Christ which surpasses knowledge, that you may be filled with all the fullness of God" (Eph. 3:19).

Let it be.

> We can choose not to exercise authority, but we cannot choose to have no authority.

4

USE YOUR AUTHORITY

FOR GOD'S SAKE

> *Jesus called his twelve disciples together and gave them authority to drive out evil spirits and heal every disease and every sickness.* (Matt. 10:1)

"JESUS DIDN'T TELL HIS FOLLOWERS to pray for the sick," Healing Prayer Rooms California director Rick Taylor has noted; "he told them to heal the sick."

Now, there's a concept!

For the record, Jesus not only gave his disciples authority, but in fact, "instructions" to "heal the sick, bring the dead back to life, heal those who suffer from dreaded skin diseases, and drive out demons" (Matt. 10:8).

What would it mean for us to exercise this authority as Jesus' followers today? Why, indeed, have we balked at doing so?

This issue became dramatically clear to me some years ago when a young ministry intern at a local church told me that his father was sick and the doctors couldn't find what was wrong with him. A few weeks later, I saw him and asked how his father was doing.

"Not so good," he sighed. "Dad's been in the hospital awhile now and just keeps getting worse. The doctors still don't know what to do. They're worried he's not going to make it."

I asked him if he had organized others to pray for his dad.

"Oh, yes," he declared. "I've got the whole church praying, and all my friends everywhere. But Dad's still getting worse."

Sensing something amiss, I prayed quietly. *Lord, do you want me to push this?* Gently, I eased ahead. "How are they praying?"

"What do you mean?" the young man snapped, knitting his brow. "They're asking God to heal him, of course!"

"That's a good prayer," I allowed, "but it may not be the best prayer. Has anyone taken authority over his sickness?"

"'Taken authority'?" he echoed, puzzled.

COMMAND SICKNESS TO GO

"Yes," I declared. "Has anyone gone to the hospital, laid hands on your dad, spoken to the sickness in the name of Jesus, and commanded it to leave him?"

Taken aback, the young man hesitated. "Well,…no, not really. I mean, I never thought of that."

"It's a very biblical way of responding to illness," I noted. "Since nothing else is working, somebody had better think of it soon—and I suggest it be you!"

A few weeks later, I called him and asked for an update.

"Well, I did go see Dad and do like you said and took authority over his sickness," the young man replied matter-of-factly. "The doctors never did figure out what he had, but Dad's out of the hospital now and doing fine."

"Halleluiah!" I exclaimed. "What a great experience for you to minister to your dad like that!"

"Well," he scoffed, "I don't think my prayer really had much to do with it—we're all just thankful that he's better."

Astonished, dismayed, I realized that this born-again Christian on the threshold of ordained ministry—together with a host of believing friends and a sizeable church in town—had no context in which to affirm this authority Jesus had given him, even to save his father's life. They could all ask God to heal someone, but to speak healing in the name of Jesus—as the Lord Himself exhorted His disciples—never occurred to them. Even when the young man did exercise that authority and his own father was healed of a life-threatening illness, he could not entertain the possibility of any connection between these events.

Little children beg Daddy and Mommy to do everything for them. But if the parental relationship is intact and vital, the children grow up and take responsibility to exercise their own giftings with appropriate authority. To do so honors the parents, as evidence that they've done their job well.

FATHER-SON AUTHORITY

Years ago when I was teaching my son to drive, I told him not to be intimidated by tail-gating drivers behind him who would push him over the speed limit toward endangering himself and others. "Let the other guy get the ticket, not you," I told him.

Later, I was riding with him as he drove within the speed limit, and watched as a car sped up behind us too close for comfort. Without asking me what to do, he glanced in the rear-view mirror and maintained his proper speed. As the other driver eventually pulled out and squealed past us in a huff, Dad sighed in satisfaction.

"Good move, son!" I declared, patting him on the shoulder.

In effect, my son communicated to the tailgater, "By the authority of my father, I tell you: If you want to speed, that's fine—go ahead and pass me. But I won't be intimidated to risk myself for your haste."

Similarly, as new, "baby" Christians, we typically present the Father with lists of what we want and are genuinely encouraged by His often gracious responses. In fact, when I especially want God to move in my behalf, I confess that I'm tempted to go find a brand new

Christian to pray for me. Sometimes, the Father seems more willing to act on a child's cry, to preserve and re-enforce their budding faith!

Maturing Christians, meanwhile, become cautious of asking God to do what He has already given us authority to do. God is not co-dependent. It's good to beg God to heal others, to expel or bind the Enemy. But we must be prepared ourselves to speak that healing, to command that deliverance in the name of Jesus.

This honors the Father—even as I felt honored when my son dismissed his tailgater—and is entirely in accord with Jesus' teaching. It's evidence that the Father has done His job well, that we're appropriating the full measure of Jesus' life, death, and resurrection by affirming His Spirit's work in and through us. Thus, we become agents of His Kingdom come on earth as it is in heaven, speaking it into being as He has called us to do—and did Himself at Creation (see Gen. 1:3ff.).

Certainly, no one knows just how much my young intern's prayer of authority contributed to his dad's healing. I'm happy to believe that everyone else's prayers also figured into God's plan. The roots of physical illness, emotional brokenness, and spiritual oppression can be complex, even mysterious; God can heal any way He wants, whether through someone's prayer or not.

NOT A FORMULA

But while authoritative prayer is not the only means for God to heal, it's a powerful and all-too-often ignored part of biblically-based ministry. **Like all genuine prayer, it's not a formula to get what we want, but a trusting relationship that allows God to get what He wants—and often more than we seek.**

Certainly, it's important in every circumstance to ask Jesus how he's praying for the person and how he wants you to cooperate with his purposes (see Romans 8:34). You may not always get a clear answer. Amid these mysteries, however, I'd rather speak with authority and have nothing apparent happen, than withdraw from it when something of God might have happened—whether in me or the person I prayed for.

Many Christians are offended when I say this. Obviously, no one wants to bear the shame of not having done something that might have helped or saved another person, especially a person who died from that need. But such self-absorbed civilian pride is not tolerated on the battlefield, where even fatal mistakes are not only made but diligently faced in order that they not be repeated and other lives might be saved.

That's why doctors do autopsies. Unlike so many Christians blackmailed by religion, **they don't allow the shame of failure to overshadow its lessons and short-circuit their calling to heal**. They use all known means to help their patients and constantly seek newer means.

As a result, medical research decreases human suffering and saves more and more lives. In fact, many diseases that once killed people are unknown today. My grandmother's twelve-year-old brother died in the 1890s of diphtheria and a friend of mine was nearly crippled by polio in the 1950s. At the time of their illness, no one had a clue how to heal it.

Instead of scoffing that it couldn't be done in order to cover the shame of their inability, medical researchers pressed on until they developed a vaccine that did it.

Yes, by the time it was available, the damage had been done; neither my grandmother's brother nor my friend with polio would've been touched by disease had they been born later, after the vaccine. Clearly, God has allowed diphtheria, polio, and other diseases to exist—as many others yet today. Countless people have suffered them and died before He prompted medical researchers to the cure.

It seems patently unfair, even cruel. Apparently, that's life in this fallen but being-redeemed world. I don't like it. But I didn't get to write this story.

The great conundrum—indeed, frustration—of faith is that **the God who allows suffering is the only One capable of overcoming it.**

Though confused and angry at times, I press on after His overcoming power. I can—and do—rail against God for allowing human suffering. As many others have done, I can curse God and turn away from Him—and find plenty of company. Yet I know from experience that debilitating spirits of bitterness, weakness, and isolation lurk here.

I've learned that the only way to avoid this trap of the enemy is to surrender not to him, but yet again to God. I can either rant and rage about life's inequities, or beat on the gates of heaven for new revelation. I have to trust that God is working to overcome the world's brokenness both in and among us all. Like the medical researchers, I can only offer myself humbly but deliberately to join Him in that work.

It's hard. The older I get, the more pain and suffering I see. But I've also seen enough healing and restoration to know that the enemy's not the only player on the field.

Over the years, the Bible character I most appreciate having with me on the journey besides Jesus is the father who brought his son to Jesus crying out that the boy had "an evil spirit in him and cannot talk." Desperate to see his son healed, this bold father confronts Jesus, "I asked your disciples to cast the spirit out, but they could not."

Throughout Jesus' healing ministry, he's most often composed and almost matter-of-fact in his authority. He can get emotional, but focuses any anger on the spirit causing the malady (see Mark 1:41ff.). Here, however, this father's cry of desperation in behalf of his son stirs Jesus to exasperation, not first with the demon, but with his own followers.

"Oh unbelieving generation!" Jesus exclaims; "how long shall I stay with you? How long shall I put up with you? Bring the boy to me."

The father tells Jesus that his son has suffered from this demon since boyhood. "It has often thrown him into fire or water to kill him. But if you can do anything, take pity on us and help us."

"'If you can'?" Jesus echoes indignantly, bursting out yet again in frustration. "Everything is possible for him who believes."

"I do believe," the boy's father "immediately" exclaims, adding poignantly, "help me overcome my unbelief!"

Without responding to the father or his disciples Jesus resolves himself to the more significant task at hand. He then "rebuked the evil spirit, 'You deaf and dumb spirit,…I command you, come out of him and never enter him again'."

At that, "The spirit shrieked, convulsed him violently and came out."

This moving scene demonstrates that the issue for Jesus in warfare is not God's power—which is matter-of-fact—but our willingness to trust Him and exercise it in His name.

When at last I meet God face-to-face, therefore, I want to ask Him in many instances, "Why didn't you exercise Your saving power?" I don't want Him to respond, "Why didn't *you* exercise the authority I gave you?"

For many Christians, the answer may lie in painful and fearful childhood experiences of authority, often with fathers.

When you know your father loves you, that is, you do what he says readily, because you know it's best for you. If the security of Daddy's love has been violated, however, as by harsh punishment, judgment, abuse, or abandonment, you grow up distrusting authority. If you don't take this father-wound to Jesus for healing, it becomes your natural default and colors your worldview. When you grow up and move into positions of authority yourself, you may simply treat others as you learned from Dad—either by judging and coercing or simply withdrawing and abandoning.

Thus, you miss the essential distinction between *authoritative*— as one called and empowered by God to effect His good purposes in others, and *authoritarian*—as one driven by self-centered desires to coerce or manipulate others for your own goals.

HUMBLE, SCHMUMBLE

When childhood wounds and their accompanying pain, fear, and anger remain unhealed, praying with authority seems arrogant and egotistical—like Dad. So we withdraw from it, like my ministry intern friend, in order to appear humble and thereby, blameless—unlike Dad.

"Humble, schmumble!" Jesus `might well exclaim. "For God's sake, pick up the sword I died to give you, and use it!" **To humbly reject the world's applause is one thing; to "humbly" reject God's call to restore His Kingdom on earth is quite another.**

Wounded children often grow up angry and unforgiving. In order not to incur themselves the judgment they pass upon their parents, their main objective in life is to not hurt anyone—like my wounded generation years ago as "Peace and Love" hippies.

This goal, however, can be accomplished simply by staying in bed. It's a recipe for passivity.

Thankfully, surgeons don't share that goal, or there would be no surgeries—and no healing in hospitals. All surgeries hurt. In fact, not all are successful. But surgeons take that risk deliberately, trusting that the pain of the operation will be balanced if not effaced by its healing. If, indeed, the operation is not successful, surgeons may well mourn, even suffer shame, but they channel that energy into an autopsy, facing honestly their unknowing and seeking ways to improve future chances of success.

How much more bold are these men of the world—and indeed, faithful to their calling—than the many timid Christians who balk at praying with authority for fear of embarrassing God if it "doesn't work"! In fact, they're afraid of being embarrassed themselves and losing their faith, by apparently believing in a God who's not active and effective. Or maybe a loved one died and they didn't pray with authority, so the thought that their prayer could've made a difference is too burdensome.

It's an awfully good thing scientists don't feel that way, or there would be no advances in medical treatment. The bedrock of scientific discovery is experimenting and learning from "mistakes" to try again differently. If you're determined to learn and grow, today's best decisions will often turn out to be seen as mistakes in the light of tomorrow's discovery. That's life in this fallen but evolving world. It's why God offers both mercy and grace to encourage a dedicated heart to press on.

In this sin-infected world, brokenness and evil abounds. Jesus himself declared, "In this world, you will have trouble." But he never said, "So don't pray with authority because I don't want to be embarrassed if it doesn't work" or "So when it doesn't work, give up." In fact, he exhorted, "But take heart! I have overcome the world!" (John 16:33NIV). As Paul reassured, "There is no condemnation now for those who live in union with Christ Jesus" (Rom. 8:1).

Exercising Godly authority over sickness and evil can give God something to bless. Certainly, it doesn't always bring about the desired change or "cure." **But if we're more concerned with God's purposes than with the shame of our own failure, we press on after**

understanding God's work in this broken world and join Him in it.

LOVE'S AUTHORITY

Too often, we abdicate to the devil speaking with authority, as if only egotistical and presumptuous people do it. In fact, it's a godly ministry to exercise authority in each other's lives. Not the kind that enforces commands with threats and punishment—as many of us learned in childhood—but the kind that empowers God's plan with blessings.

Because "God is love," that is, all love relationships bear divine authority to the lover (1 John 4:7-21). By its very nature, love opens our hearts to each other and allows, even begs, for authoritative input.

The child's heart cries out, "Daddy/Mommy, tell me that I did a good job!" and the spouse, "Honey, show me that I'm valuable, loveable, and worthy of respect."

The parent or lover who abdicates this authority abandons, and thereby deeply wounds the beloved—like a gardener who fails to water a plant. **We can choose to withdraw from, abuse, or exercise faithfully our authority over loved ones. But we cannot choose to have no authority in their lives**. What you speak or don't speak of them, speaks *into* them, often shaping their self-image.

Authority figures, such as parent, teacher, older sibling, or boss, can communicate binding curses—from "You'll never amount to anything" to "You'll always be left out." To break these, ask Jesus to identify any such patterns in your life, set the cross between you and the one who spoke that curse over you, and in the Name of Jesus break it and nail it to the cross. Pray for the blood of Jesus to cleanse you from its effects, and reclaim God's authority by speaking the biblical truth of who you are in His sight.

The opposite of a curse is a blessing—which bears even greater power, namely, to accomplish God's purposes. "This is my own dear son, in whom I am well pleased," the Father proclaimed over Jesus (Matt. 3:17). Immediately after this, He sent Jesus into the desert to battle temptation head-on with Satan—knowing that His blessing would empower His son in victory.

Dare to ask this loving Father, "Show me myself the way You see me."

Be prepared to receive His blessing.

Genuine positive input from an authority figure, whether spoken over heart, body, or spirit, bears a blessing—not only to the one who receives it, but from God, who ordained it. "You're a beautiful and capable young woman," Dad and Mom can say to their daughter; "You're a strong and courageous young man," they can say to their son. Likewise, a son or daughter can affirm "You're a great dad," or "You're a great mom." Any honest child or parent knows the marvelous power such a simple gesture bears.

In praying for someone, we can ask Holy Spirit to provide supernatural knowledge of how He's working in that person's life and how our praying with authority would facilitate His plan.

Certainly, as the Apostle noted, in this imperfect world "we see through a glass darkly" at best (1 Corinth. 13:12). **But our human limitation does not define God's possibility.** Nor should it deter us from faith that the Father wants us to see ever more clearly what He's doing and join Him in it.

May that faith lead us to exercise the authority Jesus died to give us.

> **You're a sinner like everyone else; what makes you think you should be exempt from the fallout of a sinful world?**

5

HOW PRIVATE RYAN WAS SAVED

WHY GOOD THINGS HAPPEN TO BAD PEOPLE

> *Jesus then said to his disciples, "I assure you: it will be very hard for rich people to enter the Kingdom of heaven. I repeat: it is much harder for a rich person to enter the Kingdom of God than for a camel to go through the eye of a needle."*
>
> *When the disciples heard this, they were completely amazed. "Who, then, can be saved?" they asked.* (Matt. 19:24,25)

"WHY DO BAD THINGS HAPPEN to good people?" is a common question amid human suffering, which can often seem random and patently unfair. In fact, such seeming injustice inevitably leads us to ask, "Why would a loving, all-powerful God allow good people to suffer?" Among Christians, this challenge stirs shame and a face-saving compulsion to defend our God to a doubting world.

The very question, however, reflects a cherished but false assumption about human nature.

From a New Covenant perspective, that is, there simply are no good people.

"Good teacher," a rich man asked Jesus, "what must I do to receive eternal life?"

"Why do you call me good?" Jesus replied. "No one is good except God alone" (Mark 10:18ff).

Jesus' self-deprecation here is startling, but we soon see why he's quick to make such a radical distinction. When he instructs the rich man to keep the biblical Law, the man declares, "Ever since I was young, I have obeyed all these commandments."

Jesus knows that someone so convinced that he's good needs to be jarred into humility before he can open to God's goodness. Otherwise, he thinks he doesn't need God—and will get picked off easily by the enemy. So Jesus "looked straight at him with love" and declared,

> You need only one thing. Go and sell all
> you have and give the money to the poor, and
> you will have riches in heaven; then come and
> follow me.

Here, at last, is a commandment which challenges radically the rich young ruler's identity in this world—where his money, youth, and power are paramount values. The choice overwhelms him and he's undone: "When the man heard this, gloom spread over his face, and he went away sad, because he was very rich."

If indeed, Jesus loved this rich young man, it must have hurt to see him walk away. But the Great Surgeon has inflicted a necessary wound.

Jesus is not co-dependent. He doesn't rush after the rich man to bargain for an easier deal. Whether we're rich or poor, God respects us enough to let us face His terms of reality—and the consequences of not doing so. "There is no difference at all," the Apostle Paul echoes; "everyone has sinned and is far away from God's saving presence" (Rom. 3:22-23).

Our not-good-ness stirs shame, and when confronted with it, often we walk away from Jesus like that rich young man. At best, we balk. In the grip of shame, when struck with suffering, we ask, "Why me?" Our self-centered human nature assures us that we're basically pretty good, and therefore don't deserve such misfortune.

WHY NOT YOU?

From a biblical perspective, however, God's answer might well be, "Why *not* you?" That is, **"You're a sinner like everyone else; what makes you think you should be exempt from the fallout of a sinful world?"** Bad things happen to us all—at times, simply because we live in a fallen world and that fallen-ness lives in us as our sin-nature. You don't need to do bad things in order to incur painful circumstances. He who did the very best thing died on the cross for doing it. God "sends rain on the righteous and the unrighteous" alike, as Jesus noted (Mt. 5:45).

Sure, it seems unfair. But we all know from hard experience that it's real. And if Jesus himself asserts it, then this reality—no matter how "unfair" by human standards— must beckon God's purposes.

Like the rich man Jesus upends, those of us who are doing pretty well in the world can allow our material comfort to lull us into the fantasy of our own goodness. Thus, the disciples were flummoxed when in the opening chapter scripture Jesus tells them how hard it is for a rich man to enter heaven. But if we want truly to gain eternal life and not just more comfort here and now, we need to face our not-good-ness and un-worthiness.

"Why do bad things happen to good people?" is therefore a civilian question. It's a fantasy of denial which ignores the awful reality not only of this fallen world but of our sinful human nature and the need to be crucified with the King of Kings to overcome it (see Rom. 12:1-2). Worse, it's a cover-up for the powers of evil that war against God's purposes—not just "out there" in others, but in our own hearts.

The warrior, on the other hand, sees life differently, because he experiences it within the larger reality of evil and death. The wrenching classic WWII film *Saving Private Ryan* portrays this contrast graphically.

In the film, four of five Ryan brothers are killed in battle. A platoon is dispatched to find the surviving fifth brother and remove him from battle in order to spare his parents from total loss. Amid bloodshed and carnage, Private Ryan is indeed rescued by the platoon, most of whom die in the effort.

SEVERE WITNESS

Fifty years later, we see him pudgy and gray, kneeling in a military cemetery as thousands of white crosses surround him in severe witness. No hero here, just a tormented survivor: humbled, but not humiliated; lost in the mystery, but found at last by its Author; one who has faced the awful reality of evil and death not only on the world's battlefield, but also in his own unworthy heart.

"Why me?" he whimpers.

Here, at last, are the makings of a Kingdom warrior: one who's been saved not by any virtue of his own, but by the sacrificial grace of another. He's not demanding to know, Why did I suffer? He's begging to know, Why was I spared? **He seeks mercy, not vindication.** He's overwhelmed—and properly so—by the mystery of grace: Why do I still live, and even prosper, when so many braver men more worthy than me—even Jesus Himself—have been killed, even for saving me?"

In fact, we're all undeserving Private Ryans, indebted to many, many others both known and unknown whose suffering has enabled our life today.

"Why do good things happen to bad people (like me)?" This is the question required of every man and woman who dares kneel at the foot of the Cross and call Jesus, the most worthy of human beings, "Lord." Both blessed in its truth and awe-ful in its grace, this humble question stands between every one of us and eternal life. It's the gateway to God's kingdom come on earth as it is in heaven—that is, to walking out Jesus' resurrection victory in a world broken unto death.

When no honest men or women kneel thus in the shadow of the cross, no genuine warriors are left to dare ask this question. And so, the enemy divides and conquers us. *Diabolos*, the root word for "devil" (as in *diabolic*) comes from two parts: *di* (split in two, as in di-vide) + *abol* (as in abolish or destroy).

At the political/theological extremes, the "liberal" faction declares that there's no sin and evil, that we're all good. The problem is, we just haven't been educated to realize how good we are and how to act accordingly. Under the banner of "Tolerance and Inclusivity," this heresy beckons the spirit of universalism, which fuels the current "politically correct" ideology.

It's grace without truth, shame-less-ly naive.

The opposing, "conservative" faction declares that there is only sin and evil, that we're all bad. The problem is, we haven't tried hard enough to be good. Under the banner of "Judgment and Exclusivity," this heresy beckons the spirit of religion, which fuels an exhausting "measure-up-to-these-standards-and-you'll-gain-God's-favor" life of striving.

It's truth without grace, shame-ful-ly cruel.

Both factions undermine God's purposes. Performance religion masks the shameful truth that we can't perform; gracious tolerance overlooks behavior that harms God's beloved children.

ANOTHER PLAN

Meanwhile, God's busy working out another plan: "God gave the Law through Moses, but grace *and* truth came through Jesus Christ" (John 1:17, italics mine).

Here's the truth: We were indeed created good. But through the draw of evil we lost our innocence from our very Genesis, allowing sin to enter and infect our human nature, to separate us from God unto death.

And here's the grace: Jesus has come to bear the shame of our otherwise unbearable not-good-ness, and thereby to restore our innocence and make us worthy to approach Father God. You can fall on your knees, cry out your unworthiness to Him, and let His Spirit restore you daily to your created good-ness as God's child. You can thereby become free at last to choose what's best for you and get on with your destiny, both now and forever.

The warrior is not disqualified from battle by this humility, but indeed, commissioned by it, for it positions him to rest in the Father's presence and trust His lead as Commander-in-Chief.

That's why good things happen to bad people (like us): Because the Father whose "love endures forever" (Ps. 118:2) has "created you for a life of good deeds which he has already prepared for you to do" (Ephes. 2:10). God has a plan for your life and the power to accomplish it. He wants you to come to Him so He can do that. **He therefore won't abide our being seduced away from His truth by universal tolerance, or blinded to His grace by religious judgment.**

The crafty spirit of unworthiness hosts this debate. Like all demons, it relies for its power upon our unwillingness to surrender to Jesus and attempt, rather, to save ourselves. When the Father chooses to bless us, even to give us what we need to accomplish His calling, the enemy whispers, "You're not worthy to receive that. Give it back!"

TWO OPTIONS

Human nature offers only two options here. You can acquiesce to the demon, refuse what God would give you, and go your un-worthy, un-fulfilled, un-equipped, un-productive, and often resentful way. Or you can rise up in self-righteous determination to assert, "No! In fact, I *am* worthy. Look at all my accomplishments, my righteous deeds, all of which prove that I deserve what I want!"

If you want to shake your fist at God and demand, "Give me what I deserve!" wait just a minute, please, so I can step away before the lightning toasts you!

It's like the old joke, in which a lost city slicker asks the farmer how to get to a certain town—whereupon the farmer scratches his head and declares, "You can't get there from here."

To exit this double-bind so characteristic of sinful human nature, we must turn to Jesus, the liberating Third Option and the truth that sets us free. In fact, the enemy is right. We *are* unworthy. Who among us can stand worthy of God's son dying for you—indeed, for all of us who so naturally turn away from Him?

If you have a belly button, stay seated.

Jesus' response to our dilemma is this: "Settle the dispute with your (accuser)...before you get to court" (Matt. 5:25). That is, in order to counter this demonic conundrum, speak the truth: "You're right, Satan. I'm not worthy of anything the Father would give me. Thanks for reminding me.

"God blesses me not because I'm so good, but because He's so good. It's all about His grace and not my merit. I have no earthly right to receive His blessing.

"But Jesus died so I could receive it, and I'm not about to let Jesus die for nothing. What's more, I need the resources of God's Spirit to overcome my sinful nature and accomplish His purposes. So I will receive those resources by grace alone and humbly use them to serve Him in this world."

The world's charade of "judgment *vs.* tolerance" is thereby exposed, revealing truth and grace as no longer enemies, but holy complements. Both Liberal and Conservative on their knees before Jesus are united in His calling and power. With that confession and affirmation, you're ready to cast out the spirit of "unworthiness" and invite spirits of dignity, sonship/daughtership, humility, and worship to replace it.

Do you want to get where Father God has designed you to go? Can you be honest with yourself and confess you haven't trusted Him to get you there, even discounted His larger purposes in your life and determined to get there by your own talents and effort?

If so, you can begin this journey of genuine faith with the foundational belief that good things can happen to bad people—even you. You can confess you're not worthy of God's goodness, praise Him for His determination nevertheless to give it to you, and receive it thankfully. Then "give yourselves to God, as those who have been brought from death to life and surrender your whole being to Him to be used for righteous purposes" (Rom. 6:13).

You can get there from here.

> **The role of the survivor is to tell the story.**

6

DELIVERED FROM ABORTION

HEALING A FORGOTTEN MEMORY

You will know the truth, and the truth will set you free. (John 8:32NIV)

LATE IN THE FALL OF 1943, as Nazi submarines terrorized Allied shipping, a young Navy officer and his wife faced a terrible dilemma when he deployed to an aircraft carrier in the North Atlantic.

Living in makeshift wartime housing with an 8-month-old baby girl, they had only the bathtub for washing diapers and no clothes dryer or warmth except a volatile kerosene heater in the New Jersey cold. At least, there had been time to enjoy each other on a recent Thanksgiving furlough. But now, that joy was overcome by fear when they discovered another child was on the way.

The young woman's parents—already anxious for their daughter and only child—were furious at her husband for this, refused to speak to him, and threatened to disown her. Torn and confused, at her next visit with the Navy doctor the 21-year-old wife poured out her anguish and tears.

DOCTOR'S SOLUTION

The doctor, however, had a solution to her problem. Handing her a small, dark red bottle and scheduling her for an appointment the following week, he explained that he could "fix everything" quickly and easily after she took the pills.

Days later, before leaving for the appointment, the young woman shook the pills out of the bottle into her hand and closed her fist. Shaking from both cold and anxiety, she poured a glass of water with her other hand. Uneasily, she hesitated and looked out a frost-covered kitchen window. *What if this is the son my husband wants?* she thought. Turning to her fist, she paused, then opened it and lifted the glass of water.

"Did Mother ever tell you about the time she was going to abort you?" my 17-month-older sister asked casually as we chatted one day 35 years later.

Stunned, I stared at her and shook my head in silent disbelief. My mother did mention it briefly to me later in a letter, but in that moment I stood transfixed as my sister first told me the story—which concluded with startling simplicity:

"She told me that at the last minute, she thought, 'Maybe this is the son my husband wants'—and just threw the pills away into the trash can."

This jarring revelation stirred a host of unsettling, lifelong mysteries.

I remembered my recurrent nightmare of swimming frantically underwater and, strangely, breathing while submerged—apparently an amniotic, prenatal "memory." Once, I told a psychiatrist how I felt "trapped" and panicky in close relationships with women. Fears of death had dogged me, and a pervasive, empty sense of not belonging anywhere.

"You were a colicky baby and cried awfully, night after night," my mother had said.

"Gordon's always afraid he's going to miss something," Dad often teased me as a boy.

At the time, I was pastoring my first church out of Harvard Divinity School and, during my ministry about a year earlier, had experienced an upending supernatural encounter with Jesus (see "Healing Emotional Wounds: Seeing the Past as Jesus Sees It" in *Broken by Religion, Healed by God*). Soon after my sister told me about the plan to abort me, I began struggling with headaches and anxiety, and at last, decided to invite Jesus into my fearful memory.

FEARFUL MEMORY

Lying on the floor, I curled up in a fetal position and imagined the kitchen scene 35 years earlier as my sister had related it: myself tightly bound inside my mother's womb as she held the pills and glass of water, pausing over her decision.

As I "saw" my mother lift the pills, I began to shake in terror. "Jesus, help!" I cried out desperately. "Save me, Jesus!" As I lay trapped and trembling, in my mind's eye I saw Jesus come into the kitchen and stand by my mother. With a single gesture, he reached and swept the pills out of her hand and into the trash can.

Amazed, I watched as he then turned to me. "You don't owe your life to your mother," he declared. "It was I who stayed her hand. You belong to me."

A cool sensation of release swept over me. Sighing deeply, I lay quiet.

This watershed revelation freed me to face many unhealthy dynamics in my life—most notably, feeling overly responsible for my mother's happiness and guilty for wanting a life of my own. In the years since, I've gone back into that scene with Jesus several more times to cry out my feelings toward both my mother and father—until I could forgive them in their predicament, sense their genuine love for me, and become current with my heart.

I've identified and cast out from myself numerous related demons—from abortion and death itself to worthlessness and anxiety—which entered through my shattered defenses from that pre-natal trauma (see "How Demons Enter—and Leave" in *No Small Snakes*).

Still, the proverbial "survivor's question" yet stirs: Why me? Why was I saved when millions of other children who shared my plight have been killed? Why did Jesus not stay the hand of their mothers? Certainly, I was not saved because of any righteousness on my part in an embryonic state—nor even, as Jesus revealed, on my mother's part, thankful as I am that she "just threw the pills away."

In my dismay and unknowing, I find direction in Holocaust survivor Elie Wiesel's statement, "The role of the survivor is to testify."[19]

To tell the story of God's deliverance, that is, saves you from both the presumption of deserving and the shame of undeserving. Better, it can jar others out of complacency or despair to entertain saving power far beyond their own.

In fact, honest testimony trumps both politically correct tolerance and religiously correct dogma. "Jesus saves" is for me not about religion, but reality—as unwieldy as it is exciting.

Today, 70 years later, I remain humbled by this awesome mystery, but determined to entertain it. I'm neither obligated to dwell on it nor free to forget it.

I'm privileged to testify. The more I do, the more thankful I am to Jesus, and the more determined I am to see others experience his saving power themselves.

Is that enough to compensate for the deliverance I didn't deserve? I don't know. I only know it's all I can do, and I do it gratefully.

> The awful crunch of life-threatening reality strips the façade from religious presumption.

7

RELIGION VS. REALITY

FAITHFUL LEADERSHIP
IN A SAVAGE WORLD

So far as the Law is concerned, however, I am dead—killed by the Law itself—in order that I might live for God. I have been put to death with Christ on his cross, so that it is no longer I who live, but it is Christ who lives in me. (Galat. 2:19)

SOME YEARS AGO, A PLANE carrying a Uruguayan Christian college rugby team, their families, supporters, and crew, crashed high in the remote and freezing Andes Mountains. Chronicling their 72-day ordeal with chilling tales of heartache, avalanches, and cannibalism, Nando Parrado—an otherwise undistinguished team member who eventually trekked to gain rescue for the 16 survivors out of 45—tells the riveting story in his book *Miracle in the Andes*.[20]

The essence of authentic, ordained leadership emerges as Parrado portrays how the awful crunch of life-threatening reality strips the façade from religious presumption.

The fit young rugby players, from a church-sponsored college, were all well-trained to struggle against opposition within the humanly-created boundaries of an athletic field, game rules, and church theology. Immediately after the plane crash, the upright team captain Marcelo naturally assumes leadership over the beleaguered group. As on the rugby field, he exhorts them heroically to persevere, promising amid starvation and cold that their faith will be rewarded and a rescue plane will soon find them.

"God saved us from dying in the crash," he preaches to his struggling teammates. "Why would He do that just to leave us here to die?"

NO RESCUE

Weeks later, however, their jerry-rigged radio picks up a news broadcast that all rescue attempts have been abandoned—whereupon Marcelo breaks down and withdraws into depression.

"It troubled me to see him in such misery," Parrado puzzles over this apparent contradiction in the team's otherwise resolute leader. "He had always been a hero to me":

> Marcelo was different from the rest of us, more principled, more mature. He was... devout, followed all church teachings and tried his best to live a virtuous life. He was not a self-righteous person; in fact, he was one of the humblest guys on the team. But he knew what he believed, and often, using the same authority and quiet charisma with which he pushed us to be better teammates, he could coax us to be better men.

Morally strong, even determined to remain a virgin while single, Marcelo "seemed to know his own mind well." Thus, Parrado struggles to understand his leader's emotional collapse:

> He had thought carefully about all the important issues of his life, and he knew with clarity where he stood. For Marcelo, the world was an orderly place, watched over

by a wise and loving God who had promised to protect us. **It was our job to follow His commandments, …to love God and to love others as Jesus had taught us.** This was the wisdom that formed the foundation of his life and shaped his character.

It was also the source of his great confidence on the field, his sure-footedness as our captain, and the charisma that made him such a strong leader.

It is easy to follow a man who has no doubts. We had always trusted in Marcelo completely. How could he allow himself to falter now, when we needed him the most?

Wrestling with such apparent contradictions, Parrado reaches a startling conclusion:

Perhaps, I thought, *he was never as strong as he seemed*. But then I understood: **Marcelo had been broken not because his mind was so weak, but because it was too strong**. His faith in the rescue was absolute and unyielding: *God would not abandon us. The authorities would never leave us here to die.*

UPENDED MORAL UNIVERSE

Yet the powers of the world, with all their carefully-reasoned protocols and projections, had done just that—and thereby, upended Marcelo's ordered moral universe:

This must have felt to Marcelo like the earth beneath his feet had begun to crumble. God had turned His back, the world had been turned upside down, and all the things that had made Marcelo such a great leader—his confidence, his decisiveness, his unshakable faith in his own beliefs and decisions—now prevented him from *adjusting to the blow and finding a new balance.* (italics mine)

Here lies an exquisitely fearful assessment of most Christians today, whose faith often teeters on the false foundation of religiously correct assumptions—and therefore in the face of life-threatening evil either collapses or becomes calcified and remote.

From the outset, the rugby team's stalwart captain had urged that none risk setting out over the surrounding frozen peaks to seek help, but rather, that they should trust God and the compassion of others to persevere in rescue attempts. But now, such principled religion was revealed as not merely ineffective, but deadly.

"(Marcelo's) certainty, which had served him so well in the ordinary world," Parrado realizes, "now robbed him of *the balance and flexibility* he needed to adjust to the strange new rules by which we were battling for our lives. When the ground rules changed, Marcelo shattered like glass." (italics mine)

Graphically, ruthlessly, Parrado then portrays the subtle but ultimately lethal fallacy inherent to religious constructs and all human presumption to domesticate God in a treacherously fallen world:

> Watching as (Marcelo) quietly sobbed in the shadows, I suddenly understood that in this awful place, *too much certainty could kill us*; *ordinary civilized thinking* could cost us our lives. I vowed to myself that I would never pretend to understand these mountains. I would never *get trapped by my own expectations*. I would never pretend to know what might happen next. *The rules here were too savage and strange*, and knew I could never imagine the hardships, setbacks and horrors that might lie ahead.
>
> So I would teach myself to live in constant uncertainty, moment by moment, step by step. *I would live as if I were dead already.* With nothing to lose, nothing could surprise me, nothing could stop me from fighting; my fears would not block me from following

my instincts, and no risk would be too great.
(italics mine)

The implications of this contrast between religiously-based assumptions and reality-based experience are profound for anyone who would follow Jesus on earth—this "awful place" so "savage and strange" as to murder its very Savior.

OMINOUS LESSON

This lesson speaks ominously to a generation numbed by media fantasy and virtual reality. Thus, in a simpler yet apt portrayal, an old *New Yorker* magazine cartoon pictured a car with flat tire stopped in the rain. Outside, a soaked and haggard dad holding a tire iron shouts to his kids inside the car, "Don't you understand? We can't change the channel!"

In our domesticated, cash-and-carry culture, much Christian teaching focuses on distilling the Bible down to "scriptural principles" and exhorting others to "align with" or otherwise believe in and obey them. The take-away here—whether implicitly suggested or explicitly promised—is that God's protection, provision, and blessings follow thereupon.

Within this comfortable mindset of "ordinary civilized thinking," authority accrues to those most manifestly successful within the rules, and leadership is about urging others to follow suit and benefit similarly. **It's about what I do when I try harder, not what God does when I surrender to him more genuinely.** Such control-oriented "faith" animates demonic, self-centered New Age spirituality, from meditating on hundred-dollar bills for wealth to the bumper sticker, "Visualize World Peace"—aptly spoofed in another, "Visualize Whirled Peas."

But it's not unknown among Christians.

Certainly, scriptures emphasizing God's love and provision abound. It sounds good. In fact, like an athletic contest within game rules, it may even work—at least, within the secure boundaries of a college playing field or suburban church neighborhood, where life's basic needs are not only provided but presumed.

The orderly assumptions which uphold this religion of moral performance and God's reward are seriously upended, however, by a sinful world fallen away from God— often into evil, whose powers mock civil convention and standards of decency. Indeed, those who encounter most convincingly the power of evil and death in this world realize that only power beyond this world can save us from it.

They thereby become authentic recruits for Kingdom warfare. Even as a good soldier is always on alert, they recognize the dangerous deception and false comfort in natural, man-made rationale and defenses.

A religion based upon human performance, that is, works well as long as human beings can perform—that is, within humanly designed, protective boundaries. Inevitably, however, the "strange and savage rules" of this sinful world intrude and upend this controlled charade—as through serious illness or accident, job loss, divorce, rebellious teenaged kids, or a plane crash in the freezing mountains. Such religious presumption is thereby revealed as a deadly deception, robbing us of the "balance and flexibility" which foster the un-usual, un-worldly thinking necessary for deliverance amid un-controllable circumstances.

Certainly, it's appropriate to construct a society, as did our American forebears in our Constitution, which "insures the domestic tranquility" for its citizens and provides fair economic avenues for their "pursuit of happiness." But when such human constructs become so imbedded and assumed that **they divorce from the God who inspired them, citizens forget their vulnerability to the larger, broken—and indeed, savage—world that prompted them.**

COLLECTIVE DENIAL

This collective denial spawns "leaders" who cannot acknowledge the awful depths of the world's brokenness nor lead others through and beyond it, *because they have never dared to face it in themselves.* They function well in a domesticated and otherwise civil society. But when the awful reality of the larger world's evil intrudes—from sexual temptation and financial loss to disease and plane crashes— they shatter like glass.

The seductive spirit of passivity thereby both underlies and oversees ordered human affairs, prompting a response ranging from dismay and compassion on God's side, to scorn and torment on the side of evil.

A self-serving "protective" naiveté enables the fantasy that we're saved from sin and death by our own steadfast convictions and moral achievements. **Such deception "protects" people not from sin and death, but from the truth of our utter dependence on God—and thereby, from experiencing His freedom and saving power amid dire circumstance.** When life "crashes" and we feel trapped by its looming mountains and immobilized by its freezing winds, trusting God can mean not simply waiting passively for Him to intervene, but in fact, trusting His saving power by trekking into the wind and over the mountains for help.

A desperately lost and freezing Nando Parrado thereby learned on the brink of death that his former "ordinary civilized thinking" is a lethal deception. In that process, however, he discovered the reality of life not simply in the treacherous mountain peaks, but of life everywhere in this fallen world—yes, even in our self-secured suburban islands of civilized prosperity, where often unplanned and untidy events, from cancer to divorce, yet strike.

The pressure of Parrado's particular ordeal was severe enough to crack the shell of human denial—which, painful and devastating as that process was, nevertheless released the seed of authenticity in his God-dependent heart to grow and mature. It enabled him to see the truth at last, namely, that **in this fallen world we all live each moment on the brink of death.** What's more, as we struggle to prop up our idealized moral universe, we separate not only from real life but from God—and thereby, from His power to save us from its savagery.

LARGER REALITY

Meanwhile, a larger reality encompasses our humanly ordered society.

The devil—like God—is not impressed by moral standards or religiously correct convictions, but primarily by a broken heart surrendered to Jesus (see Ps. 51:17). He's intimidated not by "leaders" who know how to do it, but precisely by those who know Who does it. That is, by men and women who openly confess they can't do it and trust, rather, in God's greater-than-human power to do it in and through them.

The destructive schemes of evil are therefore thwarted not by religious gamers but by spiritual warriors wholly alert to uncertainty not only in the world about them, but in their own hearts. They know, often by painful, terrifying experience, that they're utterly dependent upon God not only for righteousness, but for survival itself.

Leaders in this patently uncertain universe therefore rise among those who have seen it stripped of its moderated façade, and upended by unprogrammed invasions—from tragic accidents to sexual attraction. Not certain of what lies around the next corner tomorrow, they know only that God stands with us now as always, and their life purpose unfolds only insofar as they are dependent upon, surrendered to, and trusting in Him.

To lead others in this utterly broken world dominated by greater-than-human powers is to live—in Parrado's term—as if you "were dead already."

Thus, Paul's confession to the Galatians as he compares the deadly effects of Law-bound religious posturing to the life-giving freedom in surrendering to God:

> So far as the Law is concerned, however, I am dead—killed by the Law itself—in order that I might live for God. I have been put to death with Christ on his cross, so that it is no longer I who live, but it is Christ who lives in me. This life that I live now, I live by faith in the Son of God, who loved me and gave his life for me. (Gal. 2:19,20)

The Kingdom leader is thereby freed amid life-threatening circumstances to entertain the life-giving presence of God—whose power depends neither upon outward circumstances nor our own righteousness. **Leaders who bank for their salvation on ordered moral behavior, on the other hand, "save" us not only from having to trust God, but thereby, from the very relationship with God that is our only security in a dangerously insecure world.**

The rugby captain Marcelo "trusted" God to uphold a church-sponsored religious economy, whereby his own moral lifestyle guaranteed God's saving action. When dire circumstances and the threat of death required a larger economy, his narrow concept of God could not accommodate it.

As an athlete, he should have seen the flaw in believing that God will bless you with victory because you've kept the moral boundaries/ game rules. Sooner or later, every team loses. Presumably, both teams keep the rules in any case—that's why games have referees—and a win may come about through a variety of other reasons, beyond even the skill of the players. In fact, when the playbook action falls apart, often it's the best "broken field runner"—who moves more by inner instinct than outer convention—who wins the game.

Still, even Parrado's decision to leave his fellow survivors to seek help could have been as pretentious as to stay and await rescue. Just because you're fed up and want to take matters in your own hands doesn't mean that's God's will for you to do so. **The gift of faith, that is, often comes most authentically via revelation and not determination.**

Thus, when Parrado realizes the hopelessness in awaiting rescue and that no one among them would strike out in search of help, he begins gingerly to recruit others—and discovers that eventually "many began to see me as a leader":

> Never in my life had I assumed such a role—I was the one who always drifted along, riding the current, letting others show the way. **I certainly didn't feel like a leader now. Couldn't they see how confused and frightened I was? ... For my part, I had no desire to lead anyone; I needed all my strength just to keep myself from falling apart.** I worried I was giving them false hope, but in the end I decided that false hope was better than no hope at all.

Here lie the tender but sure seeds of true Godly leadership: conferred not by title of civilized performance—from team captain to pastor—but by humble self-acceptance; not assumed by virtue of skill, but confessed by virtue of necessity and indeed, anointing.

SUPERNATURAL CONFIRMATION

As in fact, on the very night he accepts leadership, Parrado experiences a supernatural encounter:

> It was after midnight. The fuselage was dark and cold as always, and I was lying restlessly in the shallow, groggy stupor that was as close as I ever got to genuine sleep, when, out of nowhere I was jolted by a surge of joy so deep and sublime that nearly lifted me bodily from the floor. For a moment the cold vanished, as if I'd been bathed in a warm, golden light, and for the first time since the plane had crashed, I was certain I would survive.

Excitedly, Parrado awakens the others:

> "Guys, listen!" I cried. "We will be okay. I will have you home by Christmas!"
>
> My outburst seemed to puzzle the others, who only muttered softly and went back to sleep. In moments my euphoria passed. I tried all night to recapture the feeling, but it had slipped away. By morning my heart was filled once more with nothing but doubts and dread.

Thus, the supernatural gift of faith. Parrado's natural relapse into depression when nothing changes afterward, only validates the *super-natural* dimension of his vision—to which he clings thereafter for hope and determination in his death-defying trek over the mountains for help.

The entire scenario suggests a holy drama: God plants a seed of hope in His chosen leader, who—driven by threat of severe pain and loss unto death—begins to voice that hope among the others. They confirm the call by acknowledging him as the focus of that hope. The newly implied leader balks, but determines to act in spite of his fear and steps out in faith—whereupon God speaks His approval with supernatural reassurance and power to accomplish the mission.

Meanwhile, starvation looms for all as time begins to run out. In the final, astonishing act, Parrado climbs icy precipice, trudges through waist-deep snow, huddles in freezing sleet at night, and presses on until finally, he meets a farmer who leads him to a military outpost. There, helicopters are dispatched immediately to rescue the survivors, who become international celebrities.

DISDAIN FOR RELIGION

In the end, Parrado does not acknowledge God—to the dismay of his fellow Christian survivors, who chastise him for not being "grateful to God." On the heels of his newfound celebrity status, in fact, he plunges headlong and without shame into hedonistic revelry, from celebrity parties to fast women, hinting that his discounting God stems from a disdain for what he's seen of religion.

It's hard to blame him. He's seen the touted religious assumptions of his mates paralyze leadership and inspire only despair and passivity, which would have meant certain death for all.

From his conferred leadership among the men to his supernatural jolt of hope to his persevering rescue trek, Parrado experienced graphically the biblical truth that "the written Law brings death." Yet he cannot embrace its counter-focus that "the Spirit gives life" (2 Corinth. 3:6). In describing the ordeal, however, he finds only the language of faith can express this marvelous story: "It was a miracle."

Certainly, the tragedy which prompted this miracle manifested most sorely in the lives lost. Yet the more far-reaching tragedy—with due respect for the deceased and their relatives—lies here: The very heroic protagonist in this miracle could not affirm its Author precisely because **his religion had mis-defined faith as focusing on what we do when we try to be right, rather than what God does when we become real**.

This presumption among Parrado's fellow Christians that salvation is about your righteousness eliminates God from the equation, and thereby, eliminates His miracles from life—even as it would clearly have led to the death of them all. The man so duly inspired and empowered by the Spirit of God to save so many lives, thereby missed out on the most abundant life of knowing Jesus.

Nevertheless, Parrado is open and real—more so than most Christians, in fact—and in that holy sense, unsettling. We Christians today dare not let our dismay at his apparent lack of thanksgiving preclude the jarring question, How many others have been deterred from real life with Jesus by the false presumptions of religion, even in His name?

Yes, the Father sent His Son to die on the cross. But He did not kill Jesus. The Pharisaic spirit of religion did the dirty work—then, as now. In today's increasingly dangerous world, Christian leaders must walk out the truth that **authentic faith is born not in right action, but rather, in utter surrender to the Supreme Actor**—trusting that it is He alone "who works in you to will and to act according to His good purpose" (Phil. 2:13NIV).

RIGHT BUT NOT REAL

In our God-created hearts, we know the truth: There's no Easter without Good Friday, no Promised Land without its desert, no genuine closeness to God and commitment to His purposes without pain and loss severe enough to force us into His arms. Without it, we may be right, but we're not real. We have truth, but not grace, right thinking without real hearts.

You don't have to be a Christian to spot dangerous naïveté in another. You just have to be real. If you're real, God can make you right. But if you're right, the enemy will make you real via his merciless rod.

A leader, that is, takes people where they need to go. The task of authentic leadership is not, like advertising, to create and satisfy temporary desires, but rather, to stir awareness of our ultimate needs and take us where those needs can be fulfilled.

You can't lead people to a place you're not willing to go yourself. Those who have not dared face their own deepest needs and the overwhelming shame of their inability to satisfy them, who have not confronted the power of sin and death in their own lives, can only proclaim a domesticated god who offers reward for good behavior. Yet this god can not meet us amid the strange and savage realities of this fallen world which so often pre-empt such behavior.

Significantly, this "miracle in the Andes" was conceived not in moral correctness, but a heartfelt cry for saving power against overwhelming odds; was confirmed and welcomed not by righteous conviction, but through supernatural revelation, and was fulfilled not by religious obedience, but by trust that the power which birthed the vision would be present to empower it as the leader stepped out.

Christians who seek God's victory and destiny in a yet strange and savage world, take note.

> Western culture scorns spiritual reality and those who embrace it.

8

SPIRITUAL IMPERIALISM:

SECULARIZATION AND WHITE RACISM

Go figure out what this Scripture means: "I'm after mercy, not religion." I'm here to invite outsiders, not to coddle insiders. (Matt. 9:13,14TMB)

EARLY IN 1966, AS A PEACE CORPS TEACHER at a European mission high school in Nigeria, I was approached by a worried student with a startling request. "My people show me that my headache and chest pain are from someone wishing to put an evil charm on me," Nwafor declared. "We know that you have very powerful native doctors in America. I beg that you tell me the name of such doctor who can give me a powerful charm to cancel my present one and cure me."

The facts behind this young man's malady would fit neatly into a psychiatrist's casebook. He had first felt pain shortly before he was to take the do-or-die graduation exam for his West Africa Secondary Certificate. One of the few local students at our rural school, Nwafor struggled against the popular conception among his more urbanized classmates that he and his fellow villagers were backward hicks. Lost among mostly middle-class boys, Nwafor was everything he was supposed to be: unsure of himself, socially awkward behind a broad defensive smile, below average as a student, and increasingly frustrated when his diligence did not produce better grades.

JUJU AND GEOMETRY

Not far from where I taught Nwafor about congruent triangles, his father was clan guardian of the *mbari* house, the temple of the local gods. His bare-breasted, loinclothed mother could be seen on hot afternoons from our shaded classroom windows, suckling her baby while wielding a cassava hoe.

If Nwafor failed academically, not only his hard-working parents would be disappointed. No fewer than four men, from local farmers to village clerks, were contributing toward his school fees and expecting significant financial returns upon his graduation and presumed employment.

Headache enough, to be sure—but even more loomed.

Nwafor and his family had seen their local juju man conjure and wield palpable supernatural power. But now at the mission school Nwafor had wholly committed his life to a Christian religion and culture whose leaders demonstrated no spiritual power. To consult his father's local pagan *juju* shrine for healing would risk expulsion from the mission school, and thereby, death to his education, hopes for future employment, and the investment of his creditors. Meanwhile, a 60-mile round trip on borrowed bicycle to the nearest hospital had cost a month's local wages and gained him nothing but a handful of aspirin—as indeed, I myself could only offer him then.

Nwafor's case, sadly, is typical wherever the Western package of Bibles and antibiotics has been delivered to the rest of the world. His dilemma, however, is rooted long before our modern era.

In the first creation account, Adam is given authority to "rule over" over all other living creatures, both animals and plants (Genesis 1:26). The second account clarifies that God created Adam "from the dust of the ground," that is, from the very stuff of earth (Genesis 2:7). In fact, the Hebrew word *adam* suggests its root in the similar *adamah*, meaning "ground."

The biblical account clearly notes that human beings are not simply in the earth, but of it. Later hubris, however, led some to balk at this lowly estimation and infer, rather, that they themselves were not just first among, but indeed, wholly distinct and apart from other earthly creatures. These more technologically inclined peoples saw themselves as ordained to rule not only the more lowly plants and animals, but also those other human beings more closely associated with the earth than themselves—as "underdeveloped" peoples, later sanitized to "developing."

Those who impelled material progress thereby allowed the inference that peoples less materially developed and thereby more a part of the natural world than apart from it, are less than genuine human beings.

Liberal humanitarianism charged that such "Third World" cultures could only watch helplessly as the juggernaut of Western industry advanced along trails blazed by missionaries. Conservative religion, on the other hand, deemed it a moral imperative to establish dominion over those uninformed by Christianity, and therefore, presumably incapable of participating responsibly in the material progress which it heralds.

Both judgments are equally narrow if not patronizing, as they neither recognize the integrity of the non-Western mindset nor allow that its peoples played any part in shaping their own destiny. In fact, the newly Christianized Nigerian Igbos with whom I lived had not accepted Westernization meekly, nor had they been tricked into accepting it.

NECKTIES AND RELIGION

Traditional African spirituality, that is, regards religion and culture as one—even as education from a Christian school insured a worldly job later. Western culture and its boons were therefore an assumed, if not anticipated concomitant to Christianity. Only after they had embraced both and discovered that forks and neckties were not endorsed by Christ, did Africans become trapped between their spiritual past and the technological future.

"Africans do not divide life into compartments—political, economic, educational, and religious—as Westerners do," Nigerian sociologist Ako Adjei notes in his significantly titled article, "Imperialism and Spiritual Freedom." "Life, in African philosophy, is a unity that cannot be divided."[21]

The African worldview, that is, does not distinguish between natural and supernatural.

The belief that all things perceivable are real rounds out this holistic view of life. For example, a farmer once told me how a "crazy man" of his clan one day shouted at everybody to look, that standing right there among them was "a spirit." Rolling on the ground, he cried out his warning and frightened everyone.

"That crazy man could see a spirit there which no human person can see," my farmer friend declared, "so you know that he has power that passes other men." In such more integrated, spirit-centered cultures, the Western concept of "hallucination" or "imagination" does not exist. All human perceptions are respected as a valid reality with a spiritual root.

Dreams, therefore, are afforded implicit authority. Some friends in my village believed that your spirit is transported to the scene of your dreams. A neighbor of mine told me of a local hunter who, returning home empty-handed one evening, complained bitterly to his wife. During the night he arose from his bed determined to return to his hunting spot. There, he was delighted to spot the goat he had sought earlier and at last, shot it.

Proudly bearing his prize, he ran to his wife's house and knocked on her door. But of course, there was no answer; she was dead. Her worried spirit had entered into the goat to visit the hunting spot, and was killed along with the animal.

"You know that if you worry over one thing before you sleep, that thing must come into you again that night," my neighbor explained.

Such African accounts of the supernatural may be difficult for the Eurocentric mindset to entertain, but they cannot be dismissed wholesale.

ΦΙRΕCΤ ΕΧΡΕRΙΕΝCΕ

"The African's belief in supernatural phenomena is not the result of sheer imagination," as Ghanaian E. A. Asamoa has noted, "but rather the outcome of the direct physical experience in the supersensible world. While this experience is no longer first-hand, it is nevertheless true that the beliefs that are maintained today have come out of what used to be a first-hand experience."[22] Asamoa therefore reproaches the Western church for viewing African beliefs "not with the impartial eye of a neutral observer, but with that of a western man whose scientific form of civilization has cut him off from the experience of the primitive man (sic)."

Until "First World" Western peoples are able to entertain a present and active spiritual reality beyond our secularized worldview, that is, we can only disrespect "Third World" peoples—even as our numeric designations First and Third imply a distinct cultural hierarchy. No matter how much humanitarian aid we pour into their society, schools we build, teachers and doctors we send, our missionaries and emissaries of relief will find themselves at odds with their Third World hosts, because we at best disregard, and more often scorn their foundational worldview.

As South African Afrikaaner Laurens Van der Post declared,

> (T)he bigoted rationalism and the fanatic adherence of Western Man to outer physical reality and his overvaluation of the demonstrable objective world around him is the cause of much of his undoing. He is neglecting all manner of invisible and imponderable values in his power ....

Writing in 1955, at the historical sunset of European imperialism, Van der Post concluded:

> The explosions which are blowing European man out of so many parts of the

world ... are caused largely by his neglect of these great imponderables in himself—and therefore, inevitably in others.[23]

Brazilian Catholic ex-priest Leonoardo Boff portrays the counterpoint in a *Los Angeles Times* article "Young may prove challenging for Pope." Brazillians, he declares, "see the presence of God in everything. God isn't an object of faith, but of experience."[24]

Culture clash signals betrayal when Third World peoples realize that **their supernatural worldview which Westerners scorn is that of the very Bible which the Western missionaries themselves have promoted.**

Years ago, my kindergartner son came to me one day with a puzzled look. "Daddy, is there such thing as 'coincidence'?" he asked. "You know, when two things happen at the same time and nobody did anything to make them happen like that?"

"There's no word in Hebrew for 'coincidence'," I offered. In fact, a secularized culture must create an entire vocabulary to accommodate its spiritual denial, with similar words like accidental, random, intuition, happenstance, fluke, fate, misfortune, and luck.

It's one thing for those who have never heard of spiritual reality to scorn it in other cultures, but quite another for those reared in an ostensibly Christian culture to do so. In fact, it's a startling accomplishment for a people to dismiss spiritual reality whose God appears in the flesh, supernaturally heals bodies and casts out demons, then dies, is resurrected to eternal life, and returns in a non-physical body to share the boons of his life with others.

Yet many Christians today in our "modern" technological culture are so wonderfully sophisticated as to do just that. "Ah, brave, new world that has such people in it!" as Shakespeare's ingenuous Mirando ironically exclaims in *The Tempest* (Act IV, Scene 1).

SECULARIZED ELITES

Today, Western Christianity's denial of the very active spiritual reality that spawned it is increasingly recognized as toxic, even—especially—by the secularists who have sponsored that denial. As Dean David Hempton of Harvard Divinity School has declared,

Peter Berger has stated that secularization, far from being the inexorable product of modernity throughout the world, is more or less confined to Western and Central Europe, and what he calls "an international cultural elite." *In the rest of the world vibrant religious cultures are the default position, not the exception.* I see this gap between secularized cultural elites and global religious traditions as potentially one of the most dangerous things in our world. (italics mine)[25]

With commendable honesty and courage, Hempton then warns his Harvard colleagues that "The consequences need to be thought about, especially since research universities like ours recruit most of our faculty and students from Berger's secularized minorities."

The fact that our secularized worldview marks us as a minority among peoples of the world startles those of us who presume that worldview. Yet, insofar as it pervades our most esteemed educational institutions—as Harvard Dean Hempton notes—**this secular cultural bias blinds our most intelligent youth to life's deepest reality.**

What's more, secularism cannot acknowledge the reality of spiritual powers because to do so is to allow that some are more powerful than others. Thus, it requires both relativism and pluralism. Rather than face the untidy business of an honest spiritual face-off, the secular mentality retreats to an ostensibly higher, ideological view, from which all faith traditions are equally valid. Ultimately, this translates not as universal respect, but rather, wholesale condescension.

"Relativism is Western and ethno-centric," as theologian Art Lindsley counters in his book *True Truth.* "Many in the Western liberal theological tradition see all religions as basically the same. (But) how could you prove that this is the case? Even more, it seems to be the imposition of Western pluralism on other cultures' religious views."[26]

Citing Alister McGrath, Lindsley then caricatures and challenges the conceit that "it is only the educated Western liberal academic who can understand all the religions":

Their adherents (of other world religions) may believe that they have access to the truth; in fact, only the Western liberal academic has such privileged access, which is denied to those who belong to and practice such a religion....

Yet is not this approach shockingly imperialist?

The belief that all religions are ultimately expressions of the same transcendent reality is at best illusory and at worst oppressive—illusory because it lacks any substantiating basis and oppressive because it involves the systematic imposition of the agenda of those in positions of intellectual power on the religions and those who adhere to them. The liberal imposition of this pluralistic metanarrative on religions is ultimately a claim to mastery—both in the sense of having a Nietzschean authority and power to mold material according to one's own will, and in the sense of being able to relativize all the religions by having access to a privileged standpoint. (italics mine)[27]

As a Euro-centric conceit, unprecedented beyond the cultural confines of those seduced by its sophistry, secularism is thereby intimately related to white racism.

The fallenness of this world, that is, has infected humanity at its core. Its legacy festers in unmitigated shame, not only from failing to measure up to God's standard, but from being wholly incapable of doing so. "I know that good does not live in me, that is, in my human nature," as Paul lamented. "For even though the desire to do good is in me, I am not able to do it... What an unhappy man I am! Who will rescue me from this body that is taking me to death?" (Rom. 7:18,24).

That's why Jesus came. "Thanks be to God," as Paul answers himself, "who does this through our Lord Jesus Christ!" (Rom. 7:25).

Insofar as we resist this humbling truth of our inadequacy before God, we attempt by ourselves to bear its unbearable shame. It's an overwhelming task which turns many away from God and drives others deeper into religious denial. A more common—albeit cowardly—defense is simply to dump your shame onto others to bear it for you.

Thus, the foundational tenet of racism: I'm OK, precisely insofar as you're not OK.

Even as physically weak white slave owners cast their burden of manual labor upon black slaves, so spiritually weak whites have cast the shame of our human inadequacy upon people of color.

During the early civil rights rallies of the 1960s, for example, white supporters were anxious to join hands with black protesters and sing, "We Shall Overcome." But we were largely embarrassed by a black chorus of "Nobody knows the trouble I've seen/Nobody knows but Jesus."

True, we could accept such graphic and unseemly devotion to "Jesus" among black people, but only because to criticize it might sound racist—even though we'd never countenance such a thing in our own, more sophisticated churches. We therefore had to dignify spirituals because they were black—not because they dignified Jesus. Duly, inclusively, we added them to our hymnals, but not without casting them in fine print as "Irregular."[28]

Indeed, because their exclusive focus on Jesus embarrassed us, we condescendingly secularized black spirituals—no longer regarding them as worship, but rather, as an American art form, like the Christmas crèche scene at shopping malls. We all knew black people just hadn't been afforded the education we had, and were thereby vulnerable to such simplistic thinking. After all, wasn't the whole liberation movement about equal education and professional advancement?

Certainly, to us educated and professionally advanced whites it was.

What's tragic, meanwhile, is that throughout centuries if not millennia of such literal white-washing, Jesus has already borne our shame on the cross and thereby, precluded the very foundation of racism. Even as "Satan cannot cast out Satan," merely branding racists as evil only increases the shame which fuels their bigotry (Matt. 12:26).

What Euro-centric cultures like our own need to hear from the Church is not only that racism is evil, but that it's unnecessary. When you've surrendered to Jesus and through him received God's mercy for your wrongdoing, you don't need to fabricate a "lower" level of humanity to bear your shame.

MISSING LINK

The missing link between the secular and spiritual worldviews can be seen in the Igbo word *ogwu*, often translated "medicine" but significantly double-edged in meaning.

For example, people in my Peace Corps village came to me in quest of *ogwu* for physical problems such as stomachaches and knife cuts. Prior to his big examination, my student Nwafor asked me for some performance-enhancing *ogwu*. Again, I was told of a native doctor, or *dibia*, who had the very *ogwu* through which I could discover who had stolen a chicken from my yard. *Ogwu* is therefore both supernatural *and* physical, and a single man, the *dibia*, administers it.

Our dualistic world of both clergy and physicians makes the very Western mistake of saying that the *dibia* provides both drugs and charms. But among my Igbo friends, drugs and charms were seen as one and the same *ogwu*. In this worldview, **both physical and emotional maladies share their source in the spirit realm.**

I hasten to reiterate that this non-Western worldview melding both physical and emotional problems as spiritual dysfunction, is eminently biblical. Did not the Great Physician who healed the lepers come "to destroy the works of the devil" (I John 3:8b), bearing not a spirit of fear, but rather, of "power, love, and *a sound mind*" (1 Tim. 1:7 italics mine)?

"The African believes that when you get ill you are making sacrifices for your failings," as Ugandan Prince Nyabonbo notes. "Sickness," he adds, "is a gentle reminder that [one] is out of harmony with the Creator since all who are in harmony are strong of mind and of body .... To be unhealthy is to be away from Nature."[29]

Your stomach may ache from excess acid, that is, but that condition emanates from something extra-physical—for example, something you have done wrong, as sin, or from someone else who has wished you harm. Similarly, any gastro-enterologist today would agree that emotional stress can precipitate digestive disorders.

In any case, only by negotiations with the spirits via the *dibia* can your body be healed. From this view, antacids are the *ogwu* which operates independent of spirituality, and in that sense, have supplanted God.

Western medicine, that is, too often addresses symptoms, but not causes. It answers the natural question, How? but avoids the nagging super-natural question, Why? In thereby diverting attention from root spiritual issues, the scientific medical view short-circuits ultimate truth and in fact can inhibit healing.

What's more, it can beckon addiction. "Just give me the pills," the Western scientific mentality demands, "so I can continue undistracted from my plans."

While a spirit-centered perspective is entirely biblical, distinctions are clearly evident and in order. Jesus saw physical illness, for example, as rooted not only in sin but in a variety of causes. Accordingly, he exercised appropriately a variety of healing modalities—from spittle on a blind man's eyes (Matt. 8:3) to casting out a demon (Matt. 9:33) to affirming the faith of a sick man's friends (Mk. 2:8).

Our secularized worldview questions whether spirituality is to be taken seriously or not. Among spirit-centered peoples, however—like those of the Bible—the question is, Which spiritual power is most primary and authentic and thereby, most authoritative and effective? That is, **Which spiritual worldview most genuinely recognizes human needs and manifests power to fulfill them?**

To Sadducees and Pharisees—now as then—it's about either political or religious correctness. To Jesus, it's about discernment and power.

LEVEL PLAYING FIELD

The God of the Bible wants deliberately to be revealed, needing no human endorsement, but seeking only—indeed, enjoying—a level playing field. From the ancient prophet Elijah's challenging Baal worshippers to a supernatural duel (1 Kings 18:20-40), to Paul's preaching to the pagan Athenians before their statue inscribed "To an Unknown God" (Acts 17:23ff), the God of the bible chafes for a chance to reveal and demonstrate authentic spiritual power—as only a winner can.

A people who fear any power greater than their own, however, will deny and dismiss all spiritual power as unreal. In order to cover the shame of their powerlessness, they tolerantly, if not condescendingly, afford every spirituality an equal place at their table. Yet the "tolerance" which sponsors this charade in fact patronizes the various spiritualities which it hosts by implying that none mediates any real power worthy of regulating.

None, that is, except Jesus. With legal impunity, public schools and business offices today can feature every spirituality from Buddhist flags, Transcendental Meditation, and Halloween witches to Harry Potter's sorcery—but not Jesus.

By definition, the only power which must be excluded in order to perpetuate a lie is precisely that of ultimate truth. Ironically, **in singling out Jesus to be excluded from their otherwise inclusive agenda, the powers of the world betray their concession that Jesus is in fact the true God.**

It would seem that—regardless of professed religion or spiritual loyalty—in our God-created hearts we know that if you let Jesus onto the playing field, the game's over. More than even the most well-crafted Christian apologetics, *nothing so clearly witnesses to the manifest power of its God as the deliberate exclusion of Jesus from public dialog, especially by those who otherwise insist upon inclusivity.*

If Jesus were just an imaginative fantasy, how could he be such a threat as to merit wholesale exclusion—unto prompting the excluders to violate their own fundamental tenet of tolerance? Even as Jesus is often banned by far-left communistic regimes, far-right fascists, and non-Christian theocracies, so this demonstrated and politically enforced fear of Jesus implicitly concedes his power and authority.

In a secularized society, the contest for authority is seen as scientific data vs. imaginative superstition. A spirit-centered people, however—from Nigerian Igbos to the Jews of the Bible—recognize the contest as between good and evil spirits.

Western secularism, that is, has hijacked Christianity *in an effort to avoid the truth it bears about spiritual reality and the shame of our human powerlessness amid it.* This false, hybrid religion-*sans*-spirituality would focus the debate either, as the tolerant Liberal universalists, on whether the supernatural biblical events ever actually happened or, as the judgmental Conservative evangelicals, whether they still happen today.

The much ballyhooed "conflict" between these supposed opponents is but a smokescreen to hide their common fear of losing control amid powers greater than themselves. In their denial of active spiritual reality, that is, Christian Liberals and Conservatives are bedfellows.

Certainly, Pentecostal/charismatics believe in and celebrate freely the supernatural dimension of Christian faith. It remains to be seen, however, whether they can resist the lure of shame-based religion and enmity-driven politics to offer a credible third option.

The worldview which emanates from Jesus, meanwhile, understands that all reality is subsumed by spiritual powers. Its adherents walk out the truth that biblically ordained supernatural activity not only happened then but also happens today among those who would surrender to and trust the God who animates and oversees it.

Ultimately, this integrated worldview requires the question of authenticity, namely, Which supernatural events reflect the work of the true God, and which do not?

Any spiritual phenomenon, that is, must be accompanied by the power to discern it from the false. Thus, the Christian revelation includes that of Holy Spirit, who "gives….the ability to tell the difference between gifts that come from the Spirit and those that do not" (1 Corinth. 12:10).

DEMONS BELIEVE IN GOD

Many among the secularized minority might nevertheless balk at calling themselves atheists and concede that they "believe in God." From a Christian perspective, however, **authentic faith is not simply believing that spiritual power—even God—is real.** "Do you believe that there is only one God?" as James scoffs. "Good! The demons also believe—and tremble in fear" (James 2:19).

Demons most certainly believe in God (see Mark 1:24). They do not, however, submit to Him. Indeed, they fear the God of Jesus because, unlike us spiritually-challenged Westerners, they know that this God is all-powerful and deliberately active even today to overcome their kingdom of darkness. As a loving Father, among other personae, God is as decisively intolerant of evil as any parents of an act that would harm their children (see Psalm 46:8-10).

Too many Christians today have less spiritual maturity than a demon.

Traditional African spirituality, meanwhile, shares the Judeo-Christian biblical worldview. "The African believes that there are two kinds of superhuman beings: the good and the evil ones," noted the late Nigerian statesman Mbonu Ojike in his book *My Africa*. "When he experiences flood, hurricane, or pestilence, he says it is caused by the evil god. The West calls such events acts of God, …[which] means disasters that by the science of today are non-preventable."[30]

From the African perspective, our secularized Western culture explains God out of bodily experience. Among us, God is not dead, but merely anesthetized and indeed, banished. The idea that divine power could be so pedestrian as to speak through a stomachache seems profane to our scientific mentality. We allow that God is "imponderable" not out of respect, but rather, disdain—in order to get supernatural power and the shameful truth of our un-Godly impotence off the radar screen.

To posit that divine power functions only in the realm of the unknown is to exclude God from what we know. **Too often, our "scientific" efforts at knowing thereby push God away rather than invite revelation of divine purpose in the order and intricacies of life.** We may even sigh with relief that since the advent of astronauts, God has retreated further into space. "I flew into space," as Yuri Gagarin, the first cosmonaut from the Soviet regime was quick to proclaim, "but did not see God there."[31]

Yet any humble observer of nature's intricate order amid life's unfathomable complexity might be led to confess, "I don't have enough faith to be an atheist."

MIND-BODY SPLIT

When Western medicine and education were first established in Africa as religious mission enterprises, anxiety over Christianity and its apparent mind-body split was temporarily eased by dramatic medical advances. In the early 1930's, for example, mission doctors in Nigeria halted virtually overnight a widespread epidemic of yaws, a painful skin disease, with a single injection.

Indigenous *dibia* had not been able to cure yaws. The white man's antibodies thereby pre-empted the *dibia* and wiped out local spiritual authority along with the disease.

In a spirit-centered culture, medications developed by Western science were nevertheless regarded as *ogwu* and their healing effects as spiritual miracles. The anti-yaws injection was therefore not forgotten. But neither was the confusion it stirred resolved—resulting in practices both unscientific and ungodly.

Years later, for example, many of my local friends held a blind faith in the injection as a cure-all. A pharmacist near my school always kept a syringe of distilled water handy to validate his "prescription." Being painful, the shot reinforced the popular notion, as one villager told me, that "without hurting or taking something from you, *ogwu* can never work"—even as children we all knew that merthiolate, which stings, must be more effective than mercurochrome, which does not.

CIRCUMCISION AND MORALITY

In a cultural example, circumcision commonly accompanies the Igbo rite of passage for boys, which makes no distinction between the physical operation and the social values which are taught during the weeklong initiation ceremony. "Circumcision," as the late Kenyan premier Jomo Kenyatta declared in his *Facing Mt. Kenya*, "is merely a body mutilation which is regarded as the *conditio sine qua non* of the whole teaching of tribal law, religion, and morality."[32]

Similarly, in the Hebrew Testament worldview, God's covenant of destiny with Abraham and the Jewish people is sealed by circumcision.

The New Covenant, meanwhile, clearly proclaims that the work of Holy Spirit has superseded the practice of bodily circumcision (see Romans 2:28,29). Nevertheless, Western Christians must learn to set aside our narrow view of pain as merely a wasteful by-product of the more functional life processes. Rather, we need to see that pain may be ordained to create sensitivity—as when, through the pain of adolescent circumcision, a young man becomes alive to his cultural heritage.

"I will abandon my people until they have suffered enough for their sins and come looking for me," as Hosea prophesied. "Perhaps in their suffering they will try to find me" (Hosea 5;15). While Christians may disavow the superficial ritual cut of males, we must be willing to allow the notion of God's working out His purposes in the midst of suffering—else we miss the message and power in the cross (see Rom. 2:28,29).

Certainly, a distinction between male and female circumcision is necessary. The former bears not only biblical antecedent but also some medical endorsement as a deterrent to disease. The female procedure bears no such endorsements, but rather, must surely grieve God in its misogynist effort to deprive the woman of sexual pleasure so she will not be tempted to stray from her husband.

In any case, when Western missionaries arrived on the scene accompanied by physicians—even as doctors themselves, such as Albert Schweitzer—they therefore did not realize that **to affect an African's body is to tamper with his or her spirit.** Whether imposed by natural malady or tribal ritual, bodily pain and other sensations are seen as reflections of one's spiritual state—even as communication from the gods.

As Western doctors were stopping pain, African gods were therefore being sterilized—and supplanted. Thus, Van der Post declared,

> The enormous power the European had over physical things—which you must remember were never merely physical things to the African, but containers of all-powerful spirits—convinced him that the European was more than human.[33]

Meanwhile, the Igbo man—though he wore a necktie to Sunday morning services —embraced Christianity with his own set of expectations. "So your own American spirits have wings to fly with, like a bird?" our school carpenter commented when he saw a picture of angels in my Bible. "Sometimes we have that spirit in Igboland ourselves," he added, and proceeded to tell me a story he had heard from his grandfather about one flying spirit which seized men's heads in the night.

Again, while African spirituality may on occasion strain Western sensibilities, **the authentic contest for African hearts—as ultimately, for all of us—is not between secularism and spirituality, but between true spirituality and false spirituality.**

HONORABLE ALTERNATIVE

While Western medicine has unquestionably brought widespread healing and relief to other cultures, nevertheless it does not address the essential spiritual dimension of reality. "What is deplorable," Van der Post laments in detailing Europeans' destruction of African spirituality, "is that, having discredited this ancient way of living, we have not put an honorable alternative in its place."[34]

This, of course, is the challenge of Western Christians today—not just in overseas missions, but within our own, secularized culture.

Long after his yaws had been cured, that is, the Igbo convert wanted to know just what sin of his own or what scheming enemy had caused such a disease to befall him in the first place. Thus, the stage was set for a profound moral crisis.

Clearly, Christ's wonderful medical *ogwu* protects us from sickness—and thereby, from both from our own sins and the ill-will of our enemies. With Christ, therefore, you can do what you like without fear of suffering. And whatever misfortune does in fact befall you is not necessarily the consequence of your own misdoing, but merely God's whim.

"Destroy...reverence and fear of the unknown, the ever-present, the all-seeing and the all-powerful," Ojike warned, "and you have severed the religious fibers that bind man to man in families, societies, and nations."[35]

Indeed, could the aggressive secularism of our "modern" dualistic culture blind us to a spiritual factor today in such otherwise apparently unrelated maladies as divorce, racism, and bodily disease?

Amid such confusion, educated young Africans are beginning to question the price of Christ's *ogwu* with bold honesty. We American Christians must listen to them. Need the sterilized needle kill spiritual sensitivity along with pain? As machines and medical science save us from so much pain and effort, is there yet no room for God's manifest activity in our everyday life?

My former student Nwafor and the millions of other Third World people simply cannot wait for the answers to these and other burning questions to filter back to Africa from the "Christian homeland" in the West. Unable to embrace either the insufficient spirituality of their ancestors nor the spiritual void in a secularized Western future, they're lost in their own country.

UNYIELDING QUESTIONS

That African criticism of the Church has been largely redemptive and not destructive is no affirmation of Western Christianity. Africans are quite aware that they cannot return to their traditional religion, any more than modern technology can inject into them a new spirituality along with its antibodies. Nwafor's traditional faith has not been totally destroyed, but stripped down to a core of unyielding questions about the imponderable world both about and within us.

For generations now, he has been in limbo, waiting for Christianity to break free of the West and admit the whole Nwafor—*not just his mind in school or his body in labor, but his spirit in all life aspects as well.* Before we can answer Nwafor's questions, however, we must listen to him. "To ignore African religion is to ignore a part of theology itself," as Ojike declared.

Listening to a people struggling to integrate spiritual reality and material technology should not seem so strange for us in the Western world, for that, in fact, is our human struggle as well. This becomes difficult only—and precisely—insofar as we have forgotten and even suppressed spiritual reality in and among ourselves.

"(Human beings) cannot achieve publicly what they have not achieved within the private bounds of their own personality," as Van Der Post notes.[36]

Certainly, we whose secularized worldview precipitated this global dilemma bear some responsibility to foster its resolution.

We may begin by confessing that our Euro-centric hubris denies the spirit realm because it hosts super-natural powers far greater than our own natural abilities. This disparity between God's power and our own has bred shame among us so desperate to hide our inadequacy. We become jealous of more humble peoples who freely embrace spiritual reality and we fear their threat to expose our charade.

Thus, we displace our shame upon them in racism.

The issue before Euro-centric cultures today is no longer whether Western religion can replace Third World spiritualism, but whether Christianity can survive Western secularism. Our resolute fear of losing control by acknowledging spiritual power has become a death grip on the Church, virtually suffocating the faith since it became lodged in Europe millennia ago.

Secularism fosters pluralism and its underlying disrespect of spirituality. In order to avoid judging one faith, that is, secularized Western culture grants no palpable reality to any. Our lofty acceptance of all religions is thereby revealed as simply a judgmental scorning of spiritual reality in all forms of expression.

Among Third World peoples, mere ideological tolerance for others' religion translates not as noble grace, but as patronizing disrespect. Thus, Harvard theologian Harvey Cox notes that in dialoging with persons of other faiths, whenever he "tried to avoid talking about Jesus too quickly," he discovered that "they did not believe they were really engaged in a brass tacks conversation with a Christian until that happened."[37]

Indeed, as other cultures reel from the intrusion and ultimate emptiness of Western secularism, our sophisticated "tolerance" is revealed as a cheap cop-out from facing spiritual reality, the vulnerability it reveals, and the fear of powerlessness which it engenders. While often others appreciate the boons of Western technology and material generosity, most have suffered enough deadly deprivation to distrust the promises of such "advances."

The struggling peoples of the world today deserve not only our compassion and material aid, but our respect for their worldview. From internal wars to starvation and disease, they experience firsthand and live daily amid spiritual warfare which commands participation of every human being as a child of God. From the front lines of battle, their ordeal compels us not to retreat from that conflict behind a more sanitary rational "higher ground," but rather, to enter it on their side, fully acknowledging and engaging spiritual reality in its promise of saving power.

Knowing that our generosity comes from an ostensibly Christian culture, **they are therefore confounded not only by our spiritual ignorance but especially by our spiritual impotence.** Why, indeed, cannot these followers of a resurrected "Savior" break the power of evil—even as their holy Bible describes—and set people like my student Nwafor free from destructive, clearly evil forces?

Furthermore, Western "tolerance of all faiths" ignores the very real consequences of religious beliefs among those who—unlike Eurocentric Christians—take the supernatural claims of their faith altogether seriously.

For example, Europe has for some time now faced an increasing immigrant Muslim population, whose core beliefs are often at odds with European social, political, and religious convictions. With virtually no spiritual moorings of its own, Europe finds itself with few resources to engage the issue beyond either atavistic racism or passivity.

Europeans, as others have noted, are attempting to engage religion with non-religion—and creating only deeper division and discord.

ANTIDOTE TO MATERIALISM

In scorning spiritual reality, secularism breeds materialism. At its root, however, the materialism which plagues secularized Western culture is not a wholesale focus on physical comforts, but rather, a denial of any reality beyond what human senses can perceive or natural power can control. **The antidote to materialism, therefore, is not frugal self-denial, but authentic spirituality.**

In our God-created hearts, from nightmares to death itself, we know the truth: that spiritual reality is not only active, but encompasses power far greater than our own. The problem is not only that Western civilization has invaded and overrun Third World cultures, but that *it has domesticated if not disowned the manifestly engaging and powerful Christian spirituality which birthed it.*

Cultures and races which accept spiritual reality and indeed, live intentionally within it, thereby become a threat to Western cultures, insofar as the former would reveal the shame of our ultimate short-sightedness—and powerlessness. Western governments have historically sought not only to deny political and military power to Third World peoples, but indeed, to destroy their spiritual acumen by schooling their children rather to focus exclusively on objective natural reality. Such spiritual imperialism has undermined respect not only for Western culture, but for the God its missionaries so faithfully and tirelessly have worked to reveal.

Today, spiritual sensibility threatens to become extinct in the Western world. Severing ourselves from ultimate reality, however, does not change the nature of that reality—nor indeed, satisfy our hunger for it.

To deny spiritual reality requires denying the innate human longing for connection beyond our natural abilities. Since that reality lies at the very root of our existence, it cannot be eliminated, but rather, **surfaces among white peoples as a jealousy toward people of color, who rather, have embraced it.** Euro-centric bias against an active, supernatural spirituality is thereby the fountainhead of white ethnic and racial prejudice.

Thus, among Europeans themselves, British disdain for the Irish—whose culture embraces a lively spirituality in music, dance, and mythology. In the film *The Commitments*, for example, a group of struggling inner city Irish youth form a band with that name and devote themselves entirely to covering black American soul music. "After all," the group's founder declares, "we Irish are the n—rs of Europe."

Abdicating its spiritual root has debilitated the Western Church—but has not changed that root, which cries out today for restoration. The credibility today in our Western Christian witness lies **not in whether we can rescue others for Jesus, but whether we can rescue Jesus from "our" Church.**

Not without irony, God has begun sending other peoples to help us.

By the mid-20th century, American hunters had wiped out the wolf population in our forests. More recently, we've imported extant Canadian wolves in order to repopulate and reinvigorate the American wilderness. Similarly, Western Christians may look today to Third World peoples to help restore a flourishing spiritual worldview to our increasingly barren, secularized landscape.

REVERSE MISSIONS

In fact, while isolated pockets of Christian renewal do exist in Europe, overwhelmingly the greatest growth of Christianity today is taking place in the Southern hemisphere—Africa, South America, and Asia. Those who have not been shamed and educated out of spiritual reality, that is, are embracing Jesus in the supernatural presence and power of his Holy Spirit. What's more, many are coming as "reverse missions"[38] to the US and Europe, founding large and successful churches which confess and move powerfully in the fullness of spiritual reality.

In fact, the fastest-growing church in England—as of this writing at 10,000 members—the Kingsway International Christian Center in London, is pastored by Nigerian Matthew Ashimolowo, who was born a Muslim.[39] Arising out of the Nigerian revival in the 1970's, he and a number of his countrymen went to Europe **"believing in the supernatural and also believing that God is able to do the supernatural."**

As Ashimolow explains,

> So when (Africans) come into a post-Christian Europe, shall I say, a very atheistic Europe, they carry the faith they've known and they stand-out and they run the church the way they believe they've seen it elsewhere (as in Africa). And I believe God honors those who are daring enough like Daniel, and the three Hebrew men, to stand-out.

Ashimolow sees himself and these other African pastors as a "living sign and wonder" to the otherwise declining church in Europe. "God has a reason for using blacks in the diaspora to start something," he declares.

Thus, even as African-American William Seymour sparked the 1906 Pentecostal Azusa Street revival in Los Angeles, today a number of Episcopal churches in America are severing ties with their US denomination to come rather under the authority of the East African

Anglican communion, which they regard as more authentically Christian in its view of sexuality.

In the American church today, deliberate, well-funded, and well-intentioned programs among liberal-universalists promote "racial equality." Conservative-evangelicals support many overseas missions and pray for people of color around the world. Yet both constituencies in the US remain overwhelmingly white—and not coincidentally, in spiritual denial.

Pentecostal/charismatic fellowships, meanwhile—which at their best focus on the supernatural work of the Holy Spirit instead of humanly-driven programs—are by far the most racially integrated.

What, indeed, caused Western civilization to abandon its spiritual roots?

No doubt our unprecedented material prosperity and advanced weaponry has infatuated us with our natural abilities and distracted us from supernatural reality. Ironically, however, the answer may lie in our very pursuit of such Christian values as individual rights and egalitarian freedoms.

Under the banner of "Liberty, Equality, and Brotherhood," in fact, the eighteenth-century European "Enlightenment" ushered a spiritual dark ages into the continent. As Van der Post laments,[40]

> When the excessively nationalistic trend
> in French history reached its social climax in
> revolution, there was an official ceremony in
> Paris at which God was deposed and a goddess
> of reason crowned in His place.

The exalting of natural human power over God's thereby became ensconced in Europe, and thereafter "was deep at work in (the European's) spirit, setting him at variance with his intuitions and instinct."[41] Today, therefore, "the European's own eye is so darkened that he can no longer see himself or the things round about him in their full reality."[42]

A tree without roots is a tree without fruits. Unto today, neither the West's consumption-oriented economy nor its "virtuous, disapproving"[43] religion can satisfy the innate human longing to connect with our authentic spiritual root and participate together in its power to overcome the world's brokenness. Failing to do so, however, will allow the shame of this failure to drive us further apart from others.

If we in the West are to become active, mutually supportive agents in the hopeful future of a broken world, we must therefore own our belonging to it in its entirety—not just in its economic, educational, and technological enterprise, but in the spiritual reality which undergirds it and infuses us all.

> When the wound becomes normative, the healed
> become outcasts and the Healer gets crucified.

9

HOMOSEXUALITY AND THE FATHER-WOUND

OUTING THE MAN-HATING SPIRIT

> *See, I will send you the prophet Elijah
> before that great and terrible day of the Lord
> comes. He will turn the hearts of the fathers to
> their children, and the hearts of the children to
> their fathers; or else I will come and strike the
> land with a curse.* (Malachi 4:5,6NIV)

MARRIED AND A GRANDFATHER AT 50, George (not his real name) had engaged in many homosexual relationships until three years earlier, when he became a Christian and renounced them all. Lately, however, same-sex desires had resurfaced, and he came to me for help.

Uncertain, I offered to pray with him in his struggle.

"Father, I'm so fed up with this," he cried out. "Please, Jesus, come and do whatever it takes to overcome these desires in me!"

Surprisingly, a memory soon came to George's mind when, at 5 years old, he huddled terrified under the kitchen table as his raging father, with fist raised, was yelling at his mother. "I was scared to death of him!" George declared, shaking even as he talked so many years later.

I invited George to hold in his mind that memory of trembling under the table, and ask Jesus to come to him in the kitchen and do whatever He might want.

"Yes, Jesus, please come and be with me in the kitchen," he pleaded. "I need you here, Jesus! Do whatever you want!"

I prayed quietly—if not uneasily. Moments later, George sat up, his eyes still closed but eyebrows raised. "Jesus is here!" he burst out excitedly. "He's right there, standing in the middle of the kitchen and....and now He's reaching down and picking me up. He's holding me in His arms! I can feel the strength in Him. He's talking to me. He says, 'It's OK. I've got you safe in my arms now'."

"Let Jesus hold you," I offered, "and receive His strength."

I looked and saw George smile, relax for a moment—and then stiffen. "But Dad's still angry and yelling at Mom!" he said, his eyes now squinting in fear.

Hesitantly, I forged ahead. "Jesus said, 'Whoever has seen me has seen the Father'," I noted. "Now that you're safe and secure in your true Father's arms, why don't you speak up and tell your dad once and for all how you feel about what he's doing?"

JUST HOLD ME

"Daddy, STOP IT!" George burst out immediately. "Stop yelling at Mommy like that! You scare me so much. Stop yelling, Daddy! Stop and...and just...just hold me, Daddy!" George's head fell into his hands and he began sobbing uncontrollably. "Please, Daddy," he managed, gasping for breath, "please, hold me...."

Later, George sat quietly amazed. **"Now I see where that desire for a man to hold me came from,"** he said. **"I did want a man to hold me—but not some other guy. I wanted my dad.** But he was so big and out of control—it was just too scary for me to let myself feel that vulnerable to him. So everything got mis-directed toward other men instead."

George noted that when he prayed, Jesus had come with palpable masculine strength—which he could feel from Jesus' arms and receive—bearing courage enough even to stand up at last to his abusive father. "I've always felt so weak as a man," he sighed. "I can see now that when I went looking to draw strength from some other guy through sex, it was just that wounded little boy in me looking to get manly strength from Dad. That's why I always felt attracted to bigger, muscular guys. But really, all they did was take from me and leave me feeling weaker and abused—just like when I was a boy with Dad."

That day, George met his true Father and experienced graphically His masculine strength through Jesus.

In order to heal his image of manhood, I knew George would need to see his father from God's perspective. So I then invited George to pray, "Jesus, show me my dad the way you see him."

As he did so, George sensed clearly that his father had been similarly wounded by his own father (George's grandfather) as a boy himself. Eventually, George was able to cry for his wounded father. "I realize now that you just hurt me the same way your father hurt you," he spoke out. "I forgive you, Dad, for not controlling your anger and scaring me so much—and **for making me afraid to be a man**."

I knew also that enemy spirits often enter by taking advantage of wounds and fears (see "How Demons Enter—and Leave," in *No Small Snakes*). As we prayed further, a deep anger surged up in George toward his father. We prayed, and sensed a demon of anger in his father, which had manifested that day in the kitchen toward George's mother and passed down to him. He renounced and cast it out.

MAN-HATING SPIRIT

As we prayed further, however, we sensed an even deeper spirit underlying the anger. Eventually, the name "man-hating" came into my mind. I had encountered that spirit before in women, especially those who had been abused by men. But how, I wondered, could a man-hating spirit enter a man?

Eventually, I understood: to stand weak and frightened before his angry, overpowering father feels dangerous to a little boy. Yet it's not natural for a boy to hate his father, so he needs super-natural power to do it. Here, the father of Lies is happy to oblige, with a man-hating spirit. The boy receives this readily, as it fabricates a sense of strength and power before men—**but it cuts him off from trusting friendships with other men and indeed, leads him ultimately to hate his own masculinity**.

Seeing this deception at last, George prayed with a boldness and strength that surprised him. "In the name of Jesus, I set the cross between my father and me, between him and his father," he declared, "and I bind you, man-hating spirit in me and command you in Jesus' name to get out of me and go into the hands of Jesus!"

We then asked that the blood of Jesus would cleanse his natural bloodline of this evil, and that Father God would replace it with a spirit of true manhood **and the freedom to embrace it in himself—instead of grasping after it in other men.**

"Father God," I prayed, "let George know the joy in his manhood that is Your joy in him as Your son."

George had much healing work yet to do—including casting out such spirits as lust, perversion, and eventually, homosexuality itself—but these powerful revelations of God's truth and grace in Jesus set the course for his struggle and spurred him later to persevere (see John 1:17).

A note: while a demon of homosexuality has emerged in most men I've ministered to struggling with same-sex attraction, this knowledge must be complemented with wisdom to know when to cast it out. Most often, it's rooted in deep wounds which have hosted the demon. To cast out the evil spirit without healing its roots only beckons more demons (see Matt. 12:43-45). Be sure to respect the man's emotionality and trust Holy Spirit's timing.

My years of ministry experience since then suggest that a man-hating spirit is the fountainhead of homosexual desire, often focusing on a father who is either abusive or absent physically or emotionally. I've noticed, for example, that the second son of such a father especially may draw this spirit by feeling less than his older brother in his father's eyes, leading him to hate both Dad and his older brother. Often, the second son takes refuge in Mom, and hides from his masculinity within a feminine worldview.

In many cases, a man has been sexually molested as a boy by an older male and hates him for it—or hates his father for not protecting him from it. Whether the boy "inherits" it generationally from his father or mother (who hated his or her father) or draws it from boyhood wounding, the man-hating spirit "broadcasts" from within him, attracting other men similarly broken—even molestors, who most often were molested themselves as boys (see "Kick Me Spirits" in *No Small Snakes*).

George, meanwhile, saw his mother as the weak one before his father—in fact, as the victim, like himself. **Too scared to identify with masculinity, as falsely caricatured in his abusive father, George instead was drawn to identify with his mother and her weakness.**

OVER-BONDING TO MOM

In fact, she had often been seductive toward him, even holding him as a boy both for his protection and for her own comfort from her husband's outbursts. So he bonded with his mother and withdrew from his masculinity, seeking an apparently safer identity in femininity.

At first, it seemed to me counter-intuitive that a man-hating spirit would fuel homosexual desires. Obviously, homosexuals are not attracted to women; why, rather, would not a woman-hating spirit be the culprit?

Clearly, however, George was drawn to his mother, not repulsed by her. Furthermore, if homosexuals were driven by a woman-hating spirit, then they would scorn and avoid beauty parlors, fashion design, interior decoration, and other largely feminine environs. But more often, they participate widely in such arenas.

Certainly, in the realm of sexuality, mysteries abound. But I would offer the following rationale to support my conclusion:

A man wants a woman most strongly when he feels good about himself as a man. When he does not, he avoids the woman, because he fears the shame when she sees his inadequacy and the likelihood that she'll reject him for it.

The man-hating spirit causes a man to hate not only other men and masculine endeavors, but eventually, to hate his own masculinity. In that self-deprecating state, he fears approaching the woman as a man.

If at the outset he can say, "I'm not a good/true man," the pressure is off; he need not measure up to any standard and thereby avoids any shame for not doing so. He can be around a woman, even be like her, but he cannot engage her with the manly centeredness, compassion, and strength necessary for ongoing emotional and physical intimacy with her.

The spiritual dilemma is this: a man cannot naturally hate his own masculinity. But a man who becomes broken and disconnected from his true masculinity knows if he tries to embrace it and move toward the woman, he will fail—and thereby, be overwhelmed with shame.

He needs supernatural power to change this.

If he takes his shame to the Father of Truth revealed in Jesus, the man will experience his true Father's grace, thereby be removed of his shame and begin the process of healing his masculinity and loving a woman.

SHAME OF INADEQUACY

If, on the other hand, the man chooses not to go Jesus, the father of Lies will oblige. Seductively, this evil father mimics Jesus and promises, "I'll save you from your shame." Unlike Jesus, however, he cannot remove shame, but only cover it up. "I'll make sure you avoid the shame of your inadequacy by never having an occasion to stir it—that is, by keeping your heart and body closed to the woman."

In the absence of the Father of Truth, the man's spirit subconsciously completes the transaction, and welcomes a man-hating spirit into him.

Stories similar to George's from many men have thereby led me to regard homosexual desire as preeminently unreal—a mis-focused distortion of otherwise genuine, but frustrated, longing for Daddy and his saving strength. It's like an addiction, generated by deep emotional pain and fueled by shame, maintained by a compulsion to cover these up.

An addict's most common defense against this truth is therefore denial, by dumping his or her shame on others. Thus, the common accusation from homosexuals that those who differ from their view are homophobic.

But this is like accusing a man lost in the jungle of fearing snakes. Certainly, in a fatherless culture like ours, gender insecurity—and thereby, homophobia—abounds. "An old man shakes at the mention of bones," goes the Igbo proverb from my Peace Corps hosts in Nigeria. Homosexuals are feared because they have capitulated to the wound which most of us men share today—and which our otherwise vaunted medical science can't heal.

But just because you're paranoid, as the saying goes, doesn't mean they're not out to get you. Same-sex attraction can be renounced wherever honest people face the truth of its genesis. **But it's feared where men deny their own wound and consequent susceptibility.**

An addictive society shuns self-honesty and instead, casts its shame upon the truth-teller. That's how Jesus got crucified.

"I'm not an alcoholic," the addict charges; "you're just judgmental!" Or, similarly, "Nothing's wrong with my homosexuality—you're just homophobic!"

Addicts are sustained largely by others so wounded themselves that they fear the addict's judgment, and are intimidated by such shame into silence and even complicity. Thus, the term "codependent," for those who—often the emotionally blinded children of addicts— **make excuses for the addict or otherwise enable him/her to avoid facing the truth that would expose the addiction and allow it to be healed.**

At a city-wide clergy meeting I once attended, for example, several local oldine denominational pastors advocating "tolerance and acceptance" promoted a seminar entitled, "Toward a Compassionate View of Homosexuality."

"You've stacked the deck with your very title," an ordained Christian therapist among us countered. "It presumes that everyone who disagrees with you is not compassionate. Some of us here don't think it's 'compassionate' to abandon a brother in his brokenness."

Is homosexual impulse inborn? My ministry experience suggests that, apart from inherited/generational spirits, it is not. Even if same-sex desires were inborn, however, from a Christian view, so is sin (see John 9:34). In this fallen world, congenital disorders abound, from hare lip to cerebral palsy. Just because you're "born that way" doesn't mean it's good or God's will. Rather, it's an occasion for medical researchers to heal it. In fact, scientific research has revealed a credible genetic predisposition to alcoholism. But even as Jesus has come to overcome the effects of sin, no one parades for "Alcoholic Pride."

HOMOPHOBIA AND THE FATHER-WOUND

The father properly confirms masculinity in a boy, stirring him by winsome example to want to become a man, like himself (see "Seeking the Brown Ooze" in *Sons of the Father*). Sadly, tragically, few men today have received this blessing from their fathers.

Yet, at a recent men's conference, I asked 150 Christian men, "How many of you did your father talk to you about your sexuality when you were growing up?" Only two hands went up. On another occasion, I asked 350 Christian fathers, "For how many of you, when you first became a father, did your own father come to offer you comfort, support, encouragement, or advice?" Only five hands.

Indeed, most men today *are* homophobic—because the father-wound that fuels homosexual desires is today so vast and pervasive that it's become normative.

The man-hating spirit in a fatherless world drives homosexuality. Today, more than 40% of boys in America are being raised without their blood father in the home. No wonder the feminized politically correct mindset—loosed by father-abandoned post-WWII boomers—has swept our culture.

When a wound becomes normative, the healed become outcasts, and the Healer gets crucified.

Co-dependently accommodating the father-wound and its destructive effects, our entire society has become an addictive system, so accustomed to being wounded that we've forgotten what healed looks like. Emotionally crippled and spiritually starved, we can neither weep for men trapped in same-sex desires nor stand and offer them hope for freedom. Desperately, we trade uncomfortable truth for manageable ideology, covering our shame with a patronizing "tolerant" or "more compassionate" worldview.

When such epidemic shame reaches a tipping point, the greatest aspiration of society becomes not to hurt anyone. It's a good thing surgeons don't feel that way! Surgery, like the truth, often hurts. **Those who want to be healed more than they want to hide their shame, however, not only submit to the operation, but determinedly seek it.**

This, at last, marks a real man—not one who's never had a same-sex impulse, but who faces the truth squarely and pushes through pain which fuels that impulse unto revelation and healing. In that process, he discovers that manhood is not about either politically correct ideology or religiously correct morality, but rather, trusting relationship at last with your true Father revealed in Jesus—the Father, in fact, "from whom all fatherhood, in heaven and on earth, receives its true name" (Ephes. 3:14 NIV footnote).

Those who by faith enter into that relationship soon discover that a good Father does command sexual boundaries—not to deprive His children of pleasure, but to protect them from pain. **Only a cruel god, in fact, would command behavior without providing the power to walk it out.**

Thus, the Father God who has told us to limit sexual expression to man and woman in covenanted relationship before Him, is present unto today in His Spirit to empower us to do so. Self-control, in fact, is defined biblically as a "fruit of the Spirit" (Galat. 5:22). It's not the natural result of your effort, but the super-natural result of God's effort.

Harry, single and a 32-year-old banker, came to me struggling with a host of sexual compulsions, including same-sex desires. Over several months of prayer, he revisited with Jesus painful scenes of being emotionally and physically abused by both his parents, and was then able to forgive them genuinely, from his heart.

He confessed his own sins and received Father God's forgiveness. He cast numerous demons from himself, from lust and perversion to man-hating and sensuality, asking Holy Spirit to replace them with respect, purity, philia (brotherly love), and sensitivity. As a result, he was even beginning to pray for a wife.

And then one day, he came to my office deeply worried.

"My boss is sending me to our Los Angeles office to meet a client," he said, his voice wavering. "I know every massage parlor within blocks of that place. I have phone numbers of neighborhood prostitutes, both male and female, branded in my brain. I'm scared I'm going to fall!"

I would not be able to protect Harry on his trip into the proverbial asphalt jungle of LA. But I knew Who would.

I remembered that when Joshua was on the threshold of Jericho, his most significant and thus most fearful mission, he did not desperately formulate a future plan for Israel. Rather, he gathered the people of God and reminded them of how He had delivered them in their past (see Joshua 24).

SOLID HISTORY

Fortified by solid history testifying to their God's saving power, the people of God remembered His presence and power, and were thereby spurred to press ahead courageously into the uncertain future.

And so I encouraged Harry to remember all the times he had gone to Jesus in his prayers, all the times Jesus had shown up to uncover truth and lead him into healing and deliverance. We did so and, gingerly, I sent him on his way.

The next week, he came into my office looking rested and in good spirits.

"How did the trip go?" I asked very casually, straining to cover my fears.

"Well, we ran into some bad traffic at first, but we just made it on time. In fact,...."

"But how did the trip go?" I interrupted.

"Pretty good," Harry declared, nodding in self-approval. "We didn't get exactly the terms we wanted for the contract, but..."

"But how did the trip go?" I interrupted again.

Harry drew back, perturbed. "I'm telling you how it went!"

"Alright," I said at last, "let's cut to the chase. What about the massage parlors and prostitutes and all?"

Startled, Harry sat up with amazement in his eyes. "Oh, I see what you mean," he murmured, with a growing smile. "Actually.... well, you know, I never even thought about all that! I didn't even masturbate!" Lost in wonder, Harry sat glowing with joy. "I guess God….just took care of me!"

Harry had more healing work yet to do, but that experience became a solid turning point in his faith that allowed him to trust his Father for whatever lay ahead. He realized that he did not choose his parents, that their abuse of him stemmed not from any defect in himself but rather, from their own childhood wounds displaced onto him. He thereby learned that it's not shameful to have same-sex desires, but only to hide them and not receive Father God's power to overcome them.

Over the years, I've been privileged to meet and minister to many heroic men like George and Harry, who have courageously faced their spiritual/emotional wound, taken it to Jesus, and determined to persevere after His deliverance and healing. **As with most brokenness in this fallen world, often it's not an instant "cure, " but rather, a process of painful honesty, terrifying surrender, and ongoing trust.**

While the Father's heart is to heal His children, He does so in order to facilitate His larger purposes. God has designed a holy destiny for each man (see Ephes. 2:8-10). Overcoming same-sex attraction enables that higher calling, but does not in itself fulfill it. Rather, that fulfillment grows in honest, trusting relationship with the God who made us male and female in His image.

The opposite of homosexuality, therefore, is not heterosexuality, but faithfulness to Jesus.[44]

> Gangs are a symptom of a deeper brokenness among us all—one that few men, no matter how socially well-situated, dare to face.

10

GANGS AND THE CURSE OF FATHERLESSNESS[45]

THE SPIRIT OF ABANDONMENT IN MEN

For if my father and mother should abandon me, you would welcome and comfort me. (Psalm 27:10 LIV)

RECENTLY IN MY HOMETOWN California beach resort, a shocking downtown gang fight in broad daylight left one young man dead on the sidewalk and our city in grief and confusion. Sadly, similar events are occurring so often today in larger cities that the press ignores them.

Amid this growing violence among young men, a *Los Angeles Times Magazine* cover story "Mothers, Sons and the Gangs"[46] suggests the source of the problem.

In the article, several mothers of young gang members pondered sadly why their sons had gone astray. As a man, I was startled by what they didn't say.

"I don't understand why he goes out on the streets," was the gist of each woman's grief. "I'm a good mother. I keep a clean house, I go to church, I don't run around with men, I cook for the boy, wash his clothes, and provide a good home. Why doesn't he want to stay here?"

INNATE MALE LONGING

No matter how righteous and fine a homemaker his mother may be, a boy is drawn to the gang by the innate male longing and need to break away from the mother, bond to the father, and be joined thereby to the company of men. Without the father to engineer that process, the choice for a young male is ominous: either to join a gang—and either get killed or go to prison—or to stay with Mom and starve in a cell of femininity.

We're not talking politically correct ideology here. We're talking about the heart of a boy and the core stuff of manhood.

Certainly, these are good mothers, wholly worthy of honor and respect. In fact, I suspect their sons genuinely know that. But these mothers are not fathers, nor can they be.

A fatherless culture hides the awful pain of this truth behind ideological fabrications. For example, a full-page *Newsweek* magazine ad for health insurance pictures a mother seated on a high school stadium bench beside her son. She gazes compassionately at him with hand on his knee, as the track-suited boy holds an asthma spray to his mouth. *I AM A FATHER AND A MOTHER,* the ad proclaims.[47]

The father of Lies is playing our unfathered culture like a piano. Only a deeply deceived culture of denial could believe that a woman can be a boy's father. Until we confess that lie and face the massive wound among us from father absence, we'll never know how sick we are—and never seek healing.

The God revealed in Jesus, meanwhile, is "the Father from whom all fatherhood in heaven and on earth receives its true name" (Ephes. 3:14NIV). A world addicted to the fantasy of its own saving power cannot recognize this God and His saving power. We lack the supernatural perspective from which not only to face the crippling wound of father-abandonment in men today, but to foster its healing.

Sadly, women as well suffer deeply from father absence today (see "Of Fathers and Daughters" in *Healing the Masculine Soul*).

The finest woman's best is not good enough to usher a boy into manhood. Our "modern" civilization has forgotten that this is men's work, properly done by the father and the community of men.

Ancient civilizations knew and respected this reality. In the last two verses of the Hebrew bible, God promises to heal relationships between fathers and sons "or else I will come and strike the land with a curse" (Malachi 4:6NIV). Jews therefore have provided to pre-empt the curse of fatherlessness with their Bar Mitzvah rite of passage for boys. After two years of studying his heritage at the feet of his father and older men, the boy stands at last before his congregation and declares, "Today, I am a man."

Years ago, as a math teacher certified by the US Peace Corps, I lived among the Igbo people in rural Nigeria, and was humbled by the dignity of my high school students. These men had no shoes and—shocking as this may sound—neither X-Box or iPod. But they had something far more valuable: a secure manhood, certified by their fathers and the old men of the village through a fearful but defining initiation rite (see "Come out, Son of Our People!" in *Healing the Masculine Soul*).

INNER-DIRECTED MATURITY

A boy who does not grow to see himself as a man among men lacks an inner-directed maturity, a sense of his own identity. He'll let anyone define him. Indeed, he seeks someone to do it. If his father doesn't do it by affirming his talents and character and by drawing the son to himself and other men, the boy will not grow up confident in his calling to become a responsible, productive member of society.

He can only yield eventually to the world's self-centered, destructive identity fostered by the media: You are someone who needs a light beer, a gun, a fast car, plenty of money and women.

When ultimately he realizes these definitions do not address his true and deepest longings—that the world has duped him—the young man becomes angry. He's spent his best energies doing what everyone has said makes a man, and yet has nothing to show for it but a hollow manhood and deeper shame for not measuring up. **The fear of being exposed as inadequate drives him to hide his shame among others who share his brokenness.**

Thus, the gangs serve as surrogate fathers. Their violence is a misdirected vengeance against males/fathers who have abandoned them. What's more, because society has also abandoned them to a false and unsatisfying manhood, a spirit of alienation enters and fosters crime.

Today, we hear much official rhetoric about getting tough on gangs and the destruction they often cause. Certainly, law-abiding citizens have a right to be protected from gang violence. But restricting behavior, while at times necessary, is not sufficient to heal the heart.

DEEPER DISEASE

Gangs, that is, are symptoms of a deeper brokenness among us all—one that few men, no matter how socially well-situated, dare to face.

This malady, which infects an entire generation of men today regardless of race, status, or age, is fatherlessness—which functions as a curse in the masculine soul. Precious few men today, however, no matter how high their social position, political authority, or religious profile have dared face **this awful emptiness in our masculine souls which makes gangs and violence so attractive.**

The media is quick to report murders, sexual abuse, and other destructive male behavior. We read little about the root of destructive male behavior, however because the father-wound that fuels it is so universal it's become normative.

Much as an alcoholic uses a drink, often we use the police and courts to avoid facing our own problem. We focus on the symptoms and dump the problem onto law enforcement because the crippling father-wound in us all stirs a shame that no one knows how to overcome.

You don't have to be young and poor to understand what drives a gang. You just have to be real.

Even as a plant dies without water, father-abandonment starves and kills manhood. Worse, it misfocuses manly energies on destruction.

In over 25 years of ministering to men around the world, I've asked men at my events, "For how many of you did your father come to you around age 12 and talk to you helpfully about girls and sexuality?" On the average, only two or three out of a hundred raise their hands. Is it any wonder men's sexuality today is out of control?

Similarly, I ask groups of fathers, "When you first became a dad, for how many of you did your father come alongside you with comfort, support, encouragement, and helpful advice?" At one conference of 350, only 5 raised their hands. No man wants to do a job he feels unqualified for; is it any wonder men withdraw from our children?

Father God has come in Jesus to meet our deepest longing for a father—in fact, to give us what no earthly father can. "My mother and father may abandon me," as the Psalmist proclaimed, "but the Lord will take care of me" (Ps. 27:10).

Let's do our part, therefore, to uproot the cause of gangs. Let's get real with Father God and with other men and confess at last our common longing for what we needed but didn't get from Dad. Let's learn to support, encourage, and hold each other accountable. Let's bind and cast the generational demons of abandonment and alienation out of us and out of our sons, and ask Father God to replace it with His spirit of "sonship" (Romans 8:14-16).

We can begin together by confessing the God revealed in Jesus as our true Father. We can receive His Spirit, form support groups and get real with Him and each other. That way, we can prepare a community of real men not only to recognize the wound in boys today, but to invite them into healing.

> Emotional depression often comes from trying to deny feelings you don't want to feel and to control circumstances you can't control.

11

DEPRESSION —OR EXPRESSION?

THE EMOTIONAL, PHYSICAL, SPIRITUAL BATTLE

> *I went down to the very roots of the mountains, into the land whose gates lock shut forever. But you, O Lord my God, brought me back from the depths alive.* (Jonah 2:6)

MOST OF US HAVE been troubled and puzzled at times by emotional depression—from a temporary sense of discouragement to a more debilitating inability to function. Popular expressions such as "got the blues," "down in the dumps," "stuck in a rut," or "bummed out" may try to explain the sensation, but still we wonder what depression is, what causes it, and how to overcome it.

Often, chemical imbalances may precipitate a depressed state, for which prescription medication can be helpful. Yet something must cause that imbalance. Certainly, emotions can cause chemical changes in your body that precipitate physical effects. Fear, for example, stimulates adrenalin, which stirs muscular tension and emotional alertness.

Furthermore, powers of evil commonly stir fear. We might therefore ask, Does depression have any spiritual component which needs to be addressed as part of the healing process?

DISCONNECT FROM GOD

As Christians, we know that we live in a broken, sinful world, and Jesus therefore noted that we "will have trouble" in it. Yet in the same breath, he also urged, "But take heart. I have overcome the world" (John 16:33NIV). In fact, he promised, "I have come in order that you might have life—life in all its fullness" (John 10:10).

The difference between "trouble" and depression is that **the former is most often about external circumstances, the latter about internal responses.** Depression which moves beyond discouragement to incapacity therefore suggests a disconnection from God-who-is-Life. While our sin-nature readily reacts with shame to such a suggestion, to those surrendered to Jesus, this possibility signals an avenue to healing.

"Depression," as Rev. Margaret Crockett explained, "is a withdrawal from joy and the capacity to love and express oneself that constitute the birthright of a child of God":

> As such, it is separation from others, and from God, and often the sufferer finds it impossible any longer to communicate with them or even with (God). (He/she) … is weighed down with a pervading sadness, a sense of hopelessness and despair,… can become ridden, with self-hate, guilt, and … may want to run away and hide, to curl up and die … (He/she) feels that there is no hope for

the future and that these unhappy circumstances will continue indefinitely.[48]

What might cause such an emotional condition? Beyond—or possibly, prior to—chemical imbalance, psychologists have discovered that **emotional depression can be rooted in not processing particularly sad or painful events.**

Certainly, we all experience painful circumstances in this broken world. We do not, however, become depressed in every instance. Significantly, the tipping point here is often not the event itself, nor even the emotions which it stirs, but rather, an unwillingness to face and experience those emotions fully.

"Patients who do not report feeling depressed may have feelings of sadness at one event or another," as one psychiatrist has observed, "but those feelings are always specific to a particular situation."[49] **A key toward unlocking the gates of emotional depression is therefore being able to connect appropriately what you are feeling to the specific event which caused that feeling.**

Often, in fact, the depressed person may not even "recall" that event. Indeed, he or she has "depressed" it below consciousness—and that in itself may define the condition. "I don't know why I'm so down like this," is a common sensation. The occasion or "reason" for being depressed is lost somewhere in the unconscious mind.

To "depress" the brake pedal means "to push it down"; to be "depressed" therefore suggests pushing down some unpleasant feeling below consciousness instead of facing and experiencing it. When people complain they "feel depressed," therefore, I first ask them, "What are you depressing?"

The opposite of depression is expression.

RETREAT FROM FEELING

Contrary to popular belief, depression can reflect not the absence of feeling, but rather, an unwillingness to feel—resulting not from an "empty nothingness" inside, but rather, a reservoir of dammed-up feelings. As the aforementioned psychiatrist continues, "Depression is a mask for very deep and painful feelings," which a person has not "connected with the event" that caused those feelings—a sort of emotional amnesia.

Depression, he concludes, "is not a feeling ... but a mood"—in fact, a "retreat from feeling."

No one wants to feel pain; in fact, it's entirely natural to avoid it. If you have no safe way to express your pain, therefore, you may try to avoid feeling the pain by suppressing or pushing it down below consciousness, where you fancy it will be forgotten. But this only insures that feeling will continue to affect you unconsciously instead of consciously—making it harder to access, and therefore, to recognize and overcome.

As that deep pain cries out more persistently to be brought forth and healed, more energy is expended in depressing it. Eventually, you begin to shut down all feeling. Hence, **the emotional numbness and exhaustion that often accompany depression.**

It's like a string of Christmas tree lights, in which if one light goes out, they all go out. You may fancy, "Well, it's just one painful circumstance, so I can suppress that without affecting the rest of my life." But that rarely works. In fact, as you turn off the "one pain," your entire system of sensitivity begins to fade and shut down. You have literally *depressed* your emotions, like the brake pedal, and by definition become "depressed."

Depressed persons monitored on an electromyograph therefore exhibit "a very high level of tension," the psychiatrist notes, which suggests that "depression is a disconnected feeling." A National Institute of Mental Health study thereby demonstrated that "depressives begin their dream activity almost as soon as they fall asleep, and the sleep is truncated and fragmented"—further evidence that "tension is involved in depression."

This tension may come from the inner struggle when deep and genuine feelings want naturally to come up and out, but are held down inside instead: "Indeed, some persons are willing to kill themselves before they would feel those feelings."

STIFF UPPER LIP

America's highest suicide rates, in fact, are in Vermont, New Hampshire, and Maine. Mental health officials have blamed this on the very personality trait which so many Americans hold dear. "It's the Yankee version of the "stiff upper lip," as Dr. Stephen Soffeff, Director of Emergency Psychiatry at Portland's Maine Medical Center, explains:

> They try to keep it all in, try to be strong; hide their feelings until they do something drastic—like kill themselves. **They feel that to get help for their depression ... is not only wrong, but a symbol of weakness.**[50]

The most dramatic example of this connection between painful events, depression, and suicide I found in a student essay for an immigrant adult education class I once taught:

> I was about fourteen years old. My father spank me real hard, because I did not do what he wants me to do. So I was really upset and angry to my father. But I didn't say any word to him, because I respect him very much in every way but the only thought in my mind, I am going to kill myself—because of my father didn't likes me.

These few broken sentences from a boyhood memory reveal the roots of depression more clearly than any psychology textbook I've seen.

This boy started with real feelings connected to a very specific event, namely, pain at being whipped, not out of simple discipline but "real hard"—implying vengeance—and then, anger at his father. But his cultural values which enforce parental authority disallow this feeling as shameful. He is convinced that his feelings, no matter how real, are therefore unacceptable. He cannot feel his pain openly and drop all defense to his father's merciless beating, nor can he show anger back at his father, who must, rather, be "respected."

The only course open to him is to suppress that genuine feeling. But his pain from and anger toward his father are so deep that, in order to suppress them he must suppress his life itself.

Such shame, and the belief that there is no release from it, is common in depressed persons. Often, they don't dare believe that the other person afflicting them—especially a larger authority figure like a parent—might be guilty of wrongdoing. And so they assume all blame themselves. In fact, this sensation of shame can be a cover-up which conceals the real—but unacceptable—feeling of pain from and anger toward the dominant other person.

Certainly, you may bear real guilt. Maybe you lashed back violently to avenge the other person. If so, you need to seek forgiveness. But healing requires facing up sooner or later to the original event, in order to forgive the perpetrator and thereby release the enemy's grip on you. "For when I forgive," as Paul declared, "...I do it in Christ's presence because of you, in order to keep Satan from getting the upper hand over us, for we know what his plans are" (2 Corinth. 2:10,11).

It's safer, of course, simply to feel guilty for what happened than to say, "You hurt me"—especially if the one who hurt you is much bigger and stronger and holds the very power of life itself, such as any parent holds over a child. In fact, often the "other person" is a parent, simply because the one who can inflict hurt most deeply is precisely the one needed most desperately—and every child is born ultimately dependent on its parents.

The child, that is, reasons: "You hurt me, Mommy/Daddy. I need you to acknowledge that and say you won't do it again, so I won't be afraid with you. But if I tell you that, you might hurt me even worse by lashing back, ignoring, or rejecting me. That makes me angry at you. But I can't show anger at you or you'll hurt me more. Therefore, I can only depress my hurt feelings, turn my anger away from you and focus it on myself instead."

SWALLOWED ANGER

Those who turn their anger from its true and external focus back onto themselves—who "swallow their anger"—often experience a physical effect in gastro-intestinal problems. Ultimately, they can be tempted into suicide, the ultimate depression of life.

Release from this destructive, even deadly charade begins with re-learning to express yourself openly and honestly. **What is expressed**

is no longer depressed. Expression is the first step in overcoming depression.

"The mental depressive," as one Christian author has noted, "is usually one who has refrained from complaining, who has put (him/herself) under such long and rigid control that (he/she) is worn out from the effort."[51]

Again, Catholic priests Dennis and Matthew Linn state that "Much psychological depression is really swallowed anger and will disappear if I can answer the question, "Who or what is irritating me?" and then deal with my anger … When I don't like my anger, I usually feel guilty about my anger."[52]

Similarly, Rev. Crockett recalls her own journey toward healing:

> I was so busy being self-critical …, blaming myself for my sorry state, that I did not realize I was depressed.
>
> When I was able to stop feeling guilty at being angry at what had happened, and to start getting in touch with my anger rather than turning it unconsciously against myself, then I began to feel better.[53]

Often, therefore, the depressed person sits on a powder keg of repressed feelings, enforced by childhood threats and fear. "Children are to be seen and not heard," as my grandmother used to say. "Stop crying, or I'll give you something to cry about," fathers told so many of us men as boys.

What began as pressure to "control yourself like a good little boy/girl," becomes an adult habit. This continues until so much pain, so many unpleasant feelings dam up inside that you become afraid to deal with any one of them for fear that pulling one log out of the dam will bring the whole flood down unto destruction.

One common response is simply to run away, to avoid commitments or intimacy of any kind that threaten to spark your otherwise pent-up emotions. Another is to dull the pain with alcohol, drugs, and other compulsive behaviors when willpower is not strong enough to hold it down.

Alcohol, for example, is a downer, a *depress*ant – not an upper, stimulant drug. Its abuse is often aimed at pushing down pains and fears. Alcoholism is therefore closely related to depression. Dennis and Matthew Linn conclude a chapter in their book titled, "Dealing with Depression" in saying, "This chapter could be summarized by the twelve steps of Alcoholics Anonymous."

SHORT-SIGHTED HELP

From this perspective, we see that many of the usual "helpful" ways of trying to bring someone out of depression are short-sighted. Often, we may want to say, "Just try harder, work more at bringing yourself out of it!" **But if depression is caused by too much self-control and effort in the first place, this advice only adds to the burden of shame and forces the person deeper into darkness.**

Again, we may want to say, "Count your blessings! Look on the bright side of things!" As one patient responds,

> So I would do, saying to myself, "I have a fine husband, and three lovely children and a comfortable home and no great financial problem ... There's no reason why I should feel this way. But I still do feel this way, so I must be going crazy!"[54]

Ultimately, the deeply repressed feelings need to be identified, felt, and at last, expressed. Often you become so used to deceiving yourself in order to suppress the feelings that another person, such as a skilled professional counselor, is needed to help re-surface those feelings.

I once received a call from a woman saying her son Fred (not his real name), a young man in his late 20's, was struggling with depression. When I talked to Fred by phone, he said that his father had abandoned the family years ago, and he was furious at his mother, whom he saw as particularly possessive of him as a boy. Eventually, the two of them came together to my office.

As his mother detailed how "insensitive" Fred was to her—why, he had gone to Europe for several weeks and hardly called her while he was gone!—Fred sat glumly until I encouraged him to tell her how he was feeling. With a deep breath, he summoned courage and exclaimed, "Let go of me! You're suffocating me! I want to get away from you and everything you say just makes me want to get further away!"

Unfortunately, his mother was so bound up in her own pain from feeling abandoned—both as a girl from her father and as a woman from Fred's father—that she became indignant and could not listen to Fred's feelings. This, of course, only confirmed her as the source of his depression. In a later meeting alone with Fred, he burst out the logical conclusion to his dilemma: "Sometimes I feel like the only way to cut myself off from Mom is to kill myself!"

I affirmed his courage for speaking up honestly to his mother, and spent some time letting him vent his anger toward her in exercises without her present. When he had done so enough to reconnect with his true self and find security in that, I helped him see how **his anger at her was co-opting his energies and life focus**. I encouraged him to start thinking about his own life calling and start moving in it.

"You're not responsible for your mother's happiness," I reassured him. "That's an issue between her and Father God. But you are responsible to honor your mother, and to move ahead in God's calling for your life." Standing in for his father, I gave him permission to leave home and become the man he was created to be. Eventually, I helped him ask Father God how to honor his mother—without capitulating to her manipulations.

Later, I met with his mother to deal with her own feelings of abandonment—which, as I had suspected, were rooted in her own girlhood and causing her to grasp onto her son.

SPEAK OPENLY

If depression can be rooted in suppressed feelings, we parents can help our children avoid depression later in their adult lives by allowing them to speak their feelings openly and honestly to us. A child's best safeguard against depression is therefore the freedom to say without fear of judgment, "Mom, I'm angry at you because I think what you did to me was unfair," or "Dad, it really hurt me when you said that," or "Mom/Dad, I'm just feeling awful and I need you to hold me and listen."

Letting your child speak his or her feelings openly does not mean "giving in just because the kid throws a temper tantrum." It means simply acknowledging that the child is a human being with real feelings—something every child needs desperately to know in order to survive in this often un-feeling, impersonal world. As an older schoolteacher told me my first day of teaching years ago, "The kids have a right to complain—and you have the right to insist. Try to keep that balance" (see "Man's Anger and God's Righteous Purpose" in *Sons of the Father*).

Sometimes, of course, the parent has genuinely wronged the child, and the child's anger must therefore be acted upon to right the wrong through apology and amends.

Of course, some discernment here is in order. At times, a responsible parent must insist when the child refuses to do something that you know is best for him/her—such as going to school in order to identify and develop the child's gifting, and honest owning-up to misdeeds. In such cases, it's important to avoid head-on confrontation by allowing your child the right to complain even as you have the right to insist.

When my son was old enough to take out the trashcans to the curb for pickup, I showed him how to do it and turned him loose. After a few weeks of doing it, he decided he would much rather play a video game, and when I asked him to take out the trash, he snapped, "I don't want to!"

Startled by his defiance, I prayed under my breath to stay centered and not overreact. "That's fine," I managed matter of factly. As he knit his brow in surprise, I explained. "I never asked you to want to do it. I asked you to do it. I never wanted to do it when I was your age either. In fact, I'd probably be worried if you really enjoyed taking out the trash.

"We all have jobs in the family," I added, patting him on the shoulder, "and this one is yours. So how about doing it right now. The sooner you get it done, the sooner you can get to your video game." With another pat, I turned and walked away. Later, I saw the trash can out at the curb. During dinner later, we chatted as if nothing had happened.

As children of God ourselves, we can allow God to save us from depression. That is, **we can dare to connect our depressed**

feelings with the persons and events which caused those feelings. Depression often stirs from assuming "There's no one I can safely share my troublesome feelings with. What I'm feeling is too awful; anyone who heard me expressing these feelings would reject me!" No option is seen but to depress the feelings—and thereby hand your heart over to the Prince of Darkness.

A trust in Father God's accepting grace undergirds the healing process. Feeling loved and safe with Him frees you to speak openly what you might otherwise have depressed in your childhood family. What's more, in Jesus we see that God's love for us is so strong that it triumphs over death itself. "For I am certain," Paul told the Church at Rome, that

> Nothing can separate us from (the love of Christ): neither death nor life, neither angels nor other heavenly rulers or powers, neither the present nor the future, neither the world above nor the world below—there is nothing in all creation that will ever be able to separate us from the love of God which is ours through Christ Jesus our Lord (Romans 8:38-39).

In Jesus, you have an alternative to either lashing out or depressing your pain. You can bring it to the surface, with the help of a pastor, professional Christian counselor, loving brother or sister in Christ, and invite Jesus into the wound to heal it (see "Healing Emotional Wounds" in *Broken by Religion, Healed by God*). At times, while driving alone, I've rolled up the car windows and shouted out to Jesus how angry, sad, or afraid I am.

Because depression is so often rooted in suppressed feelings, God's healing does not mean that you're delivered instantly from all pain and anger. Instead, by ex-pressing yourself honestly to God, you experience the gift of full here-and-now feelings, so you can know who or what is truly upsetting you.

CREATED DESTINY

God does not lift us from the hell of depression into a heaven of bliss. To connect your feelings properly to the event that caused them releases the chains, but does not propel you into the fullness of life which Jesus came to bring us. That essential process begins only when, freed from depression, you decide at last to struggle in this broken world to let God equip and empower you in your created destiny.

The story of Jonah provides a graphic biblical view of depression and God's purposes. Called to speak God's word to the pagan enemy Ninevites, Jonah balks. He boards a ship to run away from—and in that sense, to depress—his divine calling. God pursues him with a sea storm and eventually, Jonah is tossed overboard and swallowed by a monster fish—where he experiences a literal downer akin to depression:

> You (God) threw me down into the depths. I thought I had been banished from your presence … I went down to the very roots of the mountains, whose gates lock shut forever. But you, O Lord my God, brought me back from the depths alive. When I felt my life slipping away, *then, O Lord, I prayed to you, and in your holy Temple you heard me.* (Jonah 2:3-6 italics mine)

When Jonah finally cries out to God and expresses his true feelings in prayer, he is released from his depression. God orders the fish to "spit Jonah up on the beach" and tells Jonah, "Go to Nineveh, that great city, and proclaim to the people the message I have given you" (2:2). No longer burdened by bottled-up emotions, Jonah emerges from the depths energized and focused at last on his calling.

Jonah's story demonstrates that **emotional depression often comes from a compulsion to 1) deny feelings you don't want to feel and 2) control circumstances you can't control. Overcoming it, therefore, is a dual process of 1) accurately focusing and appropriately expressing your feelings and 2) surrendering your will and control to God.**

Identifying and expressing your feelings openly sparks the healing and deliverance; a lifestyle of surrendering to God and trusting His purposes fulfills it. Often, that means simply praying, "I'm so scared, Father! I can't change this awful situation that's overwhelming me."

Then, take a deep breath, exhale, and let go of it to your Father. "I give up to you, Father—not to the circumstances. I can't control this situation, so I release it all into your hands, Father, and trust You to walk me through and beyond it." Eventually, a prayer like this can become a lifestyle—and your pathway to new life in the Spirit.

By its very nature, depression beckons the powers of darkness, and overcoming it ultimately requires facing the enemy. The demon of depression is real. However—like homosexuality and addiction—to the extent that it is most often not a primary condition but rather, the effects of a deeper one, I would urge strongly against rushing to cast out a demon of depression. Instead, focus on healing those deeper wounds which cause you to fear expressing yourself. "You can shoot the rats in the garbage," as the saying goes, "but they'll come back until you get rid of the garbage."

Let the Great Surgeon lead you. Tell Father God you want Him to do this operation according to His will and the leading of His Spirit. This can be a painstaking task, requiring much patience. But you have to decide whether you want a deep, enduring healing or merely a momentary high—and a crash later.

EXPRESSING AND SURRENDERING

Insofar as depression begins with de-pressed feeling and a despair at being unable to control aspects of your life, **overcoming it is therefore a process of both expressing feelings appropriately and surrendering control to God.**

Along the way, you'll likely face spirits such as stoicism, anger, shame, abandonment, resentment, bitterness, despair, boredom, worthlessness, aimlessness, passivity, and intimidation. Each of these spirits may have entered you in different ways—from emotional wounding to generational bloodline (see "How Demons Enter—and Leave" in *No Small Snakes*). Take time to discern and process each one appropriately, and trust Holy Spirit to show you when you've undermined the foundation sufficiently to deal explicitly with the kingpin demon of depression.

Certainly, the Father's goal is to bring peace and joy. But these are fruits of His Spirit—not the product of our own determination, but the outcome of His redeeming work. Remember, the Father does not like to see His child suffering in depression. But **His purpose for our lives is greater than simply removing us from difficult circumstances.**

Indeed, He wants to equip you for your role in bringing His kingdom on earth as it is in heaven—and often tribulation forces us into becoming willing students and determined warriors. "Those who sow in tears," as the Psalmist declared, "will reap with songs of joy" (Ps. 126:5NIV).

From a biblical view, therefore, the opposite of depression is not joy, but rather, freedom to express what's in your heart and a readiness to surrender your control to God. This process beckons the vitality of His Spirit and thereby, the power to cooperate with God in the adventure of His purposes for you.

> **What God has given us, we're commanded to enjoy. Not in order to foster selfish indulgence, but rather, to inspire humble reverence.**

12

THE COMMANDMENT TO ENJOY

VS.

THE SPIRIT OF DEPRIVATION

> *Sell your produce and take the money with you to the one place of worship. Spend it on whatever you want—beef, lamb, wine, beer—and there, in the presence of the Lord your God, you and your families are to eat and enjoy yourselves.* (Deut. 14:25,26)

THE SUNGLASSES HAD BEEN STEPPED ON—the frame bent, lens pushed out, one stem hinge twisted. Righteously, if not clumsily, I pushed in, re-twisted, and resolved to live with the imbalance and discomfort. And then recently, two years later, in a blaze of spendthrift abandon I sent the glasses to the manufacturer to be fixed, without even asking the cost.

Two weeks afterward, I opened the package and was surprised to find a brand new pair. Holding my breath as I searched the invoice for charges, I was startled to read an enclosed note, "Though your warranty has expired, we have replaced your broken sunglasses at no cost, as a courtesy."

Stunned, I sighed deeply and smiled. *Amazing*!

But hold on. There's more.

The stems had always curved too short for my "X-Large" head, and on the crest of this newfound abundance, I took the sunglasses to a local store to have them fitted to my ears. When the clerk had straightened and molded them to perfection, I dutifully pulled out my wallet, noting that I had not bought them at his store. "No problem," he said; "with this manufacturer, there's no charge."

Striding down the street later in my new and for-the-first-time comfortable sunglasses, it struck me: For two years, I had determined to live in discomfort, yet all along I could've had a brand new, fitted pair simply for the asking!

HERO OR FOOL?

As a strange mixture of thanksgiving and dismay overtook me, I had to ask: Father, is there anything else I'm needlessly living with, tolerating, or enduring in my life now that makes me **not a righteously thrifty hero, but an unbelieving fool**? Indeed, Is there anything else you want to give me that I haven't asked for?

At home later, in my prayer closet, I fell on my knees—and wept as the Father revealed a host of blessings He's been trying to give me, but I haven't trusted Him enough to receive—from knee-protecting new running shoes to a greater capacity to enjoy my family. In that moment, I recognized the demon of "deprivation" which had kept me from seeing the Father's heart for me.

As I prayed for understanding, I saw how that spirit had worked overtime in my father's generation, robbed of childhood by the Great Depression and of adolescence by WWII. I remembered how hard it was for Dad—even when he had the money—to go on a vacation or even enjoy a tasty ice cream that cost as much as fifteen cents.

Seeing how this demon had stolen so much renewal and enjoyment from my father and me, I hated it—and determined to receive my full spiritual inheritance (see Galat. 4:1-7)—that is, "the spirit of Sonship" **(Rom. 8:15NIV) and the abundance of life which He sent Jesus to give me.**

Still later, I balked.

Where is the line here between humble faith and "name-it-claim-it" presumption, between overcoming demonic deprivation and indulging selfish greed? Where is the balance between today's shameless, pleasure-centered culture and our shame-full Puritan ancestors—who outlawed the popular frontier sport of bear-baiting not because it harmed the animals, but because it gave pleasure to the spectators?

Indeed, how do we escape the demonic trap between a pleasure-worshipping licentious spirit and a pleasure-renouncing ascetic spirit? Certainly, in order to discern Holy Spirit's view, you must be free of evil spirits that would cloud it. When I asked God whether those two apparently opposing spirits were in me, both emerged, and I cast them out.

Yet another dilemma: what right do I have to ask for more material blessings when others in the world are starving?

Searching the Scriptures, I was drawn to a surprising Word of God that upends not only the modern hedonists, but the Puritan killjoys as well:

> Set aside a tithe—a tenth of all that your fields produce each year. Then go to the one place where the Lord your God has chosen to be worshiped; and there in his presence eat the tithes of your grain, wine, and olive oil, and the first-born of your cattle and sheep. Do this *so that you may learn to have reverence* for the Lord your God always. (Deut. 14: 22-26, italics mine)

WHATEVER YOU WANT

If this sounds extravagant, even unrighteous, hold on again. There's more:

> If the place of worship is too far from your home for you to carry there the tithe of the produce that the Lord has blessed you with, then do this: Sell your produce and take the money with you to the one place of worship. *Spend it on whatever you want—beef, lamb, wine, beer—and there, in the presence of the Lord your God, you and your families are to eat and enjoy yourselves.* (italics mine)

Amazing! Could this biblically-ordained feast of enjoyment really constitute your tithe? If the goal of tithing is to draw your heart to God, could that goal be accomplished more surely by the blessing of enjoying your money than by the duty to give it away, even to the church?

While questions remain, sadly very few Christians understand this upending biblical truth: **What God has given us, we're commanded to enjoy. Not in order to foster selfish indulgence, but rather, to inspire humble reverence**. A little boy, that is, may obey a father who enforces severe discipline, but he will revere the one who not only teaches him safe boundaries, but who can also enjoy an ice cream with him—and in that foundational sense, to teach him to enjoy the goodness of Father God.

We think, "If I just don't turn away from God, He'll bless me"—and burn out striving to stay focused on Him. But that's not the God revealed to Jeremiah:

> Israel, I wanted to accept you as my son and give you a delightful land, the most beautiful land in all the world. I wanted you to call me Father, and never again turn away from me. (Jer. 3:19 TEV)

The more you let God accept you as you are, that is—the more you call Him Father and receive His blessings—the less likely you are to turn away from Him. **Not because He'll punish you if you do, but because He's so good you don't want to.**

God is not an exacting Scrooge who frowns on fun, but a grace-full Father who loves and therefore enjoys His children. Thus, He introduces Jesus to the world with the heartfelt blessing, "This is my Son, chosen and marked by my love, *delight of my life*." (Matt. 3:17TMB, italics mine).

Scorning pleasure is no more promoted by God than worshiping it. That's not because He's morally lax or callously unconcerned with human pain. "He was despised and rejected by men," as Isaiah describes the Messiah, "a man of sorrows, and familiar with suffering" (Isa. 53:3NIV).

In fact, God's "Thou shalt not" Commandments are no moralistic discipline, but rather, the plea of a loving Father, "Please, my child, don't to that, because it will harm you!" God's laws, that is, are designed not to deny us pleasure, but to protect us from pain. It's not the goodness of the world that we celebrate and enjoy, but the goodness of our Father. And we do it within His boundaries because that's best for us.

It's true that Jesus did not come to bring us the good life. In fact, He came to bring us the best life. **The question, therefore, is not, Why do the pagans have all the fun? but rather, Why is it so hard for me to receive my Father's blessings and enjoy His goodness?**

Sadly, tragically, when we deny ourselves God's pleasure, we not only reject His goodness. Ultimately, we deny it to others as well, with precisely the harsh judgment which we mete out upon ourselves.

Thus, Holocaust survivor Elie Wiesel—himself no stranger to the world's suffering—tells the story in *Souls on Fire,* an anthology of Hasidic Judaism, of a wealthy man trying to impress his rabbi by fasting on just bread and salt:

> "That's very bad," said the (rabbi). "I order you to eat white bread and cake, and also to drink sweet wine." – "But, Rebbe, why?" cried the astounded Hasid. – "If you are content with black bread and water, you will think that the poor can subsist on stones and spring water. If you eat cake, you will give them bread."[55]

As the writer of Ecclesiasticus put it, "How can a man be hard on himself and kind to others? His possessions bring him no enjoyment.

No one is worse than the man who is grudging to himself; his stinginess is its own punishment" (14:5-6 NEB Apocrypha).

In receiving the blessings of this world as a gift from Father God, we not only praise Him for His goodness, but are inspired to extend that goodness to others. **Material pleasures, that is, are good insofar as they are seen as the undeserved gifts of a graceful, loving God, and evil insofar as they separate us from the needs of others and blind us to their suffering** (see "Of Jogging and Cat Food" in *Broken by Religion, Healed by God*).

DEPRIVATION AND OVEREATING

Some years ago, I saw a surprising "side-effect" of deprivation when I was trying to curb my compulsive eating habits and lose weight. I never had an eating problem while growing up, when my youthful energies burned up every calorie. Later as an adult, however, my metabolism slowed down, and I began battling extra pounds—and a powerful urge to eat even when I wasn't hungry. Forced thereby to look into my heart for healing, I saw that deprived little boy in me, as it were, demanding to have some pleasure and thereby make up for lost enjoyment by over-eating sweets.

To break this stronghold, I imagined myself as a boy standing before my father, and called Jesus into the scene. There, with my heavenly Father beside me, I told my dad how angry I was at him for depriving me of simple pleasures, how that made me shut down my capacity for joy and judge others who enjoyed such pleasures themselves.

I then asked Jesus to show me my dad with His eyes. In my mind, I saw Dad as a Depression-era boy, so deprived of simple childhood pleasures that he was not only unable to enjoy them when later available, but ashamed of his very desire as it angered his own overworked, deprived father to express it.

When a child asks for an ice cream, it's one thing to deny or postpone the request directly, as, "Not just now" or "We'll have one later after dinner for dessert." **It's quite another thing to shame a child for wanting an ice cream as, "You want *what*?"** The latter beckons the demon by causing a child to distrust his or her own natural desires—which require super-natural power to suppress (see "One Ice Cream at a Time" in *Do Pirates Wear Pajamas?*).

Again, I'm not urging that those desires be indulged wholesale, but rather, submitted to the Father for His way of fulfilling them.

The spirit of deprivation had infected generations of Dalbey men. But in that moment when I saw Dad as a deprived boy himself, it was called out into the light and I could expel it at last from our bloodline. I wept for my dad's pain and disappointments as a boy and forgave him for denying me simple pleasures as his own father had denied him. I set the cross between me, him, and his father, spoke to that deprivation in the name of Jesus, and cast it out of myself at last and into the hands of Jesus.

I then asked Father God to restore my appetite to its created purpose, that is, to stir it when I genuinely needed food—and to enjoy a feast just for its pleasure when appropriate. Much work has been required to root this healing—I still struggle with my appetite—but uprooting the "kingpin" demon of deprivation has allowed it to proceed.

As often happens once a demon is expelled, revelation followed. I saw how demons often work together in polar extremes. Ironically, the deprivation in me had fueled a spirit of gluttony—which would speak loudly when I harshly disciplined myself not to have sweets. I named and cast it out, and asked Holy Spirit to heal my hypothalamus gland, which controls appetite.

Eventually, I saw that the Scandinavian/Norwegian culture of my Dalbey surname—in spite of its many other, admirable traits—can elevate deprivation to an art form.

In his *Pretty Good Joke Book*, humorist Garrison Keillor of *Prairie Home Companion* radio show fame, tells the joke of aging Norwegian-American Ole lying on his deathbed surrounded by his family: "Is my wife here?" he asks. "Yes, Ole," Lena replies, "I'm right here." – "Are my children here?" – "Yes, Daddy," the children all say. — "Are my other relatives also here?" —

"Yes," they say comfortingly, "We're all here" — And Ole says, "Then why is the light on in the kitchen?"[56]

A righteously disciplined light switch-offer, I cringe in dismay. How, I wonder, has my own compulsive deprivation not only distracted me, like Ole, from my Father's goodness and deprived me of His joy— but indeed, disallowed it in others, especially those in my own home?

Father, forgive me for not enjoying your goodness. Help me to receive your blessings so I can likewise bless others.

It's a big order. I'm asking my Father for a new heart.

But I'm not worried.

With this Manufacturer, there's no charge.

> Unmet emotional and spiritual needs trigger a bodily sensation of hunger which only God can satisfy.

13

BETTER FAT THAN SAD

GLUTTONY
AND SPIRITUAL HUNGER

Why spend money on what does not satisfy? Why spend your wages and still be hungry? Listen to me and do what I say, and you will enjoy the best food of all. Listen now, my people, and come to me; come to me, and you will have life! (Isaiah 55:1-3)

SOME YEARS AGO WHILE DRIVING across the country, I began nodding before the endless plains at dusk when far off on the horizon a tiny pulsating light caught my attention. Driving closer, I watched curiously as a towering sign emerged blinking like a lighthouse beacon in a vast sea of waving grain. At last, three massive letters proclaimed high above a roadside prairie diner, "EAT…EAT…EAT…"

Insofar as a beacon points to safety amid danger, this primal message from the American heartland suggests a national consensus that security is found in eating. Indeed, it portrays the relentless call of the world to satisfy every sensation of hunger with food.

It seems simple, even common sense: if you "feel hungry," just eat food, and that will satisfy you. All too often, however, it doesn't work. We eat, eat, eat, and yet remain strangely, if not profoundly, unsatisfied.

Thankfully, the ancient prophet Isaiah offers hope in a different call promising to satisfy the sensation of hunger. Unlike the world, he proclaims that the deepest human hunger--for fullness of life itself— can't be satisfied by eating, but only by drawing closer to God.

Certainly, having nothing at all to eat causes genuine and profound insecurity, since we eventually starve without food. Yet such physical insecurity can't be the cause of our eating so much, because lack of food, while a reality for some, is simply not the common experience in our affluent society. Indeed, our most dreaded illnesses--heart disease and cancer--as well as a host of other maladies from diabetes to sleep apnea, can be linked to diet and overeating.

DEATH THROUGH EATING

The irony, if not outrageous tragedy today, is that while death stalks most of humanity through starvation, it stalks the wealthy minority through overeating. This awful conundrum recalls a grade-school joke book in which a large, obese man mocks his rail-thin companion, "From the looks of you, there's been a famine!" The skinny man counters, "From the looks of you, you caused it!"

In fact, our unchecked, affluent appetites contribute significantly to world hunger. Today, farmland in countries where people starve is often pre-empted for tea, coffee, tobacco, cocoa, sugar, and other non-nutritious crops for export to overfed First World consumers. Surely, it's no coincidence that all these foods are damaging to the human body, since they bear death not only to us who consume them, but also to the people who grow them (see "Of Jogging and Cat Food" in *Broken by Religion, Healed by God*).

While food may be *necessary* to life, however, Isaiah notes that it's not *sufficient* to life. Thus, the devil's first shot in tempting Jesus away from the Father aims at his bodily appetite:

> After spending forty days and nights without food, Jesus was hungry. Then the Devil came to him and said, "If you are God's son, order these stones to turn into bread."
>
> But Jesus answered, "The scripture says, 'Man cannot live on bread alone, but needs every word that God speaks'" (Matt. 4:2-4; see Deut. 8:3).

Jesus declares soon afterward, "Blessed are those who hunger and thirst after righteousness, for they shall be satisfied" (Matt. 5:6 RSV). And yet again, "I am the bread of life. He who comes to me will never be hungry" (John 6:35). Jesus clearly implies that not every sensation of hunger originates in physical need, that emotional and spiritual needs may also register as "hunger" in the human body.

Most of us know we can eat more than enough food to meet our physical needs and yet, as Isaiah notes, "still be hungry"—that is, wanting something more, but unable to name it. Following the call of the world, you can keep eating yet more food--only to discover that you simply gain weight instead of satisfaction.

Thus, spirits of greed and gluttony, beckoned by misfocused and thereby, unsatisfied desire.

Certainly, it's not necessarily wrong to eat in response to a non-physical desire. In fact, God has ordained feasts--like the wedding feast at Cana, the fattened calf killed when the prodigal son returns, and the Passover meal to remember Israel's deliverance from slavery in Egypt. In that sense, a desire to celebrate God's goodness can register as a sensation of hunger.

Feasting on such occasions honors God. As noted in the above chapter on Deprivation, the Old Covenant therefore includes a commandment to "eat and enjoy yourselves...so that you may learn to have reverence for the Lord your God always" (Deut. 14:22-26).

Eating can enhance joy.

But it can't eliminate sadness.

Nor is God against eating from purely physical desire; if He were, he would exalt the poor for their hunger instead of exhorting us to feed them (see James 2:15-17, Luke 3:11).

Responding to a sensation of hunger with proper discernment therefore requires a sensitivity not simply to authentic bodily needs, but in fact, to both emotional and spiritual reality. Our secularized minds and over-indulged bodies, however, make it hard to distinguish between your body's desire for physical satisfaction and **God's desire to satisfy you by drawing you to Himself and fulfilling your created destiny**.

When the joy of eating good food becomes divorced from God's blessing and His intention for us, we learn to have reverence not for Him, but rather, for our flesh and its desires. It's easy to substitute food for God when you take for granted His gracious provision. "The Lord's people grew rich, but rebellious," as the ancient biblical historian warned:

> (T)hey were fat and stuffed with food.
> They abandoned God their Creator and rejected
> their mighty savior. Their idolatry made the
> Lord jealous. (Deut. 32:15,16)

God's concern for our eating therefore focuses on idolatry, namely, that we might look to food for the security and satisfaction that only He can provide. Insofar as food can thereby turn you away from God, it can become a weapon of the enemy, as via greed and gluttony.

You can begin countering the enemy's plan by giving humble thanks to God when you sit down to eat and by dedicating an appropriately generous portion of your tithe to world hunger ministries. You can also rein in your lifestyle and cut back, for example, on the expendable non-nutritious crop-foods mentioned above. If you have a pet, make sure you donate as much to a hunger ministry as you budget for pet food.

SECULARIZED SOCIETY

In our secularized society, we've largely forgotten God and are therefore unable to recognize or even to allow His saving intention among ourselves and among the world's hungry. The dominant focus of our Thanksgiving holiday, for example, becomes the turkey and not the God who provided it. We see pictures everywhere of turkeys and quaintly attired Pilgrims, but no sign of the Red Sea's parting, Mt. Sinai and the desert crossing, the cross of Jesus, or any other symbols of God's saving power--which the Pilgrims affirmed as the bedrock of their identity and of Thanksgiving itself.

When we have so thoroughly cut ourselves off from our roots in the God who created us, we have no assurance either of God's presence or His power to save us. We no longer recognize our spiritual nature, nor therefore, our spiritual needs. When they surface, our emotional/spiritual transmitters find no connection on the radar screen and short-circuit to food. Our God-created spirits want to celebrate His goodness, but we have no idea how to do that. We regard every sensation of hunger as purely physical and can imagine no way to satisfy it beyond eating.

This emotional disconnect which misfocuses our desires recalls Pavlov's experiment with hungry dogs. When he brought food to his dogs, their saliva increased. Later, he began ringing a bell before feeding them. Eventually, he simply rang the bell without giving the dogs any food—and found that the dogs' saliva increased even when no food was present.

What, that is, are the "bells" that stir a sensation of hunger even when no apparent physical need is present?

One graphic answer to this question was framed poignantly above the door of a Boston ice cream parlor near where I lived years ago while in seminary:

IT'S HARD TO BE SAD
WHEN YOU'RE EATING ICE CREAM

Its happy-face ice-cream scoops notwithstanding, this sign clearly acknowledged that often we eat so much food in order to hide pain and insecurity, that is, to suppress sadness and other uncomfortable feelings.

In his classic *The Celebration of Discipline*, Richard Foster agrees, and notes how the spiritual discipline of fasting challenges this natural tendency to suppress and hide works of the enemy within us:

> More than any other single Discipline,
> **fasting reveals the things that control us.**
> This is a wonderful benefit to the true disciple
> who longs to be transformed into the image
> of Jesus Christ. We cover up what is inside us

with food and other good things, but in fasting these things surface. If pride controls us, it will be revealed almost immediately…Anger, bitterness, jealousy, strife, fear – if they are within us, they will surface during fasting. **At first we will rationalize that our anger is due to our hunger; (but when fasting) we will know that we are angry because the spirit of anger is within us.** We can rejoice in this knowledge because we know that healing is available through the power of Christ.[57]

(see "The Weapon of Fasting" in *No Small Snakes*).

SADNESS AND COOKIES

At a healing prayer conference I once attended, an overweight woman psychologist told similarly how at thirteen she had felt ugly. One day a popular boy came up to her at school and said, "You look good today." Her heart leapt for joy--until shortly afterwards she heard the boy laughing with other boys at the dare-joke he'd played on "that ugly girl." Crushed, she ran home and fell on her bed in tears.

Hearing her cries, her mother came in and urged her to stop crying and cheer up, but to no avail. Soon, the mother left, and returned later with a large plate of freshly baked cookies. "These will make you feel better," she said.

The wounded girl gobbled up every cookie on the plate.

"I did feel better for a little while," she recalled, "but I continued in my adolescent years to overeat, especially sweets, as a way of not dealing with my inner hurts. I know my mother was just trying to save me from my sadness, but **I wish she could've just held me and walked with me through the pain.** Years later, I had to let Jesus walk me through that whole scene again, as part of my ongoing healing from overeating--to cry out at last all the awful pain which I had literally stuffed down with food" (see "Healing Emotional Wounds" in *Broken by Religion, Healed by God*).

We may well want to eat less, but we do not want as readily to deal with the pain, fear, and shame which our eating often hides. This marks the difference between fasting, which aims at revealing inner spiritual or emotional hunger, and dieting, which aims at suppressing appetite, even that which doesn't come from lack of food. "Appetite suppressant" pills and programs can in some cases suppress God's voice.

That's why diets so often fail. You've eaten too much for a reason, often to suppress unfulfilled needs and uncomfortable feelings. When you remove the food covering, that unsettling need surfaces at last, and you become desperate to anaesthetize yourself yet more deeply with yet more food—even as an alcoholic panics when the bar closes.

This inner conflict is reflected graphically at Christmas, when book publishers report that the largest gift book sales are both cookbooks and diet books.

In fact, women's magazine covers often reflect this cognitive dissonance in side-by-side article titles focusing on both dieting and high-calorie desserts. One *Family Circle* magazine cover, for example, featured "Easy to Fix, Hard to Resist: Chocolate Supreme 3 Layers" right alongside "Lose Weight/Get Fit."[58] Another issue proclaimed across the top of the cover, "Super Card-A-Day Diet: Lose 6 lbs. In 12 days." Below, a large, full-color strawberry shortcake with fluffy whipped cream beckoned, "Guaranteed to Please: Old Fashioned Strawberry Shortcake."[59]

The phrase "to please" preys upon the cook's desire for affirmation, which in itself could contribute to her hunger for food. It also allows her to pretend she's baking the desert for someone else and therefore will have none of it herself. Yet anyone who has cooked such a delicious-looking shortcake would be sorely tempted to eat it— along with the three Chocolate Supreme layers--and gain six pounds.

No need to worry, however; the magazine has graciously provided for that with the accompanying diet stories.

I leave it to women themselves to sort out the pathology here. In any case, such deception begs the question, Wouldn't it be better for me to face my emotional and spiritual hungers and aim at being pleased with myself--that is, simply to eat healthy, exercise regularly, seek emotional healing and deliverance--and find satisfaction in God's calling? That way, I wouldn't want to look at the magazine at all and would neither be tempted by its cakes nor need its diets.

VICIOUS CYCLE

This seems so obvious that to consider it at all forces the more basic issue, How did I become so bound up in that vicious cycle in the first place?

Certainly, we all know that eating too much--whether sweets or other foods--is not good for your body. When you do it, you feel a negative effect: stuffed, sluggish, even self-critical. Yet, just as people continue to smoke in spite of the dire health warning printed clearly on the package, we judge that the perceived benefit from too much eating outweighs its damage to our bodies.

Given its manifest negative consequences, the perceived benefit of overeating must be highly significant. Clearly, as per the ice-cream-parlor gospel, we would rather be fat than sad. This misperception reflects the father of Lies, manifested when overeating in fact does not eliminate your sadness, but only compounds it with guilt and remorse.

Since the physical effects of overeating are all negative, doing so is clearly aimed rather at gaining some non-physical benefit. That is, the fact that we would eat so much as to injure our bodies, indicates clearly that our eating is in response to something other than a genuine, bodily need.

SUCROSE BABE

What, indeed, are we most often truly seeking when instead we eat food?

A further clue lies in how we address loved ones with popular nicknames often related to sweet foods, such as Sweetheart, Sweetie, Sweetie Pie, Honey, and Honey Bun. The most blatant, of course, is simply "Sugar." A 1950's rock 'n roll romantic hit "Sugar Pie Honey Bunch," by The Four Tops, underscored the point.

It makes you wonder: Why not just cut to the chase and call your lover "Glucose"?

Such names clearly imply that we see food, particularly sweets, as the bearer of affection, intimacy, caring, and love. Again, this misconception may stem from early experience with the mother, who is often the first, most foundational focus of all these emotional needs.

She not only brings the infant milk, which has a high sugar content, but also traditionally comes bearing food and desserts to the child.

In that sense, your need for affection and caring can become a "Pavlov bell" which when unmet can short-circuit to misfocus on food instead of its origin in Mom. This phenomenon is so common in our culture as to require the term "comfort food"—which is often more likely to include mac 'n cheese than a more healthy spinach salad. The pathology here reflected tragically in 1960s rock star Janis Joplin, whose often screaming voice betrayed a deep loneliness unto suicide, while touting "Southern Comfort" as her favorite whiskey brand.

Jesus said that human beings can "hunger for righteousness"—that is, to be centered in God and flowing in His purposes; that we live "not by bread alone" but by what God says, and that we will "never be hungry" when we come to him. Why then do we misfocus our appetite on food instead of seeking to be in sync with God, listening to Him, and coming to Jesus? When food doesn't satisfy, why don't we go directly to God, as Isaiah declares, and trust Him to meet any deeper need which our hunger truly indicates--rather than wasting time, energy, and money turning to food?

Obviously, a secularized culture like our own cannot recognize a need for God. But performance religion lures many Christians into a similar deception. When we strive to earn His blessing, ultimately we fail and become desperate to cover our shame, often with food. We fear that God will not overcome our shame and remove our un-right-ness before Him as readily as a soda and French fries will cover it, that His word will not invigorate as convincingly as a three-layer chocolate cake, or that Jesus will not receive us in our brokenness and fulfill our need as convincingly as a pizza.

Such un-faith translates in the human body as a compelling sensation that something necessary is missing from your life. That emptiness translates organically as hunger.

If not focused appropriately on God, this sensation leads you to trust rather in food, saying, "Food will save me from the awful emptiness within me." Insofar as you thereby attribute saving power to food instead of to God, it becomes an idol.

The food industry appreciates this denial all the way to the bank. In his *Salt, Sugar, Fat: How the Food Giants Hooked Us*, *NY Times* writer Michael Moss documents how companies scientifically design foods to keep you eating—such as adding extra salt and sugar to Doritos chips. Similarly, Connecticut College neuroscience students recently "found that eating oreos (cookies) activated more neurons in the pleasure center of rats' brains than did consuming cocaine or morphine."[61]

Clearly, the powers of the world lose money when you begin to recognize your true hunger for God and focus on Him instead of buying their food. This suggests more fingerprints from the father of Lies on our overeating.

A people of excess, among whom starvation is unknown, can only wonder: Is it really possible to feel a "hunger for righteousness" or, as another translation, a "desire" to "do what God requires" (TEV) even as for a strawberry shortcake? Indeed, can finding righteousness—that is, rightness or favor with God—via listening to what God says or coming to Jesus and trusting Him, be as satisfying and fulfilling as steak and potatoes?

Certainly, as the discipline of fasting implies, we'll never know until we dare set aside our fries and shortcake long enough to find out.

Indeed, does your sadness truly evaporate altogether when you eat ice cream? Does your shame disappear? When you eat, eat, eat, are you stirred to become all God created you to be? If so, we Christians should be exchanging our crosses for sugar cones and our Bibles for chocolate chips, and gathering Sundays at the ice cream parlor instead of at church.

But if your sadness returns when your ice cream is gone, if you struggle with aimlessness and not measuring up even after your double cheeseburger and cola, it's time to ask, as Isaiah, "Why spend your money on what does not satisfy?"

PERSONAL EXPERIENCE

Of course, it's easy just to point out idolatrous behavior, even to condemn it and those who indulge it. This is religion at its worst. It's truth without the grace which enables us to hear it. As Jesus charged the Pharisees, "You put onto people's backs loads which are hard to carry, but you yourselves will not stretch out a finger to help them carry those loads" (Luke 11:46).

It's therefore fitting for me to say here that I speak from personal experience.

Let's face it: it's hard to overcome a compulsion to overeat. I know, because it's in my family bloodline. I've struggled with overeating most of my adult life. In fact, simply commanding myself not to eat so much rarely helps, and often stirs me to rebel and eat more. (see "The Procrastinator, the Rebel, and the True Son of God" in *Sons of the Father*).

Like alcoholism and other compulsive behaviors birthed in an effort to cover pain and shame, eating can become an addiction. Thus, the Twelve Step Programs include "Overeaters Anonymous."

I've already pointed out how the spirit of deprivation colludes with gluttony. The Depression/WWII era framed my father's youth, and he faced considerable deprivation. As a boy myself, I learned quickly not to ask Dad for an ice cream at the outrageous cost of fifteen cents. (see "One Ice Cream at a Time," in *Do Pirates Wear Pajamas?*)

This legacy drove me to indulge sweets when I grew up and left home, especially as a reward, at last to "get the pleasure I deserve."

The human body, via the hypothalamus gland, is created with a natural chemical boundary which causes you to know when you've eaten enough to satisfy your physical need. But if you continue to overrule and violate that protective warning by indulging non-physical hungers with food, eventually your hypothalamus not only loses authority, but is superseded by the enemy through a spirit of gluttony.

Indulgence invites demons (see "How Demons Enter—and Leave" in *No Small Snakes*).

Toward overcoming my compulsion and restoring organic boundaries, I've found the addiction model apt. For me, it's a blending of emotional healing, casting out the demons which have preyed upon my wounds, a physical discipline of moderating the urge to eat, choosing healthy foods, exercising regularly, and crying out for Father God to keep me on His track for my health.

Still, I must confess to no heroic willpower on my part in this process—which began only when overeating eventually pressured my stomach valve to overflow with acid reflux. Only when that pain became unbearable and the consequences so damaging to my body, did I get serious about stopping it.

In that process, I've faced numerous root emotional wounds and cast out many spirits, including gluttony and deprivation. At times, as Richard Foster suggests, I've fasted in order to smoke out other related demons. I've prayed hard and begged God to heal my digestive tract.

Above all, I've learned to cooperate with Him in order to overcome my overeating. In fact, no other life challenge has caused me more diligently to work together with God after His healing. **More than any other personal struggle, overeating has taught me that victory in spiritual warfare often requires much more than just going head-up against a demon.**

Instead of large meals, I now eat more often in smaller portions. I've slept on an inclined wedge so any excess stomach acid stays out of my esophagus at night.

I'm learning that just because you don't feel any immediate stomach pain when you're eating doesn't mean you can continue eating. Your stomach takes time to expand and accommodate what you eat, and may reach its comfort limit before you've eaten enough to feel pain. I can stop eating, feel fine, and then half an hour later the pain comes. Gauging ahead to know how much your stomach can comfortably accommodate and when to stop eating takes a lot of practice—as well as failure and frustration.

When I slip up and eat so much as to feel my stomach expanding unto pain, a digestive enzyme pill can help, and also plain Aloe Vera juice, which soothes any acid bite in my throat and settles my stomach. When emotional stress threatens to churn my stomach, I try quickly to surrender the situation to God. I ask Holy Spirit what's causing the stress. Often, it's from trying to control situations beyond my control, not expressing sadness or joy, or a demon. I ask God how to overcome it, trusting Him to lead me with His power and wisdom. I have four prayer partners around the state whom I call, one each week, and meet regularly with my men's prayer platoon here in town.

It's a battle. But through setbacks and struggles, I've begun to see genuine progress. After ten years of struggling, I'm now down to my college weight, my stomach valve pain has diminished, and my cholesterol is dropping. In the month before writing this chapter, I had no sugar desserts, and my craving for them faded, slowly but surely.

Soon after that month, I had a piece of pie a la mode at a party—which I can genuinely say was delicious. I'd been afraid that to have any sweets at all would push me over the slippery slope to indulging again, but the compulsion to eat sweets just didn't happen. I'm experiencing grace, learning to respect the body God gave me, and trusting Him more and more to guide my appetite as I surrender it to Him.

Still, I struggle. In fact, it's likely no coincidence that since I began writing this very chapter, I've slipped up enough times overeating to stir stomach pains again like I haven't felt in months. I try not to beat myself up, but rather, remind myself that the enemy knows my weak spots and that my Father is not only merciful but graceful to restore me.

And so yet again, I surrender, trust, and step into a new day—knowing that the more I give of myself to Father God, the less I have left to give to the enemy. The more I surrender control to God, that is, I can enjoy food without feeling as if it controls me.

As Isaiah exhorted, the more I long to flow in God's purposes, listen for and trust His living word in my heart, and come closer to Jesus, the old cravings seem to lose their draw. I'm beginning to experience a new and deeper sense of satisfaction.

Actually, that satisfaction without the nagging compulsion to eat felt strange at first, and I've had to tell myself, "This is what healthy feels like."

I recognize that many people have had a tougher battle than I have, and others not so difficult. In any case, I'm grateful to God for meeting me in my battle—especially for the respect to let me do what I can and for the grace to do in me what I cannot.

> When you want something from people, you give them power over you.

14

BEYOND BITTERNESS AND RESENTMENT

RECEIVING PRAISE FROM GOD, NOT OTHERS

> *Guard against turning back from the grace of God. Let no one become like a bitter plant that grows up and causes many troubles with its poison.* (Hebrews 12:15)
>
> *After all, who is a real Jew, truly circumcised? It is not the man who is a Jew on the outside, whose circumcision is a physical thing. Rather, the real Jew is the person who is a Jew on the inside, that is, whose heart has been circumcised, and this is the work of God's Spirit, not of the written Law. Such a person receives his praise from God, not from man.* (Romans 2:28,29)

SOON AFTER *HEALING THE MASCULINE SOUL* helped pioneer the Christian men's movement, I was dismayed as shame-based ministries hijacked Father God's heart by exhorting men to a variety of unattainable performance standards. Painful personal experience had convinced me that most of us today have been crippled by shame from not being given by Dad what we need to be men. I knew that **telling men what's right to do without facing the wounds that keep us from doing it would not only increase our shame, but ultimately discourage yet another generation of broken men from trusting the Father's healing.**

What I didn't know was the power of my own shame to hamstring my witness to that truth.

Wanting to counteract this performance-oriented religion in churches—even as I had suffered it as a boy—I tried to gain entrance to the growing circle of men's ministries. One of the largest invited me to keynote at their opening conference, and I spoke about the debilitating father-wound among men and how Father God has sent Jesus to heal it.

I was never invited back, even as that ministry expanded around the country.

Stung, I became angry and tried harder to be heard and validated. Yet my second men's book, now titled *Sons of the Father*, was scorned by the largest circulating Evangelical magazine as I emphasized Father God's love over our performance as the foundation of faith. "According to Gordon Dalbey," their book reviewer scoffed, "real men don't need the Ten Commandments."[57] Real men, I countered in a letter to the editor, need the Commander more than the commandments. In fact, when we dare to know His heart for us as our Father, we'll beg Him to tell us what to do—not as obedient slaves, for fear He'll punish us for not doing it, but as trusting sons, because we know it's for our own good. What's even more, when we become real enough to confess we can't do it, He pours out His Spirit to empower us to do it (see Ezek. 36:26ff).

Soon after that review, however, *Sons of the Father* went out of print. My third men's book *Fight like a Man*, focused on how Father God overcomes the crippling shame in unfathered men. Widely regarded as my best men's book, it lasted only a year.

Booking fewer events, maxing out credit cards, fearing for our mortgage, and losing sleep, I became even more angry, and more determined to be heard. Grasping a stack of appreciative letters from men around the world, I fumed at the Father, "This is your word of healing to your sons! Why don't you get my books back into print and book me more conferences to get this word out?"

YOUR PROTECTION

His response was as simple as it was upending: "For your protection."

Humbled, I laid down my fan mail—along with my books and speaking events—at Jesus' feet. The Father, it turned out, was neither impotent nor disengaged, but caring and wise.

Clearly, my ministry was significant enough to His purposes that the enemy had marshaled forces against it. For its effectiveness and my very survival, I would have to trust His timing to walk it out. I asked Him to forgive my pride, thanked Him for enlisting me in His healing work among men—however and whenever—and released all aspects of my ministry back to Him.

In order to prepare for my uncertain future, like King David I begged Him to "search my heart and find out what wickedness there is within me" (Ps. 139:23,24). At last, I became frustrated not so much at the rejection from other ministries, but at my own compulsion to make them recognize and affirm me—and my growing bitterness as they did not.

Confused and spent, I went to a prayer partner desperate for revelation—and got it, big time.

"When you want something from people," he noted matter-of-factly, "you give them power over you."[68]

In that moment, I realized that looking for other ministries to affirm me was co-opting my focus and energy. The enemy was baiting me, insinuating that other men were taking power away from me—whereas in fact, I had been giving it away to them.

The pattern, I saw, was all-too-familiar and rooted far more deeply than my present conflict. **Even as I had unsuccessfully sought praise and encouragement from my father as a boy, I had been**

seeking it from other men. As a boy, I made an idol of my dad; as a man, I had made an idol of other men and their affirmation.

Father God, meanwhile, stood waiting for me to trust Him to give me everything I sought from others, especially from my earthly father—and more. Not because I was more correct than them, but simply because I'm His son.

FOUNDATIONAL VALIDATION

The Law, I realized, is about what we do. Authentic ministry, on the other hand, is about whose we are. And this foundational validation comes only through revelation by Holy Spirit, as we give up on our own work and trust God's.

"Who is a real Jew?" as Paul asked—that is, What defines a real man of God? "A real Jew is not the man whose flesh has been circumcised," he declared. "Rather, a real Jew is a man whose heart has been circumcised, and this is the work of God's Spirit, not of the written Law. **Such a man receives his praise from God, not from man**" (Rom. 2:28-29).

I remember the day I went into my prayer closet determined to forgive the ministries and individuals who had rejected or ignored me. I did forgive them and released all expectation of their approval. I brought boyhood wounds of abandonment and shame to Jesus for His healing, cast from me related spirits such as unforgiveness, bitterness, immaturity, division, enmity, vengeance—as well as abandonment and shame—and asked Holy Spirit to re-occupy that territory in my heart.

Congratulating myself, I ran triumphantly to tell my wife Mary.

"That's great that you've forgiven them," she smiled graciously. "Now you need to bless them."

Busted, I balked—and went back to my prayer closet to bless those ministries.

The more I began surrendering my ministry to the Father, asking Him to correct or bless it, the less I sought recognition from others. As I thereby allowed Holy Spirit to "circumcise" my heart, He replaced my bitterness with the Father's heart for His lost and broken sons.

Beyond my own fading agendas, I saw simply a generation of men blackmailed by shame—even myself—longing to live surrendered to the Father and trusting His grace. In fact, I recognized that shame—even my own—as the fountainhead of the very performance-oriented religion I fought.

It's one level of faithfulness to recognize harmful teaching. It's another **to respond to it with grace as well as truth—the only real hope to stop the wounding, by healing not only the wounded, but ultimately, the wounders as well.** True, Christians must hold each other accountable—but only insofar as we balance truth with grace (see John 1:17).

In fact, it's entirely possible to become religiously anti-religious. In one case, I had to call another author and apologize for attacking ungraciously his lack of grace!

"We teach best what we need to learn most," as another has said.

LETTING GO

I now believe Father God will hold me accountable primarily not for whether my ministry was widely affirmed or whether I correctly rebuked a brother. Rather, it's about whether I surrendered to Him, listened for His truth, trusted His grace, and wrote/preached what He put on my heart—whether published and recognized or not. The ultimate letting go and trusting the Father was beckoned as one praying brother offered, "Your ministry's greatest impact may come after you've passed away."

Jesus, that is, bore our shame on the cross, so we could go to the Father cleansed and open, able to receive His heart and to manifest His Spirit in this world. Efforts to fabricate righteousness by presuming to follow religious behavior standards co-opt that saving work of Jesus and short-circuit the Father's call. But what breaks His heart, is a son's or daughter's seeking human validation instead of trusting His.

Sure, you can't isolate yourself and say you're only going to receive approval from God and discount input from others. That's a slippery slope to arrogance and alienation, if not fanaticism and cultism. We need to be—and I am—accountable to other, trustworthy Christians and seek their discernment. But it's one thing to seek others' discernment in an effort to open your heart to God, and quite another **to seek their approval in order to cover your shame—something Jesus has already done on the cross**.

Are you angry and bitter toward others—parent or spouse, boss or colleagues? Do you resent that they don't recognize and affirm you in spite of your many efforts? If so, you want something from them—which they're very likely not capable of giving you. Something, in fact, which your Father God wants to give you Himself.

Certainly, He may call you to speak a word of truth into your circumstances, but **prepare yourself to be heard by doing it with grace.** Don't waste your valuable time and energy stewing as I did. Stop complaining that others don't acknowledge you—when you're giving them power yourself to define you.

Instead, give up and grow up. Seek your identity not in others, but in Father God.

Bless the others—even "those who persecute you" (Matt. 5:44)—and crucify your agenda.

Ask the Father to forgive you for turning to others for the validation only He can give you, and turn back to Him to get it. Let Him heal the wounds and deliver you from enemy forces that would trap you in resentment and sabotage your destiny. Let Him show you what it means to "receive praise from God," instead of from others. Ask Him to show you the way He sees you.

Above all, remember that the Father "has created you for a life of good deeds, which He has already prepared for you to do" (Ephes. 2:8-10)—and go for it as He leads.

Your true Father awaits—and so does your destiny.

> We abdicate supernatural reality to the devil rather than face our desperate need for God's saving power.

15

UNMASKING HALLOWEEN

A PAGAN REVIVAL

You yourselves used to be in the darkness, but since you have become the Lord's people, you are in the light. So you must live like people who belong to the light.... Have nothing to do with the worthless things that people do, the things that belong to the darkness. Instead, bring them out to the light.... And when all things are brought out to light, then their true nature is clearly revealed.... So be careful how you live. Don't live like ignorant people, but like wise people...because these are evil days. (Ephes. 5:8-10, 15)

AMID BLACK WITCH HATS AND ORANGE PUMPKINS, the darkness of fall crept in with the trembling voice of a pastor, calling me from his hospital bed the morning after Halloween.

The night before, Jeff's (not his real name) oldline denominational church was "celebrating" their annual "Haunted Sanctuary Night." As part of the "decoration," he had been tied up and hung in a fake noose from the rafters. Below, church members and their children stepped warily through a black-walled "graveyard" maze of pews while costumed skeletons and ghosts jumped out at them. Amid spooky howling and morbid organ music, suddenly Jeff's supporting noose rope inexplicably snapped and he fell twenty feet, striking his head on the concrete floor and narrowly escaping death.

Listening on the phone, I muffled a deep sigh and prayed for wisdom. Some years before, Jeff had confided in me that he had received the baptism of the Holy Spirit, but had never told his congregation, for fear they'd reject him.

During our phone conversation, I told him how thankful I was that he survived his fall. As I realized how much I cared about Jeff, however, I knew that brotherly love required truth as well as grace.

"You've been baptized into the supernatural reality and power of God's Spirit," I reminded him. "The enemy of God, who animates Halloween, has been after your life ever since. Please, brother," I begged, "don't hand it to him on a silver platter. This is not a matter of church theology but of life and death!"

HALLOWEEN VS CHRISTMAS

From drugstore racks to office parties, this annual invasion of sinister masks and images heralds a showcase for evil, as deliberately dark spirituality takes center stage among us. In our money-driven culture, this "season" has in fact become so popular that Halloween marketing sales now rival those of Christmas.

The graphic contrasts here frame the cosmic contest: **death, dark masks, and the effort to conceal vs. birth, bright lights, and the effort to reveal;** "pranks" and bad deeds as powers of destruction are given rein vs. gifts and good deeds as the saving power of the Creator is extended.

Not that long ago, Halloween was seen simply as an occasion for children to have fun dressing in costumes and hitting up neighbors for candy. More recently—with office parties, racy outfits, and even parades—adults have taken over the occasion, co-opting its innocence. In fact, Halloween's increasing profile today among adults has been traced to its popularity among homosexuals—for whom same-sex attraction is a mask for deep wounds. "Halloween: America's Gay Holiday," as one news feature headline proclaimed.[64]

"It has been the Gay community that has most flamboyantly exploited Halloween's potential as a transgressive festival, as one that operates outside or on the margins of orthodox time, space, and hierarchy," declares Nicholas Rogers in *Halloween: From Pagan Ritual to Party Night.* "Indeed, it is the Gay community that has been arguably most responsible for Halloween's adult rejuvenation."

The word Halloween comes from an abbreviated "all Hallows Eve," a day before All Saints' Day, instituted when the early Church decided to commemorate past Christian heroes of the faith. Bowing to pagan sensibilities—even as Jeff to his spiritually blind congregation—the ancient Church coordinated the date with November 1st, New Year's Day on the ancient Druid calendar in Western Europe.

In a secularized culture like ours, this unashamed syncretistic effort to make Christianity more palatable to pagans has only accomplished the reverse, making pagan spirituality more palatable to Christians.

On their October 31st New Year's Eve, Druids extolled the "Lord of the Dead," who was believed to summon on that night the spirits of all wicked persons who had died in the previous year and been condemned to live in animals—as the proverbial black cat. On this one night, it was believed, those departed spirits returned to their original bodies and homes expecting to be honored by the living with gift offerings. Otherwise, those evil spirits would spread curses, cast spells, cause damage, and torment the populace.

Hence, "trick or treat."

Saints, it would seem, are not as much fun to emulate as demons.

HOMAGE TO EVIL

At its root, therefore, Halloween is a wolf in sheep's costume, an occasion which purports to honor Christian saints but which in fact pays homage—and extortion—to evil spirits.

God's plans are not achieved by placating evil, nor did Jesus negotiate with demons. Today, however, our blindly secularized, materialistic culture effectively does this—even as churches like Jeff's—in not daring to acknowledge the active reality of evil among us.

"This present age since the coming of Jesus is a new dispensation," goes the conservative/evangelical rationalization. "The spiritual dynamics of biblical times no longer apply. Supernatural phenomena happened then but not now."

While the latter eviscerate the faith with denial, liberal/universalists, on the other hand, prefer condescension. "The demons, miracles, and other supernatural phenomena portrayed in the bible are just literary figures of speech to accommodate an ancient, less educated readership," they avow. "It didn't happen then and it doesn't happen now."

Christians foster this "liberal vs. conservative" charade because it distracts us from the humbling fact that the greatest of our natural human powers is no match for the least of spiritual powers. We all know this because we all experience it, from unbidden nightmares to death itself.

The shame of this primal human inadequacy stirs an addictive denial that keeps even the most sincere Christians, whether liberal or conservative, from facing the reality of evil—and thereby, from recognizing its handiwork in Halloween unto today. Intoxicated with worldly conceit, we dismiss it all as "nothing but superstition"—and then we're startled when "treats" for children dressed as witches and demons begin to include razor blades in apples and drugs in candy.

Thus, we sacrifice our children's innocence on the smug altar of human pride and control. In fact, **we'd rather abdicate supernatural reality to the devil than face our desperate need for saving power**. The enemy, of course, knows this, and focuses his attacks on offering us ways to cover up our shame rather than take it to Jesus and be rid of it altogether.

As the "Son of God," that is, Jesus "appeared for this very reason: to destroy what the Devil had done" (1 John 3:8b), and to demonstrate thereby that "the Spirit who is in you is more powerful than the spirit in those who belong to the world" (1 John 4:4).

ENFORCED IGNORANCE

The enforced ignorance of our "modern" secularized worldview offers neither protection nor excuse. Those who fancy similarly that smoking is just a harmless pleasure, as the early tobacco company ads assured, nevertheless contract lung cancer—and indeed, infect others with their second-hand smoke.

"For you were once darkness, but now you are light in the Lord," as Paul exhorted the early Christians, then immersed in a pagan culture not wholly unlike our own today. "Live as children of light (for the fruit of the light consists in all goodness, righteousness, and truth) and find out what pleases the Lord. Have nothing to do with the fruitless deeds of darkness, but rather expose them" (Ephes. 5:8-10NIV).

Those called to reflect God's Light in Jesus, that is, face greater consequences for accommodating the darkness—as Pastor Jeff discovered in his Halloween brush with death.

Granted, it's hard to maintain Christian boundaries in our spiritually blind culture, which cannot recognize the need for protection. Yet the consequences of not doing so fall upon non-Christians as well.

"Man dies after botched hanging stunt," as the Associated Press headlined a story about a Texas physical therapy clinic Halloween party. There, a technician wearing a rubber monster mask hung himself from the ceiling and his hidden bracing wire broke, choking him to death.[65] Pastor Jeff was blessed indeed, to have survived his own charade.

BAD ANGELS

When my son was around three or four, I taught him about the "bad angels" who "make Halloween scary." He still wanted very much to participate in the costumes and parties, so I said I would take him to a local church for a suitable alternative: a "no bad guys" party to celebrate historic Christian heroes.

Very early that evening, however, he was already dressed in his Peter Pan outfit, and begged to go trick-or-treating around the neighborhood. I balked, but he persisted. "It's not even dark yet, Daddy!" he pleaded. Eventually, I relented and agreed to let him visit only our two closest neighbors "and no more!"

Later, after the second house, he clutched his bag of candy happily. Mary and I hustled him past the cobwebbed porch and piped-in howling sounds, down the sidewalk toward our home next door. For a brief moment, the two of us pulled ahead of him and sighed.

Suddenly, we were startled by a dull THUNK behind us, followed by a loud scream. Turning, we found our son sprawled out on the concrete. Confused how he might have tripped, nevertheless we rushed to pick him up and saw his upper teeth had cut into his lower lip, which was now bleeding profusely.

Quickly, we dashed him home and into the bathroom. I had barely wiped the blood from his whimpering mouth when it hit me like a ton of bricks. As Mary—a nurse, thankfully—took over, I ran out to the living room and fell to my knees, crushed.

Oh, Father, please, please heal my son," I begged, *"and forgive me for not maintaining protective spiritual boundaries for him!*

The enemy of God hates children because, like Jesus, they restore innocence to this fallen world. But in order to destroy the children, the enemy must first deceive the adults.

The Bible was written for evil days, even our own. Let's stop bowing to darkness and ignorance and speak the truth to a world held hostage by shame and fear: Jesus came to bear our sinful nature, so we could receive God's Holy Spirit and faithfully exercise His power over unholy spirits, even those which sponsor Halloween.

It happened then, and it happens now—to all who choose to live in His light.

> **And so I opted out of the pagan men's agenda. Yet I remain dismayed by a Church that so often refuses to opt into God's agenda for His sons.**

16

LET THIS (SOLSTICE) CUP PASS

OLD DEMONS IN THE NEW AGE

Worship no god but me. (Exodus 20:2)

FOR SEVERAL YEARS, I HAD WORKED together with these men dedicated to bringing helpful resources to fathers in our city. Now, all my efforts to collaborate had come to a painful crossroads.

They were not Christian, but knew that I am. Most were New Age enthusiasts, including several who proclaimed themselves as "practicing pagans." Others preferred more established religions. Once, while riding to a meeting, a fellow Board of Directors member mentioned that he had "graduated from seminary in town." The only seminary I knew in the area is Catholic; naively, I asked him, "Oh— are you a Catholic priest?"

"No," he replied matter-of-factly. "I'm a Buddhist."

NO CHRISTIAN COMRADES

Alongside these committed volunteers in our organization, I had braved young male offenders in juvenile hall, visited a maternity hospital to encourage young unmarried fathers, spoken about the challenges of fathering at our conferences for social workers and other health care professionals. **How often in those pioneering endeavors I longed for Christian comrades-in-arms and grieved that none of the almost 130+ churches in town were doing anything to heal the awful father-wound in local men.** In fact, these non- and some deliberately un-Christians had often been more accepting and respectful of my spirituality that many Christians.

Once, during my "Sons of the Father" weekend church conference out of state, the host pastor came to look over my book table. When he spotted my CD "Receiving the Holy Spirit," he summarily seized it and tossed it into a box under the table. "This is not something we want for our church," he snapped.

When I first told the fatherhood group Board of Directors that I'm a Christian, the president Jim (not his real name) asked me, "So where do you tend to focus most in your ministry work?"

Cautiously, I paused—then decided to be real. "I try to help men get emotionally healed, by moving in the supernatural gifts of the Holy Spirit."

Puzzled, he knit his brow. "What does that mean?" he asked, genuinely interested.

"Well...frankly," I noted hesitantly, "it means inviting Jesus to come and show us how to cooperate with him in the healing process." And then, in what felt like a leap of foolishness, I sucked in a deep breath and plunged in. "A lot of times that means identifying and casting out demons."

To my surprise and amazement, Jim drew up in respect and smiled approvingly. "Hey, that's real wild man stuff!"

Exhaling in relief, I shook my head in dismay as I received from this avowed pagan a blessing such as few churches were capable of giving me.

Some time later, I sat in Jim's home with a dozen-odd other Board members at the opening of our monthly meeting, circled amid

Buddhist flags, Native American feather poles, and a variety of other New Age icons.

"Why don't we start with prayer?" Jim offered.

Startled, I leaned back uneasily as those on either side of me took my hand. As one by one the others then prayed to deities ranging from "the spirit of the earth" to "the great power of love," my mind raced ahead anticipating my turn.

Father, I cried out in my heart, *what should I say?* Some of these people, I knew, had been raised in church-going homes; one, in fact, was the child of a pastor. They had accepted my being a Christian with characteristic tolerance, and some even with respect. **But how explicitly in a public prayer could I dare express my faith among non-Christians who were clearly beckoning demons?**

Father, should I water down my words to avoid offending anyone? Feverishly, I prayed to set the cross over me, asked for the blood of Jesus to cover and protect me. *Or should I go ahead and...* but then the hand next to me squeezed to signal my turn.

I sucked in a quick breath. "I...I'd like to offer a prayer to... the God revealed to Israel, and to the world through Jesus," I began cautiously. "Thank you, Jesus, for your love for us, and for the love you give us for each other. Come, by the power of your Spirit, and open us up to your heart for the fathers and children of our community, and give us wisdom how to recognize and promote your purposes for them."

With a measured sigh, I squeezed the hand on my other side. At least, I told myself, I can work with these men on basic humanitarian projects to help fathers face our brokenness and find resources to change.

Soon after the prayers had closed, however, Jim asked for agenda items—and I was forced to wonder.

WOLF SPIRIT

At once, a particularly bright and energetic Board member declared that what young men need—"especially those we're trying to help"—is "to receive the spirit of the wolf." In fact, he had designed just such a ceremony to instill that spirit in them, even as he had done with his own sons. "I move that we set up a time for the wolf spirit ceremony," he declared enthusiastically, "and invite all the young fathers we work with to come and receive it."

Immediately, I drew back. *Oh, no, Father!* I prayed under my breath. *What do I do now?*

Clearly, a major fork in the road loomed ahead. On the one hand, the path of acquiescing and participating in the wolf-spirit ceremony was out of the question. But speaking out against it as demonic would destroy my hard-wrought relationship with these men, who had absolutely no way to process that truth.

Stunned, I sat uneasily as a lively discussion followed, in which everyone agreed that such a "worship service" would indeed be helpful for young men. In fact, one exclaimed to excited nods, "Wouldn't it be great for the entire Board to participate and receive the wolf spirit ourselves!"

Struggling to conceal my chagrin, I prayed furiously for wisdom—to no avail. Finally, it struck me—not without relief: *How about if I just sit this whole thing out, Father?* I offered. *Is there really any need for me to make a point here? I mean, I could just not say anything, let them do their New Age thing, and not show up.*

Sure, I reasoned, this explicitly spiritual ceremony was rife with demons. But I could make some excuse and just not attend it. Indeed, **was challenging it worth risking years of credibility I had gained among these men?**

That's it! I thought, exhaling at last. *There's my solution. No problem—I'll just opt out! I'll wait until they pick a date and then apologize that I "unfortunately" had already made other plans at that time.*

Eventually, the discussion waned, and Jim suggested we break for coffee before voting. Relieved and satisfied in my decision, I arose with the others, stretched, and headed for the kitchen area.

There, Jim approached me to chat and gestured toward a number of coffee mugs gathered on the table. "Would you like some coffee?" he asked hospitably.

Not much for hot drinks, I was about to pass, but then decided to be more sociable. "Well..., how about maybe some herb tea?"

His wife, who was standing just behind us at the stove, overheard. "No problem!" she declared affably, reaching for a cup with one hand and a steaming teapot with the other.

"So…" I offered, looking back at my host. "Looks like we've got a good group here today."

"Yes," he replied, "it's good to…"

TICH! "AHH! Ouch!" A distinct cracking sound interrupted, followed by a loud outburst from his wife and the clash of glass on the countertop.

As everyone stopped and turned to see, Jim reached over in alarm to embrace his wife. "Are you OK?" he asked.

SOLSTICE CUP

Shaking hot water from her arm and seizing a nearby dishtowel, she wiped her hand. "The water was pretty hot, but at least it didn't really burn me," she offered with a grimace.

And then, she pointed in surprise to the countertop at my prospective tea cup. "Well, now, would you look at that!" she exclaimed, shaking her head in amazement.

Everyone crowded into the small kitchen to look. There, sliced cleanly down the middle in two halves, including the handle, lay my cup amid a pool of steaming water. A colorful collage of stars, crescent moons, and suns covered each surface.

"Oh, no!" Jim exclaimed. "That was our Solstice cup!"

"We got that at the Solstice Festival a few years ago," his wife explained, picking up the two halves by their split handles, one in each hand. "We've used it each year for our ceremony of thanksgiving to the sun."

"It was so special to us!" Jim lamented, shaking his head tight-lipped at the loss. Then, he knit his eyebrows, both puzzled and amazed. "Now, how could that cup just split so cleanly right in half, top to bottom, like that—even through the handle?"

As the others joined in a chorus of "Wow!" and "How about that?" murmurs, I eased back amazed—and afraid. Indeed, God had honored my petition in our prayer circle earlier. He had come, as I asked, even as a mighty Divider with a sword to enforce His holy division. Clearly—graphically—He was not only present, but commanding an audience to hear Him speak.

The message was as clear as it was unsettling. In that moment I knew that during the imminent voting discussion there would be no opting out or "inclusive" waffling. Any justification for my evading the wolf-spirit issue had evaporated like steam off a cleanly divided teacup.

"The word of God is alive and active, shaper than any double-edged sword," I remembered:

> It cuts all the way through, to where soul and spirit meet, to where joints and marrow come together. It judges the desires and thoughts of a man's heart. There is nothing that can be hid from God; everything in all creation is exposed and lies open before his eyes. And it is to him that we must all give an account of ourselves. (Heb. 4:12,13)

Nor had I any doubt whom He had appointed to wield that sword at the meeting.

In splitting their Solstice cup before us, the Father had proclaimed His testimony to the pagans. In that moment, the choice had been made for me. Now it was my turn to act.

As eventually the gathering began to circle up once again in the living room, I prayed quickly, desperately. *OK, Father, you've drawn the dividing line and made it abundantly clear that your sword of truth is here and you want me to speak your case. I promise I'll do my best. But please, you've got to help me with this. I know your truth about the demons being entertained, but give me wisdom and grace so the others will listen.*

GENUINE RESPECT

I realize that these men don't know the truth about the evil they're dealing with, and can't recognize it when I speak. I don't want to patronize or alienate them. I want them to hear You in my words. If they're going to hear me at all, if I'm going to be a part of this ministry in the future, I've got to demonstrate my genuine respect for them even as I say No to their program.

In your name, Jesus, I bind any spirits of judgment, religion, shame, and timidity over me and trust you with the outcome.

"So let's see," Jim began as everyone gathered and settled once again in the living room circle. "Is there any more discussion on the wolf spirit ceremony, or are we ready to vote on it?" Scanning around the circle, he lifted his eyebrows in open invitation.

A raised hand. "I think this is great, and we should all go for it!"

Nods, murmurs of agreement.

Amid the apparent consensus, clearly no one was about to offer any alternative view.

My time had come.

"Well," Jim offered, "it looks like we'll be—"

Gingerly, I raised my hand at last and leaned forward. "Actually," I broke in, "I personally have a bit of a different take on the issue, and I'd like to share that with the Board." Pausing for an even breath, I sensed the same openness among us that I'd experienced in all our previous deliberations.

"Let me begin by saying what a privilege it's been for me to work with all of you over the years," I offered. "We've done some really significant service together for dads and for our community—and I respect every one of you for that.

"In fact, I especially respect your spirituality. I don't scoff at any 'wolf spirit' or any of the other spirits you occasionally talk about. I believe they're real, active, and have a genuine effect on people's lives.

"What's more," I said, nodding with a smile, "I like you all. I've really enjoyed the camaraderie we've shared. I want that to continue, but…that will depend on you, if you can hear what I need to say here."

As evenly as possible, I drew another breath, and leaned in further. *Help me, Jesus!* I prayed quietly.

"You all know that I'm a Christian. The God I worship has given me every blessing I have—my wife, son, ministry, health, provision—everything. I owe it all to Him. He's forgiven me all the harm I've ever caused so I can do now what I believe He created me to do. In fact,

He's flat-out saved my life more than once. Without Him, I'd be dead. No question about it."

With that statement, a strength filled me, and I knew it was true. **In fact, without Jesus and His saving acts, I was already dead. What could I fear from any man?** Encouraged, I looked around the circle into the other men's eyes, and at last, leaned back.

"In fact," I continued, "while our work together focuses on helping fathers, my God is my true and only Father. All my work trying to help other men be better dads, everything I've done with you here, comes out of what my Father God has done for me. He's shown me that He wants the best for me, and He's done everything He can to make sure I have it—including a lot of painful operations to heal me of some really deep wounds."

JEALOUS FATHER

For a brief moment, I looked away—*Father, help!*—then turned back to the group, which sat attentively. "So because He's invested so much in me, my God is a jealous Father. He doesn't want me worshipping or opening myself up to any other spiritual powers."

I paused, sighing with determination.

"From that much of my story, maybe you can see why it'd be really hard for me to join up with the wolf-spirit ceremony. To offer myself to and bond with another spirit besides my Father's Holy Spirit would be like having sex with some woman besides my wife. I just can't do it."

Spreading my arms with hands up and palms open, I shrugged matter of factly. "I'm not into judging anyone else, just trying to be honest with you about who I am. I really want to keep on working together. But in this case, if you go ahead with the wolf-spirit ceremony, I can't go with you."

I lowered my arms and sat silently as the others digested what I had said. Finally, the Buddhist seminary graduate spoke up.

"Gordon," he offered with measured tolerance, "We wouldn't want to do anything to offend your god."

Oh, Father! my spirit cried out. *I appreciate their courtesy, but they don't have a clue how deeply this 'wolf spirit' business offends you!* I opened my mouth to speak—and paused as a flush of grace swept over me.

"Well...," I offered, nodding awkwardly, "I...I appreciate that."

A few minutes later, the wolf spirit ceremony was tabled—and never arose again. I never felt any disrespect from the others and continued to work with the organization until it ceased operating a few years later.

Even today, however, I wonder: should I have said more? Should I have said less? I really don't know. All I know is that I did my best to speak as my Father asked me and to trust His leading in precarious territory.

He had split the enemy's cup so I could not drink from it, indeed, that it might pass not only me, but from all others for all time. In that act, he beckoned me to wholeness, to unite my split and conflicted heart with His grace and truth. In that process, He protected me from both judging the others and being judged by them—and the hearts of many young fathers were saved from being given over to demons in a wolf spirit ceremony.

Certainly, I'm thankful for having been used thereby to deliver those men from such evil. That day of the Solstice cup brought closure to my fears and integrity to my ministry among men of the world.

And so I opted out of the pagan agenda. Yet today, years later, I'm dismayed by a Church that refuses to opt into God's agenda, leaving an unholy vacuum in our lost and broken world which cries out for the saving, delivering witness of Jesus. This group of pagans knew something that churches should know but have turned away from: Young men need to be awakened spiritually, even blessed by older men who can lead them into the full supernatural reality and power of Holy Spirit. But no churchmen in my town understood either this need or the heart of Father God to meet it. And so the enemy of God was using pagans to steal this territory from Christians.

On the one hand, the conservative religionists among us speak the truth of demonic influence with no grace, and their judgmental spirit turns others away from Jesus. On the other hand, the liberal universalists offer only grace with no truth, and their tolerant spirit abandons others to demonic oppression.

Meanwhile, Jesus—in whom God brought both "grace and truth" (John 1:17)—awaits His warriors.

> I stood expectantly, yea reverently, before the glowing overhead screen, where The Numbers gazed down upon me from on high.

17

"PLAYING" THE LOTTERY—

A GAME FOR LOSERS[61]

> *But all those things that I might count as profit I now reckon as loss for Christ's sake. Not only those things; I reckon everything as complete loss for the sake of what is so much more valuable, the knowledge of Christ Jesus my Lord.* (Phil. 3:7,8)

I HAVE A CONFESSION TO MAKE. I'm an ordained minister, author, and speaker at Christian conferences—but I'm also a man who knows how easy it is to fall under the spell of rainbows promising a pot of gold.

Years ago, as a 50th birthday gift, a non-Christian friend gave me several "Big 50" California State Lottery tickets, each beckoning a

$50,000 jackpot. The year before, I'd left my pastorate to write a new book, moved, and bought a house for the first time.

By my birthday, the book wasn't finished, conferences had tapered off for the summer, and the mortgage company hadn't forgotten my address. **With my bank account needle bouncing on "E," those big, silver-coated "50"s on the tickets just seemed to wink at me** from my desk—where I'd tossed them, near the wastebasket.

The good news in getting older, however is that you rack up enough sins to get humble and learn something.

For me and the Lottery, it began years before, when I'd given up a full-time teaching job and moved to Boston for seminary. I thought I'd saved up enough money to keep me going, but within the first year I'd spent my entire savings and was more than $1000 in debt—in 1974 dollars.

JUST A GAME

As my worries grew, I began paying more than casual attention to the cheerful TV commercial guy who proclaimed that every day someone won hundreds, yea thousands unto millions of dollars in the Massachusetts State Lottery. All over town, billboards, bus, and store ads beckoned me to "Play the Game!"

Eventually, I decided to buy two 50-cent tickets with my carefully allotted lunch money—for fun, of course. After all, it was just a "game."

On the other hand, it could solve my debt problem in a flash.

Like the TV guy said, it was easy. I got off the subway on my way to Church History class and just handed over my dollar right there at the newsstand. Later that night at home, I pulled the tickets out of my pocket and hesitated—then laughed at my foolishness, tossed them into the wastebasket and forgot about them.

Yet, when the next day came for the winning numbers to be announced, I had second thoughts. With a nod to thrift, I retrieved my tickets from the trash. No sense wasting a good dollar, right?

Soon, I found myself hurrying through my New Testament homework. Jumping off the subway car that afternoon, I ran to the newsstand, my heart beating much faster than that short sprint would merit.

There, at last, I stood expectantly, yea reverently, before the glowing overhead board, where The Numbers gazed down upon me from on high.

Quickly, I examined my tickets. Again, I looked up.

But just as quickly, it was over. Not even close.

*Maybe, though, if only the third number could have been first and the second had been....*I caught myself as a strange, aching sensation crept over me, and sighed in self-disgust. Pitching my tickets into a nearby trash can, I rushed off to Christian Ethics class.

A few weeks later, I cashed my student loan check, paid my tuition for the next semester—and found that I had about $50 left over. Just that week, this shivering Californian sojourning in Boston had received a monthly fuel-oil bill for over one-third my monthly rent.

WIN FOR SURE

Almost as soon as the cash settled into my hand, the thought crossed my mind: *At 50 cents apiece, I could buy 100 Lottery tickets. With that many, I'd win something for sure!*

A few days later, still bruised from my earlier loss and undecided about this "investment," I ran into a casual friend at church, a self-employed house painter with a wife and two young children. Business had been terrible for weeks, he complained. And then, just as I was about to chime in with my own problems—and my Lottery solution—he laughed gently and shook his head.

"Would you believe, things got so bad last week I was about to play the Lottery?"

'Wh-what?" I blurted out—and then, catching myself quickly, forced a lame smile. "Uh, wow—no kidding?"

"Yeah, my faith was at a pretty low ebb," he sighed. "I don't know how, but I got hold of myself one day and decided that all my panicking was only making things worse. I realized that I'd taken a lot for granted. So I decided instead just to begin giving thanks for what the Lord's given me—my health, my wife, my kids, everything."

I stood there transfixed as he shrugged his shoulders.

"I can't explain it," he went on, "but not long after that, a pretty fair contract came through for me. Not lots of money, but enough to put us back on an even keel again."

I couldn't believe it. There I was, studying at perhaps the finest university in the world to teach others about faith, listening to a struggling house painter preach the most convincing sermon on faith that I've ever heard. Embarrassed—and genuinely hopeful at last—I confessed my own story, and we both shared a good laugh at ourselves.

I never bought another Lottery ticket. I couldn't do anything after that but confess my little faith and praise God for what He had given me. I can't say that the very next day piles of cash fell into my hands from heaven. In fact, I went further in debt before finishing seminary. But often during those years of need, I was lifted up by a personal gift, a part-time job, an award—each of which became an inspired part of my ministry that no Lottery win could have provided.

Today, from my comfortable study, in the shadow of my seminary diploma and published books, that season of desperation is painfully embarrassing to recall. Yet I'm thankful for it, even—especially—for not having won the Lottery. For I was taught then to live with an enduring faith through trial and time, not with the fleeting fantasy of Lottery magic to spirit me out of life's pain and uncertainty.

This very struggle, I came to realize, marked the trail Jesus walked. "Though he was God's son, he learned trusting-obedience by what he suffered, just as we do" (Hebrews 5:8TMB).

My compulsive hope in the Lottery to save me testified that I had not learned that lesson myself. That is, whatever you attribute saving power to besides the living God revealed in Jesus, is an idol—in this case, the demon of mammon, defined by Webster as "riches, avarice, and worldly gain, as personified in the Bible as a false god."[62]

INNER WORTHLESSNESS

What's more, I know now that it wasn't primarily a financial problem that had led me to worship the Lottery, but rather, an inner sense of worthlessness—which fuels the spirit of mammon.

Often, for example, we might say about a person, "He's worth millions." With no money, from that perspective I was worth nothing. The demonic lure of the Lottery, therefore, was that **while promising to deliver me from my feelings of worthlessness, it served only to confirm them—as I and millions of others became "losers" yet again.**

A "loser" spirit thereby partners with spirits of gambling and addiction, which impel the gambler not to win, but to lose. Losing confirms the demon's condemning definition of you, and drives you to gamble more in hopes of overcoming that.

Gambling beckons addiction insofar as you look for a "big win" to cover the shame of worthlessness. But Jesus has already done that decisively on the cross. The world's abundance of counterfeit shame-removers, from guns and money to status and stardom, are eventually seen as such insofar as they not only fail to remove shame, but indeed, foster it—as when casino odds eventually bear out and most often you lose your bet.

State lotteries betray their nefarious spiritual origin in the pitch that they contribute money to public education funds and therefore "benefit the children." **To Father God, however, children are not stakes in a poker game. Jesus did not say, "Let the kids wait for whatever's left over from the casinos."** He said, "The greatest in the Kingdom of heaven is the one who humbles himself and becomes like this child. And whoever welcomes in my name one such child as this, welcomes me" (Matt. 18:4,5).

Those who value children as Father God does—that is, who welcome them in Jesus' name—make appropriate sacrifices to provide for their education. Those who abandon their children's welfare to the compulsions of gamblers have cursed the Kingdom of God—and need not waste their time awaiting His blessing.

The loser spirit is exposed when you realize that through Jesus' sacrifice, you're already a winner. "It is finished!" He proclaimed on the cross (John 19:30). Not because the Wheel of Fortune has stopped spinning, but because the Lord of all fortune has given you His power to overcome all obstacles to your appointed destiny. Not only have your sins been forgiven, but in fact, the Spirit of God is within you making you His son/daughter and empowering your destiny.

That's a winning combination.

JACKPOT MAGNET

And yet....that cash jackpot remains a flesh magnet.

OK, I confess: I did scratch my birthday "Big 50" tickets. I mean, you never know—you might be a winner. The fact that I'm writing this article instead of vacationing in Tahiti should tip you off: Once again, the Lottery said I'm a loser.

I never bought another lottery ticket. In fact, I renounced the spirits of mammon and gambling in me and cast them out. Sure, temptations remain. But I'm more free now to make my choice—and pray for the strength to choose a winner's lifestyle.

You never know about the Lottery. But you can be sure about Father God, whose name is not "I might be," but "I Am." You may not win cash from the casino or lottery. But you can bank on Jesus, who has already won for us today the security of eternal life as His beloved children and victorious fellowship as brothers and sisters. The world offers no jackpot like that.

No, I'm not on a Lottery-provided vacation. But I'm awfully thankful for what my Father's given me—including my work.

Unto today, I occasionally hear materially comfortable folks scoff in disgust about "how terrible" it is that "poor people gamble away what little money they have." I can only acknowledge sadly that the Lottery is indeed "a tax on the poor," as others have noted, since most participants are low-income.

Having experienced myself the deeper human brokenness and demonic pull that underlies that truth, I can't share in the judgment of those whose riches isolate them from temptation.

Instead, I'd rather challenge those of us who have more food, clothing, and shelter than we really need to give thanks for what God has given us by sharing it with others. Let's become a faithful community, caring and supporting each other as brothers and sisters—not a mass of individuals clinging desperately to our Lottery tickets.

We have nothing to lose but our fear—and the Kingdom of God to win.

> If "my" team loses, I'm a loser. If "we" win, I'm a winner. The game bears either the curse of condemnation or the blessing of redemption. This is the province of the gods.

18

IF THEY DON'T WIN, IT'S A SHAME

BALL GAMES AND

THE BATTLE FOR MEN'S SOULS

But Lord, you are my shield, my glory,
and my only hope. You alone can lift my head,
now bowed in shame. (Psalm 3:3LIV)

A FEW SEASONS AGO, thousands of enraged Cleveland football fans at the Browns-Jacksonville game pelted the field with beer bottles—stopping the game and sending players, referees, and coaches running for cover—after a last-minute botched call by officials which gave the game to Jacksonville.

"I like the fact that our fans care," the Cleveland Browns' president affirmed later.

Below a five-column headline "Trashing the Game," the next morning's *Los Angeles Times*[68] ran a telling photo of high-fisted, team-jerseyed fans shouting in the stands above a home-made banner:

MAKE US PROUD
GO BROWNS

These simple words, emblazoned in brown-and-gold team colors, state quite simply why a man can become so invested in his team and allow its performance to determine his very life outlook and priorities.

Similarly, a popular shipping supply catalog, below a spec chart for its "Brute" brand of containers and lids, pitches its "NFL WORK GLOVES" by exhorting, "Show your team pride on the job."[69]

UNSPOKEN CONTRACT

The fan, that is, enters an unspoken contract with the team: I identify with the players. In fact, I become a virtual team member, unto wearing not only their official logo from hats to work gloves, but the ultimate identification in an individual player's name jersey. As my "home" team, they're family; I watch "our" games and cheer my loyalty. I invest in them my money, my time, and my devotion.

In return for my investment, the team's job is to make me "proud"—and in that profound sense, to cover my shame. I may be confused as a husband, challenged as a father, eat, drink, and watch TV too much—but if my team wins, I'm OK.

Clearly, a lot's at stake here. Since it's my team, how they perform reflects upon me and my town. If "we" win, I'm a winner. If "we" lose, I'm a loser. The "game" offers not just fun and fellowship, but my team's performance bears either the curse of condemnation or the blessing of redemption.

This is the province of the gods, entered at every kickoff, first pitch, and tipoff.

No wonder energies ran so high at the Browns-Jaguars football game and the miscall reaction was so violent. The team's job was to make their male spectators proud by winning and thereby, to cover their shame. The officials, however, had sabotaged that effort. **Shame was left exposed, even before a nationwide TV audience, and the man-made gods designed to cover it were unmasked as impotent.**

Among men who don't know the grace of a father, this means war. In an extreme example, El Salvador and Honduras sent their armies to war in 1969, when rioting at a disputed World Cup soccer match ignited existing tensions between those nations.[70] In Cleveland, a shower of beer bottles and trash was sufficient to cover the emptied football field that exposed spectators' shame.

Let me say here that I enjoy ballgames. Living in Southern California, I'm a Lakers fan, own hours of NBA videos, go to local football and basketball games, both college and high school. My heart pounds when the action comes down to the wire. I cheer at great plays and groan when "my team" misses a chance to score.

Wins pump you up, no doubt about it—and losses are a bummer. As the old baseball ditty "Take Me out to the Ball Game" so poignantly urges, "Root, root, root for the home team; **if they don't win, it's a shame.**"

Sport contests, meanwhile, are man-made, synthetic battles. At best, they simulate the components of real-life conflict and thereby offer opportunity to learn skills for fighting and winning life's larger, more authentic battles.

THEATER OF WAR

A materialistic culture like our own can only define "ultimately real" conflict in military terms, because apparently only in the contest of guns and bombs is the ultimate value of physical life at stake. In our era of volunteer soldiers, however, the average man will never take up a rifle or enter such combat. If he's not introduced to the eternal and thereby ultimately definitive battle in the spirit realm, athletic fantasies must serve by default as his theater of war.

In the absence of the Real, however, the fantasy becomes normative. The ball game becomes a man's stage in which—fully exposed, even before a national viewing audience—he's displayed vicariously as either winner or loser, hero or fumbler.

For modern sports fans, in fact, "a thirst for group membership and superiority of their group can be satisfied even with symbolic victory by their warriors in clashes on ritualized battlefields."[71] Thus, when the Boston Celtics defeated the Los Angeles Lakers for the NBA championship one year, a social psychologist in Boston commented on "the aftermath":

> The fans burst out of the Garden and nearby bars, practically break dancing in the streets, stogies lit, arms uplifted, voices screaming.... It did not seem to me that those fans were just...empathizing with their team. They personally were flying high. On that night each fan's self-esteem felt supreme; a social identity did a lot for many personal identities.

In ancient, gladiator days, contestants fought for their very lives. Today's sanitized games may be more humane, but the cost of that safety to a man's self-respect is yet high.

Men are hard-wired for true battle. We who play and/or watch athletic games are haunted by the shameful truth that in fact, sports are but a contrived shadow of the authenticity we long for, and their consequences therefore fleeting. Chicago Bulls megastar Michael Jordan confirmed this sobering reality check in his retirement speech when he declared simply, "I just want to give some working guy a little entertainment."

There's nothing wrong with being entertained by an athletic contest. It's engaging because we respect hard work and skill. It bears hope because we all want to overcome adversity. Indeed, it's inspiring—**as long as it's not confused with real-life engagement**.

CONFUSED BOUNDARY

That boundary, however, is easily confused. For example, when Los Angeles Dodgers CEO Jamie McCourt's bitter divorce with husband Frank began to bleed over into team morale, a *Los Angeles Times* sports section headline read, "McCourt: Wife not interested in team."[73]

The fact that Frank's pouting might serve in court to justify his case against his wife signals an astounding blindness among men to what the other half the world's population has always known, namely, that sports are not as important as—that is, bear little consequence compared to—marriage and family relationships. In a nation where Mom & Dad are either divorced or fighting at home, the next generation will rise ill-equipped for their life calling—often angry and either passive or violently aggressive—no matter how often the home team wins.

Amid life's larger struggles, the family is by definition the "home team." **In today's era of widespread family conflict and broken homes, athletic teams often bear the burden of victory where families so often choke.**

Spiritually numb men cannot recognize the authentic, spiritual battle at hand. Like a boy hiding behind Mommy's skirts, we retreat from life's most significant battles and remain trapped in the shamefully comfortable womb of spectator sports. When the pressures of real life call us out—as in family conflicts, financial needs, and health problems—we come forth stillborn.

Still, my own and other men's heartfelt engagement with The Game leads me not to discount athletic contests as mere distraction from the more important things of a man's life. Rather, they may well reflect, albeit dimly, the most important thing. If so, then we had better not short-circuit our vision and allow passion—or disdain—for the game to eclipse the larger contest which it reflects.

In fact, something archetypal beckons at every athletic contest, a faint echo of a vast, cosmic contest between powers of good and evil. As lion cubs wrestle and "play" together in anticipation of the vital hunt to come later in maturity, to "play" a ball game can reflect and even stir you after the larger life struggles which every man faces.

Teams fight to win. But why do we want to win? If it's just about external exigencies, that urge should dissipate when no life-or-death military conflict lies at hand. But thousands, nay tens of thousands of cheering, even bottle-throwing "peacetime" sports fans testify to the contrary.

MOST NOBLE DESTINY

Could it be that a man's urge for victory stirs not simply from ignoble pride, but rather, from his most noble destiny?

As human beings, that is, we all have natural shortcomings. We're not gods. When a man has an image of who he should be, he strives to achieve it. Inevitably, however, he falls short. The gap between his natural self and his perfect self-image then fills with shame—which only *super*-natural power, rooted in truth and released in grace, can overcome.

In a man, shame stirs a crippling, burn-in-your-gut sense that "I don't measure up." What's more, if I reveal my true self, the other men will see my weakness and kick me off the team into outer darkness, banished forever from masculine identity and fellowship.

Evil, as the seductive genesis of lies, lurks here in the contradictory belief that, "If I'm real, I'm excluded from the company of real men." The conundrum both begs and mocks the definition, as terrifying as it is obvious: **A real man is a man who's real.**

The fear of being real, and thereby exposed to others' rejection, breeds a desperation to deny and expunge your human inadequacy, and in that idolatrous sense, become like God. Thus, we idolize winners, and fear losers. The powers of evil prey upon this fear, promising to remove your shame and elevate you to a humanly designed, counterfeit glory.

Thus, the ancient Psalmist reminds, "But Lord, *you* are my shield, my glory, and my only hope. *You alone* can lift my head, now bowed in shame" (Psalm 3:3LIV, italics mine).

Powers rooted in deception, however, cannot make you real. Evil therefore urges you rather to dump your shame on others and fabricate a dignity by diminishing others in comparison to you. Hence, racism, sexism, nationalism, sectarian fundamentalism, and a host of insidious "I'm OK-You're not OK" ideologies and fellowships.

SPIRIT OF SHAME

This spirit of shame can animate athletic contests as well, especially among younger players and fans who have not matured enough to find centeredness in their higher calling beyond the cheers of other men. If my team beats your team, that is, I'm OK—because you're not.

I'm not saying here that rooting for your home team makes you evil. I'm saying that looking to a group of athletes to "Make Us Proud" and thereby cover your shame, is idolatry—a false spirituality which diverts a man from his larger life focus and destiny. In a fan, it transforms excitement into desperation.

No matter how exciting the play action or entertaining the commercials, beyond the promise of victory and the bonding with other men, here is the truth which fan frenzy threatens to drown: *No ball team, no matter how winning, can deliver you from the human condition of not measuring up to your created purpose and the shame which that stirs.*

Men who have not faced the pervasive spiritual battle in their own hearts cannot recognize it in the larger world, and therefore, will not responsibly take up their positions to win it. "Team spirit" thereby becomes a self-defeating distraction from authentic spirituality, genuine fellowship, and the battle that infuses it. What's worse, it can delude a man into believing, "My team—like me—is good, and all others are evil."

Sooner or later, however, the playful wrestling lion cub has to grow up and wrestle with deer for dinner.

The cosmic war between good and evil is not won by those who mistake Boot Camp for field combat and thus, sit riveted and paunched before TV ballgames while their families and communities wait bereft in the background. We've seen enough of these AWOL men—and not just in cartoons. They haven't outgrown the passion for a ball game—not to dismiss it, but to re-focus it at last on their definitive calling to fight against evil in the real world, even in themselves.

Often, spirits of aimlessness and passivity need to be renounced here, cast out, and replaced with destiny, focus, purpose, and vitality. "God has created you for a life of good deeds, which He has already prepared for you to do," as Paul declared (Ephes. 2:8-10).

A true warrior—like an athlete—deliberately and diligently wants to know his weakest spots in order to strengthen himself, and thereby, prepare himself to defend against opponent attacks and win the battle. **When a man shouts desperately for his home team to**

win because their loss would point to his own inadequacy, he has
defined himself as a war casualty, seduced from his post by shame.
Living from game to game, he doesn't learn from the experience,
doesn't grow in his discernment of life's battles and his ability to fight
them successfully. In defeat he sees not a chance to learn and improve,
but only shame; victory bears but a hollow pride that only lasts until
the next game.

ANTIDOTE TO SHAME

Among real men, therefore, the antidote to shame is not pride
before others, but humility before God.

Too many men today, no matter how physically buffed, remain
spiritually untrained and flabby, preferring to bleep out the unmanageable reality of evil—and remain blind to its effects.

May they live happily ever after.

From the Holocaust and 9/11 to drive-by shootings, from
widespread addictions and disease to warmaking and divorce, I don't
have time to argue the point. I'm too busy struggling to overcome the
evil in my own heart and fighting alongside other men to overcome it
in this broken but otherwise marvelous world.

Those of us who live in the real world have been scarred by its
evil. We've been forced thereby to recognize the conflict at hand, both
within us and without, and we want to win it. We like to see a well-
fought ball game not because it blinds us to the reality of our own
conflicts, but rather, because it reminds us that they're real, that we're
not alone in a world filled with conflict.

So let's team up and train for the battles of life. Let's meet
regularly for training prayer and support, get real together, and face
our fears, so we can face confidently the enemy who's out to defeat us
on our home field.

And while we're at it, let's catch the home team this weekend.
They, too, are fighting hard this season, and it'll be a great game.

> **Today's hybrid horror films beckon a spiritually abandoned generation.**

19

fROM DINOSAURS TO DEMONS

HOLLYWOOD'S
X-RATED SPIRITUALITY

The world...hates me because I testify that what it does is evil. (John 7:7)

YEARS AGO AS A BOY IN THE 1950'S, I enjoyed gathering excitedly around the TV on Friday nights with my friends for *Shock Theatre.* There, vampires, mummies, robots, and dinosaurs joined creatures from lagoons, jungles, cemeteries, and haunted mines to thrill us week after week over popcorn, screams, and laughter.

No more.

Since those innocent days, a new psychic/supernatural horror film has arisen with a different kind of antagonist: one which harms human beings, yet is neither visible nor limited by material reality. Spawned in the 1970's by the intensely engaging *The Exorcist*, these films began plainly to identify the antagonist as a demon, as in *The Omen, Damien,* and *The Shining* of that era.

A particularly disturbing example was *The Entity,* in which a woman is repeatedly raped by a non-physical being. Producer Harold Schneider, who refused to let his 14-year-old daughter see his film, said that many actresses turned down the part because "they were terrified of doing a role where they had to play being raped without a human (assailant) around."[74]

When these films were becoming popular, a distraught mother asked me as her pastor for help when her six-year-old daughter began having nightmares. I asked if she could remember when the nightmares began.

"It was the night she'd been visiting a friend," the mother replied. "She said all they'd done was play in the yard awhile, and then watched the movie *Poltergeist* on TV later." The mother paused and knit her brow. "Actually, she did say the movie was pretty scary for her. Do you think a movie like that could have affected her so strongly?"

I said Yes, indeed—and urged her to invite the child to talk about the experience.

PLAIN WEIRD

A few days later, the mother called and reported that her daughter "got all strange and nervous" whenever the movie was mentioned, and would say nothing. "It's just plain weird," the mother declared.

That Sunday, she asked the entire congregation to pray for her daughter. After worship, I went to the home and prayed for the child, asking for the love of Jesus to surround and protect her and overcome all fear within her. At that, I bound a spirit of fear in the girl and in the name of Jesus, cast it out. Soon afterwards, the nightmares ceased.

Today, decades later, these hybrid horror films are fully ensconced among us, with an unprecedented power not simply to frighten the viewer for a brief thrill, but in fact, to instill an abiding spirit of fear. Unlike the old films, they portray forces which are not physical per se, but manifestly spiritual. Follow-ups like *Poltergeist II* and *Firestarter II* demonstrated that these films were here to stay.

Christians, meanwhile, represent a particular spiritual perspective to the world, and we must therefore exercise discernment as other spiritual views are introduced among us. Jesus valued children supremely as the very gateway to the Kingdom of God (see Matt. 18:1-7). In fact, because He was so deliberate and forceful in his exhortations to protect their innocence, **often the true nature of any particular spirituality is revealed by its effect upon children.**

When a virus enters a community, for example, the weaker members—often children—are the first to manifest symptoms of its presence. Similarly, when harmful spiritualities are introduced, we may see their effects upon children, such as my parishioner's daughter, as an indication of their larger destructive intent.

The added dimension of fear in these horror films is revealed in contrast to the earlier variety, in which the agent of fear threatens by its larger or more powerful body, such as King Kong or the dinosaurs of *Jurassic Park*. Frightening as these creatures were, nevertheless they could be stopped simply by greater physical power—which human enforcement agencies commonly wield.

That knowledge provided a buffer between natural and supernatural fear, allowing the viewer to be only temporarily frightened, and thereby, entertained by the film. Airplane machine guns, that is, could shoot King Kong off the Empire State Building, and human firepower similarly dispatched the Creature of the Black Lagoon, the mummies, Frankenstein, and the Jurassic Park dinosaurs.

HUMANLY APPLIED FORCE

In the 1950's classic *The Body Snatchers*, the antagonists come from outer space in large "pods" to replace feeling human characters with unfeeling clones—a story with frightening implications for our increasingly de-humanized technological society. But the viewer's fear is properly contained by the fact, clearly portrayed in several scenes, that the pods can be destroyed by fire, pitchfork stabbing, or other humanly-applied physical force.

The drama here hangs upon the simple question, Will people recognize the threat in time and apply sufficient force to overcome it before others are harmed?

When indeed they finally do, we need not see them burning, shooting, or using whatever physical means necessary to destroy the pods. We simply trust they can take care of it. We therefore leave the theater entertained, if not instructed, through this catharsis and return to business as usual, reassured of our human power to save and deliver ourselves from evil.

A major component of this reassurance is the fact that, although the antagonist is unseen—as the body snatchers from outer space—it nevertheless remains subject to the natural laws of the physical world, which we can largely manage for our own security. *The Invisible Man*, in another example, was unseen, yet he could not walk through walls or zip instantaneously from place to place.

A corollary to this consensus insisted that any character invulnerable to humanly designed power was required to be good, such as Superman. As science fiction novels took center stage following WWII and its many technological advances, physicist/sci-fi author Isaac Asimov therefore promulgated his "Three Laws of Robotics." Designed to counter a fear of technological advance in what he calls "The Frankenstein Complex" —namely, "man creates robot; robot kills man"[75]—the first and overarching Law states:

> A robot may not injure a human being, or, through inaction, allow a human being to come to harm. [76]

A generation ago, sci-fi authors and fans welcomed and abided these Laws. The new evil antagonists of our more "liberated" culture today, however, respect no human convention—much as the demons which animate them. Unlike the manufactured robot, for example, an evil spirit is not obliged to obey any humanly conceived laws such as Asimov's—nor even natural law.

CLASS AND COMPLEXITY—?

Bowing to their box-office draw, movie critics in 1984 hailed author Stephen King's contributions to these new horror films, citing his *The Dead Zone*, in which a schoolteacher is driven uncontrollably by a power which enables him to see the future, and *Firestarter*, in which an eight-year-old girl can cause flames through psychic concentration. One interviewer praised King for bringing "a measure of class and complexity to a genre dominated by crass scare films."[72]

"Crass" though many of the older films may have been, the "scare" which they prompted was held securely in check by a trust in human power to save. In that sense, they reinforced a blindness to spiritual reality. The "complexity" of the new films, meanwhile, lies precisely in **their portraying evil as a non-physical reality which mocks human power and thereby upends our otherwise secure worldview.**

One especially troubling aspect of this "complexity" is that to youth, "human" power" translates as the "adult/parent power" to which they are often grudgingly subject. To mock it is therefore to invite a spirit of rebellion.

Physical limitations are a frustrating though often necessary part of growing up; what child would not want to overcome the gap of physical power in his or her parents by having psychic power—such as to foretell parental decisions or make Dad turn over the car keys? To an eight-year-old, such power over the adult world as to start fires simply by thinking is glorious indeed. As *Firestarter* child star Drew Barrymore declared in the aforementioned interview, "I set a lot of people on fire, but they deserve it."

NEW DISNEY

Indeed, these films are often aimed explicitly at youth. As author Stephen King's producer proclaims:[73]

> King creates youthful protagonists who are very much in tune with what's going on in the contemporary world of adolescents. In books, he is the new Disney.

We adult Christians must begin to ask how our faith speaks to this aspect of "what's going on in the contemporary world of adolescents." In doing so, we shall discover at last that the materialistic worldview of our "modern scientific culture" has kept us from seeing the essential spiritual reality upon which our faith is based—and thereby, the evil loosed among us in these films.

It's too late condescendingly to disdain spiritual reality. People who walk away from the new horror films are genuinely scared, not just in the theater, but long afterward. **They have experienced and been manifestly affected by something powerful and real there—often more powerful and more real than anything they've experienced in church.**

Our "modern" materialistic worldview, which allows for no reality beyond the sensory and physical, severely handicaps our ability to respond to any suggestion of non-physical reality, whether good or evil. Even attempts to fantasize such larger powers must limit them, as the old sci-fi protocols, within the greater human potential to overcome them. That is, in a society which refuses to allow any but natural law, to introduce powers which are not limited by natural law is to precipitate a profound crisis of fear—which largely drives the newer, spiritually driven sci-fi appeal.

Similar crises have occurred in history whenever technology prompts a quantum leap in weaponry. Our fear response to the new psychic horror films, that is, may be compared to that of the bow-and-arrow society upon confronting guns or a gunpowder army facing rockets. We're at the mercy of powers which we cannot understand and, therefore, cannot control. If these powers are evil, as in fact they're often explicitly portrayed in the films, we're in grave trouble, indeed.

Furthermore, the "reality component" of the fear generated is heightened by the fact that many of these films are based on actual events—such as *The Exorcist*, The *Amityville Horror*, and *The Entity*. No one has ever seen in the natural world a King Kong, Superman, walking mummy, and the like. But demon possession, for example, though rare, has indeed been reported. More significantly, demons themselves are clearly portrayed in the Bible, and in fact, most of us human beings—though not possessed—are oppressed in some way by demons, albeit unknowingly.

DEEPER SCARE

Something is out there, even—*could it be?*—within us all, capable of generating a fear far deeper than mere "crass scare." Indeed, people sense that with sufficient conviction collectively to pay hundreds of millions of dollars to have Hollywood tell us what it is. Blinded by the culture's materialistic worldview, however, Hollywood is incapable of defining that "something," and therefore, cannot tell us how ultimately to overcome it.

The old films allowed for no such problem. King Kong, for example, was himself portrayed as the destructive force. When he's killed, the battle is finished and the viewer may leave him lying dead on the movie screen. But even if you kill the fortune-telling schoolteacher or the demon-possessed child, the destructive force which animated them remains—indeed, to animate you.

King Kong is dead; long live the Air Force! The exorcist priest is dead—*but when will the demon that attacked him attack me?*

In thereby shattering all natural protective boundaries and professional protocols, the new films have forced into consciousness what for our modern scientific mind is a radically new worldview. They portray evil not merely as human choice, but as essentially spiritual—that is, literally an Entity of itself which, though it may inhabit and affect physical things such as bodies, has no locus in the material world.

The battle against evil within such a definition is therefore fundamentally a spiritual warfare, and requires spiritual maturity and wisdom to win. Unlike the Air Force vs. King Kong, mere technology cannot save us from the enemy portrayed in these new films. Indeed, **any person limited to a materialistic, rational world view such as our own is not only helpless against its schemes, but often an unwitting accomplice.**

"The scientists come across looking pretty dumb," as one fourteen-year-old girl commented to me about *Poltergeist*. You can't bust ghosts with guns, nor exorcise demons with Valium; attempts to do so only mock human powerlessness.

Hence, our profound and abiding fear upon viewing these films. They proclaim that science—which has saved us from so many diseases and, through its improved weaponry, from armed enemies—has no saving power in the face of spiritual evil.

At this point, Christians must confess that the new supernatural Hollywood horror films have performed a profound service in challenging our materialistic worldview and opening the stage for powers greater than human, albeit evil, to perform among us.

GREAT PROMISE

Indeed, in the pit of this new and defining terror, we may become ready to entertain Christian spirituality, for only when we despair of our own human powers are we ready to entertain God's power. Here, great promise beckons our witness as His people—but also great warning if, as it would seem, the comfortable Western Church is not prepared to face spiritual reality. Among us, the temptation to spiritual denial is overwhelming—especially among the well-educated and materially secure, whose accomplished natural abilities blind us to any larger reality.

Those who press on courageously and faithfully into their fear, however, discover that what seems so radically unusual to our modern-scientific minds is in fact quite old, and basic to the biblical faith itself. **Anyone familiar with Christian spirituality will recognize at once that the spiritual worldview presumed by the new genre of psychic-oriented films is precisely that of the Bible.**

As Paul reminded the Ephesians,

> We are not fighting against human beings but against the wicked spiritual forces in the heavenly world, the rulers, authorities, and cosmic powers of this dark age. (Ephes. 6:12)

And again, the Corinthians:

> It is true that we live in the world, but we do not fight from worldly motives. The weapons we use in our fight are not the world's weapons but God's powerful weapons.... We take every thought captive and make it obey Christ. (2 Cor. 10:3-5)

Certainly, older fans of the early *Star Wars* space genre—wholly tame by today's standards—would be at home with this basic worldview, as the adventures of its protagonist Luke Skywalker often reflect a deliberate spirituality.

In *Return of the Jedi*, for example, Luke's fighter craft has crash landed in a swamp and his mentor Yoda tells him to lift it out by the psychic power of his mind. Obliging, Luke knits his brow and struggles; the plane quivers, raises slightly, and then falls back as he gives up in exhaustion. Whereupon Yoda stretches out his hand, focuses his mind, and the plane lifts out of the swamp to settle down nearby on solid ground.

"I...I don't believe it!" Luke exclaims in amazement.

"And that is why you couldn't do it," his robed guru-dwarf intones.

Compare this to the words of Jesus to His disciples:

> Have faith in God. I assure you that whoever tells this hill to get up and throw itself into the sea and does not doubt in his heart, but believes that what he says will happen, it will be done for him. (Mk. 11:23)

Again, the protagonist in *The Dead Zone* is tormented by an ability to foresee the future. Compare this to the experience of the apostles in Philippi:

> One day as we were going to the place of prayer, we were met by a slave girl who had an evil spirit that enabled her to predict the future. She earned a lot of money for her owners by telling fortunes. She followed Paul and us, shouting, 'These men are the servants of the Most High God! They announce to you how you can be saved!'
>
> She did this for many days, until Paul became so upset that he turned around and said to the spirit, "In the name of Jesus Christ I order you to come out of her!" The spirit went out of her that very moment. (Acts 16:16-18)

COUNTERFEIT SPIRITUALITY

Biblical faith proclaims that, while natural human force is helpless against a non-physical, spiritual antagonist, the power of God becomes authoritative in Jesus Christ—and thereby, both necessary and sufficient to dispel it.

Clearly, the spirituality proclaimed in these new films is a counterfeit, a false and dangerously misleading copy of authentic, Christian spirituality. We are creatures of the God who "is spirit" (John 4:24) and as such, we have a spiritual nature which hungers to be nurtured in relationship with that God. Our Western rational materialism, as a pathetic effort to cover the shame of our sin nature, has denied and forgotten this fundamental reality of human life.

But the enemy of God and humanity has not. Nor have the makers of these films. That's why they now flourish among us, seizing territory ordained for, but abdicated by Christians.

A famine stirs not only hunger but a willingness ultimately to eat garbage. Similarly, when we deny an innate longing to connect with our authentic spiritual root via Jesus, we become subject to attractive, but ultimately destructive counterfeits. When the truth is not allowed, the false becomes alluring, and indeed, so widely entertained that it becomes normative and regarded as truth.

A friend of mine in Los Angeles once took his little boy to visit a farm for the first time. An old farmer milking a cow offered the boy a taste—and both men were taken aback when the boy refused to drink it. "That isn't real milk," the boy exclaimed. "Real milk comes from the store!" The new horror films, that is, have been providing the major spiritual education for modern culture, and to that extent, we may not expect our children to recognize authentic, Christian spirituality when they grow up.

Far eclipsing its purported goal of fantasy entertainment, Hollywood's new horror films have sparked a quantum shift in the locus of reality. **Youth who endure church with a yawn are emerging from movie theaters with chills and nightmares.** Indeed, sermon illustrations and pulpit power-points now include film clips so often that Jesus is recognized insofar as, for example, He's "like Neo in *The Matrix*" or "He suffers like Superman" when the latter's body postures as a cross.

To paraphrase the milk carton story, for the current generation, authentic spirituality—the kind that touches bodies and changes lives—comes from a movie theater, not from a church.

Believing Christians today may well lament this distortion. But to be part of the truth-telling, we must look again—this time, with humble openness—at the spiritual heritage of our biblical faith.

WORSHIPPING AT THE MOVIES

It's too late for Christians to continue matter-of-factly discounting every aspect of our faith which challenges our natural human perception and power, such as dreams, healings, demons, prophecies, and miracles. Our children—who have not yet been so educated out of supernatural reality—have already been worshipping for some time at the local theater, seeking to be spiritually aroused by such phenomena where we in our fear and pride have abandoned them.

As a sixth grader, my son received the baptism of the Holy Spirit with an accompanying prayer language. Later that year, he won the spelling bee at his school and competed in the larger County Bee against over 100 winners in other schools. After months of studying and reviewing the 20-page word list, he knew them all—but grew increasingly nervous as the day arrived.

Reminding him that he knew the words already, I told him to center himself by praying quietly under his breath in his prayer language during the bee if he became fearful or forgetful.

He did—and won the county spelling bee.

It's time we told our children clearly that the spirituality of Jesus reflects the truth of the Creator God who, unlike demons, does not invade, possess, or overcome human will, but rather, frees us to make choices consonant with his saving, healing, fulfilling will for us. We need to recognize that **a spirituality—such as that which animates *Poltergeist*—which instills fear in a child that a mother's loving comfort cannot dispel, is not of God and must be repudiated and actively evicted.**

Certainly, to do this with integrity, we must take our proud rational materialism to the cross and leave it there to die—before it kills us by severing us from our spiritual root and leaving us wholly vulnerable to counterfeits. At last, we must dare humbly to begin studying and practicing the fullness of our Christian spirituality, using the Bible as it was intended, **not as a moral rule book, but as a handbook for the supernatural dimension of life** and for overcoming powers of evil among and within us.

An outspoken contemporary exponent of this view from within the historic church was Pope Paul VI, who in a 1972 General Audience declared,

> Evil is not merely a lack of something, but an effective agent, a living, spiritual being, perverted and perverting ... it is contrary to the teaching of the Bible and the Church to refuse to recognize the existence of such a reality ... or to explain it as a pseudoreality, a conceptual and fanciful personification of the unknown causes of our misfortunes ... Some people are afraid of falling into old Manichean theories again, or into frightening divagations of fancy and superstition. Today people prefer to appear strong and unprejudiced ...[74]

Even as federal counterfeit detectors are trained by examining genuine bills, the false is exposed only by the clear presence of the real. To overcome the evil generated by today's media, we worldly-educated followers of Jesus must dare to take our own biblical spirituality seriously and begin both humbly and powerfully to live it. Our youth—and our spiritually hungry society—will then see in us the truth against which Hollywood's new spirituality can be recognized as a fraud. Furthermore, we'll become so focused on true Christian spirituality and the broken world it's designed to serve, that these films will no longer have any appeal among us.

Some churches may indeed be boring. But Jesus is not.

Few can yawn while someone is raising the dead, healing the sick, and casting out demons. As we dare to embrace the fullness of super-natural biblically-certified spirituality, we will discover that we are indeed engaged in a spiritual battle—even as our courageous Christian forebears of the first century.

BEYOND HOLLYWOOD

What's more, we'll at last experience life in fellowship with Holy Spirit as exciting, terrifying, joyous, suspenseful, wondrous, dangerous, renewing, and adventurous beyond anything Hollywood can offer.

Who needs to watch E.T's battery-operated finger-light heal when we can lay hands on one another and see the Spirit of the living Christ light up human hearts and heal us?

Who needs to speculate and fantasize with *Heaven Can Wait, For Heaven's Sake, Fringe,* and other life-after-death celluloid fantasies, when Jesus has told us that the kingdom of Heaven is at hand right now, beckoning us to receive and embrace it with the power of the very King who rules it?

Who needs to watch Harry Potter cavort with demons on a movie screen when a host of destructive demons is fast at work all around—and even within us—that a command in the name of Jesus can dispel?

The answer is clear: spiritual dropouts, people so fearful of authentic spirituality and its witness to both our human powerlessness and Almighty God's strength, as to prefer being a spectator rather than a participant.

I sympathize, but it's too late to concede. **In fact, there are no spectators of the battle Jesus came to fight and win, only deluded victims and persevering victors.** Whether we choose to acknowledge it or not, we live in a spiritual world around and within us just as surely as a fish lives in and draws sustenance from water. Either unwittingly or deliberately, we participate in the spiritual battle raging now as always, between the true and the false, the light and the dark.

False and dark spirits do not hesitate to occupy the vacuum left when we withdraw from an active Christian faith. Nor, indeed, is it enough for us simply to recognize the demons among us and cast them out. Jesus came not simply to empty us of evil spirits, but indeed, filled instead with God's Holy Spirit and actively engaged in bringing His kingdom on earth as it is in heaven.

As Jesus therefore warned,

> When an evil spirit goes out of a person,
> it travels over dry country looking for a place
> to rest. If it can't find one, it says to itself, 'I

will go back to my old house.' So it goes back and finds the house empty, clean, and all fixed up. Then it goes out and brings along seven other spirits even worse than itself, and they come and live there. And so when it is all over, that person is in worse shape than he was at the beginning ... (Matt. 12:43-45)

To follow the crucified and risen Lord is to discover that a life of eternal significance lies in being animated by God's Holy Spirit and engaged in the battle to restore this broken world to His authority. Believing, as Pope Paul aptly scoffed, that you are "strong and unprejudiced" enough to remain aloof from spiritual warfare is sophistry at its deadliest. Indeed, to be "empty, clean, and all fixed up," as it were, is the most dangerous spiritual state, insofar as it beckons other powers competing for the property.

NO NEUTRALITY

Neutrality is not an option in spiritual warfare.

We therefore witness most convincingly against the false spirituality in today's horror films not as we merely scoff at them, but only and precisely as instead we model active, authentic Christian spirituality in our own lives.

Amid Hollywood's powerful spiritual seduction, we owe this to our children.

These new supernatural horror films confront the Western Church with an understanding of evil radically new for our secularized culture—but fundamentally old and well recognized in ancient cultures. It remains to be seen whether we will dare seize this opportunity to re-discover a radically new and powerful understanding of good as manifested in Jesus—and thereby enter the battle already taking place within and about us.

Certainly, such commitment must begin with a confession that we Christians, rooted in a 2000-year-old legacy of spiritual warfare, have so abdicated this essential focus of our sacred heritage **that the revelation of such a battle's taking place has come not from our churches, but rather, from Hollywood.**

Precisely in that sense, these films will continue to challenge us Christians either to put up or shut up. It's time today to demonstrate the spiritual power we profess in Jesus Christ. Otherwise, we can go back to playing church and abandon our children to rush excitedly from the ticket booth into this brave new world of dark powers emerging among us.

Jesus has lived, died, and been resurrected that we might receive His Spirit today and demonstrate for generations to come the real and powerful coming of His Kingdom among us. May we dare even now to take our place as legitimate heirs to that Kingdom so like the Apostle Paul, we can say to our children and the world,

> For we brought the Good News to you not
> with words only, but with power and the Holy
> Spirit and with complete conviction of its truth
> (1 Thess. 1:5).

> **Media viewers want distraction. When you forget what it distracts you from, however, the media settles in as definition.**

20

TV OR GOD?

PRINCIPALITIES OF FANTASY AND PASSIVITY

You went along with the crowd and were just like all the others, full of sin, obeying Satan, the mighty prince of the power of the air, who is at work right now in the hearts of those who are against the Lord. (Ephes. 2:2LIV)

YEARS AGO AS A YOUNG MAN, I once took a fatherless, twelve-year-old suburban boy on his first backpack trip. For two days we bushwhacked through scrub brush, cooled hot feet in crystal streams, and slept out under sparkling stars in the clear night sky. On the return trail, we rounded a mountain peak and were rewarded with a blazing orange sunset over the entire Los Angeles basin.

"Wow!" the boy exclaimed, drawing in the magnificent view. "This is even better than TV!"

With a jolt, I short-circuited back to 1951, at age seven outside the local appliance store window. Straining tiptoed among adults packed on the sidewalk, I gazed in awe at the dancing six-inch black-and-white picture screen inside a large, refrigerator-sized cabinet.

By the authority of my age and experience, therefore, I hereby seize the Universal Remote and push "Pause."

You'll forgive an old man for interrupting the show. But as a father now, six decades later, I've become increasingly worried for youth in this Brave New World of media entertainment. Not simply because of its often crude and ugly content, but for how the media intervenes god-like into our lives to proclaim identity, direction, and vitality to an otherwise unguided generation.

KINGDOM OF THE AIR

The Apostle Paul never saw a single deodorant commercial—a decided blessing of ancient life. He nailed the modern spirit, however, when he reminded the Ephesians that, before Jesus made them alive, they had wandered as "spiritually dead" (Ephes. 2:1TEV) and "followed the ways of this world and of the ruler of the kingdom of the air" (Ephes. 2:2NIV). Just read "airwaves" instead and you'll see what Paul's talking about here, namely, **the unseen power in the world to seduce the children of God away from our true spiritual identity, direction, and vitality.**

"Fast-Forward to Passivity," a *Los Angeles Times* editorial, sounded the prophetic warning: "It would be unfortunate if the technologies we embrace for making our lives more efficient ended up freeing us to be merely passive viewers of virtual worlds rather than engaged participants in the real one."[75]

Amid today's media onslaught, the battle of our time is for the authority to define the real world, and therefore, how to participate in it. Christians know it's not about being tough enough to face squarely what you see and "call a spade a spade"—courageous as that may sound. Indeed, the real world is not even the one we face, no matter how squarely, with natural eyes.

The world which our natural senses perceive is simply not our home. We don't come from there, nor do we end up there. Rather, for

Christians reality is defined by the God revealed in Jesus. The real world is the *super*-natural theater in which God is busy accomplishing His purposes among us—a notion which often seems as "foolishness" to our natural human vision (1 Corinth. 1:18).

This battle to define ultimate reality is therefore determined largely by where you focus your attention and grant authority.

Not long after its invention, in 1975 the national PTA president startled the nation by declaring that "TV has truly become a member of the family." Today, however, television—with its concomitant DVD player, X-Box, Game Station, iPod, and Cloud—has clearly become not simply one among other family members contending for an equal voice. Rather, the entire family gathers at its feet.

In the new millennium, it's not about whether we admit TV to the family or not, but about which of its many and mighty outpourings we will imbibe. Before the Media's throne, all human authority becomes second-hand if not virtual, belonging to whoever holds the Remote Sceptre.

In 1975, long before the advent of video players and videogames, the *Detroit Free Press* newspaper offered the modern equivalent of about $2000 to any family who would disconnect its TV for a month. Would your family today dare take such an offer—even limiting your online use to emails and no video content at all?

In fact, nearly 80% of those contacted refused. Doctors reported that the 20% who did stop watching TV for a month experienced "serious withdrawal symptoms," from nervousness and headaches, followed by sleeping pills and increased smoking.

MEDIA ADDICTION

"There really did seem to be an addiction to TV," researchers concluded. "Some of those people almost literally went crazy. They didn't know how to cope."

Even in that early era, the Nielsen Media Research agency reported that the average American TV was on 44 hours per week. That's over 6 hours a day. In a national census, 30 per cent of adults said that TV was their favorite pastime.

Even more ominous, the average pre-school child was spending almost one third of his or her waking hours in front of the tube. In fact, a 7th grader in my Sunday School class back then told me that the TV was "always on" at his house. "When the TVs off," he explained, "the house seems so empty. You feel lonely and scared."

A more recent 2006 Nielsen survey[76] revealed that in the average home the TV is on for 8 hours and 14 minutes per day, up from seven hours and 15 minutes in 1996. The average amount watched daily by an individual is four hours and 35 minutes. "Despite growing competition from then Internet, iPods, cellphones, and other new media, Americans are watching more television than ever," the report concludes.

Even today, if someone spent almost five hours a day in church or praying, we'd brand that person as a religious fanatic. To spend that much time watching TV, however, is simply normal.

TV and its concomitant video media has not entered our homes as a new baby to learn from the rest, but in fact, has intruded as the Dominant Focus, which commands the attention of the entire family. The media, in fact, has become the unchallenged Virtual Parent who presides over even Mom & Dad. **It selects what families see and portrays what's acceptable—and thereby, confers blessing and provides guidance. As such, it replaces God in the family.**

In an earlier time, the prophet Isaiah scoffed at the pagan woodcarver—the image craftsman of his day—who fashions a wood idol, "and then he bows down and worships it":

> He prays to it and says, "You are my god—save me!"
>
> Such people are too stupid to know what they are doing. They close their eyes and their minds to the truth. The maker of idols hasn't the sense to say, "…here I am, bowing down to a block of wood!" (Isa. 44:17-19)

Similarly, we bow down today before a box of semi-conductors we have made and say to it, "You are my god—save me from loneliness and pain, from emptiness and confusion!"

HIGH RESOLUTION FANTASY

In effect, the advent of video media has spawned a new religion among us. To paraphrase the ancient hymn,

> Yea, though I surf through the valley of the shadow of boredom, I will fear no loneliness, for visual media art with me. Thy commercials and thy weekly dramas, they comfort me, thy ball games and thy sitcoms exciteth my soul. Surely, happiness and sound-bite solutions will follow me all the days of my life, and I will dwell in high resolution fantasy forever.

The media today is literally *media*ting reality.

In our increasingly alienated, fast-forward society, the extended family has disappeared and busy schedules serve as a convenient excuse for avoiding the messy business of personal relationships. We're left craving for community, desperately seeking the shared experiences, values, and goals that foster it.

In "TV & Religion: The Shaping of Faith, Values & Culture," former National Council of Churches Communications Director Wm. Fore traces the root of the problem. We long for a common sense of belonging, he declares—in fact, a common Story which tells us "who we are, what we have done, and what we can do,... **a Story which expresses ultimate reality—another term for a people's religion."**[82]

This defined the myths of ancient societies, and they were true insofar as they dealt with "power—who has it and who doesn't; with values—what's valuable and worth-while and what's not, and with morality—what's right and permissible and what's forbidden."

From its beginnings, America's Story was about God's work in this world. Told in a context of humble Thanksgiving, it highlighted a Pilgrim people, who sought freedom from the oppressive powers of this world, suffered rejection and hardship, cried out for God's saving hand, and prevailed.

Yet even these pioneering Americans saw their Story as precisely that of God's ancient people, who left slavery in Egypt (as the English king forbade worship outside the state-sponsored Church), endured the wilderness ordeal (crossing the turbulent Atlantic ocean in winter), and were delivered into the Promised Land (the American shores) to proclaim their God's deliverance from the world's bondage. Even the pagan Native Americans seemed aptly to represent the Gentile pre-occupants of Canaan.

PRIME-TIME PULPIT

Today, the media is pre-empting our Story—and God's. Told in a context of commercial greed and consumption, it informs a people gathered faithfully around its prime-time pulpit what is powerful, valuable, and permissible. On Sunday mornings, the national news magazine in every local paper commonly features a cover interview about life's deepest issues—with a popular media celebrity preaching.

Whether it's teaching us that power lies in a gun, that money and sex appeal make you worthwhile, that it's OK to belch like a Simpson child or engage in same-gender sex like Ellen, the media is no passive mirror offered to reflect reality. Rather, its ad-jingle hymns and push-the-envelope catechisms reflect a power determined to shape and define reality for us.

The sad effects in many viewers' lives—from violence and addictions to passivity and sexually transmitted diseases—increasingly reveal the media Story as a seductive, two-dimensional ruse.

Media viewers want distraction from life's pain and struggles. When people forget the true Source of saving power, however, the media settles in as definition. The "powers of the air," that is, want to rule and destroy us. Their primary stratagem is to make us forget our true Story, and thereby, the Father God who has authored it. We therefore don't know Whose we are, so we can't know where we're designed and empowered to go.

Here lies the breeding ground for principalities of fantasy and passivity—which blind human beings to the real world Jesus died to save and deafen us as He calls us to join Him in that enterprise.

GLAMOROUS AND DISFIGURED

Enmeshed in virtual reality, we can't see what God's doing among us. Unable to affirm the ultimate reality of His world, we miss its compelling drama and rich vitality that actively engages every human being—both the glamorous and the disfigured, the rich and the poor, the celebrity and the scorned.

Jesus did not come to bring us to heaven, but to bring heaven to us—that is, to re-establish the Kingdom of God here "on earth as it is in heaven"—and thereby, to restore His authority and life-giving power to a lost and dying world. **Those real enough to beg Him to do that in their own lives will have a Story to tell. Not just theirs, but God's.**

As they tell it, the curtain between the natural world and the real world of His Spirit at work, rises. Not just in their lives, but in the world itself.

As on tiptoes, "all of creation waits with eager longing for God to reveal his sons" (Rom. 8:19). God—Playwright, Prompter, Director, Producer, and yes, Audience—leans forward. As the heavenly hosts applaud, we, the actors, take a deep breath—and step out into the real world.

Lights! Camera! And for God's sake, ACTION!

> Those wounded by shame-based religion take refuge
> in "tolerant" ideology—even as sheep beaten by the
> shepherd flee to the wolf.

21

BUT IS JESUS THE ONLY WAY?

THE SPIRIT OF UNIVERSALISM

I am the way, the truth and the life;
no one goes to the Father except by me.
(John 14:6)

YEARS AGO, WHEN I FIRST RECEIVED JESUS AS SAVIOR and
Holy Spirit as God's power to fulfill His calling, my faith journey
leapt into overdrive. Yet, even as I praised Jesus and marveled at Holy
Spirit's healing gifts, I balked at the above scriptural statement that
Jesus is "the only way" to Father God.

I was not anxious to seek God's truth on this issue. In fact, I feared
being rejected by my many universalist oldline denomination and
seminary friends—even as they denied the very biblical spirituality I
had already experienced to be true. Tactfully, in my prayers I allowed

that any such truth about Jesus would have to be communicated to me by God alone, and I was quite willing to wait for Him to do that.

And soon enough, He did.

As for me personally in those days, few scriptures have been more troublesome for Christians who espouse "toleration of differences" than the above, in which Jesus says explicitly that he is the only way by which human beings can fully access God the Father. Since my Harvard seminary training, I had discounted this text altogether for apparently reflecting the same narrow-minded exclusivity as racism, sexism, and other mean, small-minded prejudices.

As I began palpably encountering Holy Spirit, however, I could not so easily dismiss it. If, as Jesus said, the Spirit "reveals the truth about God" (John 15:26) and "will take what I give him and tell it to you" (John 16:15), then clearly He would be able to witness the truth—or falsehood—in this text.

I had reasoned that the God who created the universe is surely the epitome of universalism. By definition, therefore, God is a Liberal. **How could the path to the all-encompassing God-who-is-love be so narrow as to exclude those outside one particular faith, even my own?**

I try to be accepting of all persons. In fact, I've met Jews, Buddhists, Muslims, those of other faiths, and even atheists who are as loving human beings as any Christians I've met—and not a few even more loving.

Surely, God would not turn these people away in life or in death. How, indeed, could I reconcile this particularistic statement by Jesus with the universal God who sent him—who loves all of his human creation, regardless of their "religion"?

RIGGED ARGUMENTS

Certainly, I had heard many evangelical declarations to "prove" this text. Yet, in virtually every case the arguments were convoluted, if not rigged—that is, posited on a prior belief in the authority of Christian scriptures.

A representative evangelical magazine article, "Is Christ the Only Way?," for example, bore the subtitle, "Answering Objections

(When We Witness)."[83] In response to a college student who asserted that "there are many paths which lead to the top of the hill and each one is correct," the author lists "five reasons why Christ is the only way to God":

> 1. Because of who God is. The Bible teaches that...his perfect standard must be met.
>
> 2. Because of the sinfulness of man. The Bible teaches that all of us have done things that are wrong and...(therefore) cannot come into God's presence.
>
> 3. Because of the need for a "go-between." Jesus Christ, who is both fully divine and fully human, is the perfect mediator between God and man.
>
> 4. Because of the cross. Christ's death on the cross provided the payment for all the sins of the world.
>
> 5. Because of Christ's own claims. Jesus said that he was the only way to God.

Clearly, such myopic "arguments" are meaningless to anyone who isn't already a Christian and therefore doesn't accept the authority of Scripture. Number five epitomizes the startling naiveté in the others as it essentially declares, "It's true because Jesus said so."

To an outsider—or even an inside seeker like myself—this argument sounded like, "The Bible says it's true, and if you don't believe the Bible is God's word, then you're not a Christian anyhow." I felt manipulated and boxed-in with shame—neither of which I associate with Jesus. Such an ingrown approach, in fact, seemed to me suspect, as **to betray the insiders' fear that outsiders might reveal something which would destroy their argument, or even unmask their faith as a lie.**

"Go figure out what this means," as Jesus challenged the Pharisees, 'I'm after mercy, not religion.' I'm here to invite outsiders, not to coddle insiders" (Matt. 9:13,14TMB).

"Religion," as entertainer Bono puts it, "is what's left when God has left the building."[84]

Fleeing the religion police, I refused to associate the words of this "troublesome text" with Jesus—who I knew came to humankind not in a spirit of judgment, but rather, to demonstrate God's grace. "For God loved the world so much that he gave his only Son," as John proclaimed, "so that everyone who believes in him may not die but have eternal life. For God did not send his Son into the world to be its judge, but to be its savior" (John 3:16,17).

Reading this text, so often hailed by Evangelicals, I wondered: If God loves humanity and sent Jesus out of His love, then Jesus bears not judgment of the world, but rather, caring for it. Certainly, Jesus spoke harshly to the hypocritical Pharisees of his day, and I could cheer him on. **But the notion that not even the most sincere person of integrity can reach God fully except through Jesus, offended my sense of compassion for all people, regardless of religious affiliation.**

Still, apart from the orthodox evangelical view, I was left with few options. Maybe Jesus never in fact spoke those words, but instead, they came only from John's imagination or some later, misled scribe. If they were in fact Jesus' words, it would be difficult to impute some creative, alternative meaning to them besides what they say quite directly.

"He is the only way," as the *Jerome Biblical Commentary* states succinctly.[85]

Meanwhile, my experiences praying for both physical and emotional healing had led me to attribute to the Bible stories a present-day reality beyond what even most Christians today would allow. In fact, my palpable encounters with the Living, Risen Lord were leading me to believe His teachings as well.

I was reluctant, therefore, simply to declare that, since particular words in the Bible attributed to Jesus troubled me, he must not have said them. It's one thing not to understand a text, but quite another to discount it as fraudulent or otherwise misguided.

In my ongoing debate with Christian conservatives over such issues as social justice and reversing the arms race, I had often highlighted texts on peacemaking and serving the poor, which I knew would be troublesome for them. I would not have let them off the hook so easily if they'd told me, "But biblical scholars don't believe Isaiah ever really said those words scorning military power." Staying close to the Bible keeps us all humble, and thereby, able to hear God.

LARGER MOSAIC?

I was willing to allow that, like most founders of all the great faiths, Jesus brought something new to the stage of world religions. That is, he made his particular contribution to the overall picture, like one piece in a larger mosaic containing the unique wisdom in the many other, equally valid faiths. This inclusive ideology of universalism seemed altogether noble and more refined than the often discriminatory and exclusive views of conservative believers.

Thus, the *Interpreter's Bible*—often cited at my oldline denominational seminary—describes what's different about Jesus:

> Both Buddha and Lao-tzu claimed to have discovered "the way," but Jesus' unique role was to reveal "a new and living way" to God, to what is not an alarming judgment seat as (people) had supposed, but a throne of grace...(before) One who is not cold and hard and implacably just, as they had feared, but a Father, wise, understanding, tender, and most gracious of all...with a divine pity that cannot rest till it has done to the uttermost all that even God can do to save and rescue them.[86]

Still, while other religious figures might point to "the way" as some set of principles, teaching, or "path," only Jesus said that He Himself is the way. The person Jesus—the one named "God Saves"—therefore seemed to me central, unavoidable, and essential to the Christian faith and its revelation to humankind (see "Are You a Christian?" in *Broken by Religion, Healed by God*). And indeed, my own personal life crises had led me to the limits of my human power to save myself, where I had discovered that Jesus is indeed the One who saves me.

Yet the issue simmered unresolved: **Is Jesus the way for everyone, or just one way which suited myself and various others?** For one schooled in the universalist tradition, calling on Jesus alone to save me from my sin was radical enough. I was doing fine with my own revelation of Jesus—and content, therefore, to avoid the larger question, with its confusion and threat of rejection among colleagues.

WINGS AND ROOTS

Amid these thoughts, I was discussing my faith journey one day with Carl (not his real name), a lay pastor who had recently left his evangelical church because he found it "too rigid and authoritarian." In fact, we "met in the middle," as I had the liberal wings of freedom and he had the evangelical roots of conviction, and each of us was growing in the other's strengths.

Eventually, as we talked, the Troublesome Text came up, and he asked in a threatening tone, "Don't you believe those words of Jesus, that He's the only way?"

Gingerly, I shared with him my own deep and growing faith in Jesus, but drew up short of affirming that He alone is the way to Father God. As I dodged his accusations, the discussion heated up, and finally broke off in the wee hours of the morning from sheer exhaustion, leaving us both unsatisfied.

The next day, I felt angry at Carl. As I prayed about it, I knew **I'd been afraid to answer him directly because I didn't want to suffer the shame of his judgment.** Ashamed at my own weakness, I called him and explained my feelings.

"No," I declared, "I do not believe that Jesus is the only way to God. There are many other things in the Bible that at one time I didn't believe, but through experience later came to believe—and maybe this will be another of them. But for now, the answer is No."

Carl accepted my words resolutely, if not graciously. Yet as we closed the conversation, I sensed clearly that a loose end remained.

Soon afterwards, I happened to walk past a room where Carl was meeting with two other men. He came out to greet me, and invited me to come pray with them over some of the things we'd talked about. I hesitated—three-to-one were not good odds—but I decided to show my strength and go ahead in.

As soon as I sat down, he closed the door and spoke directly. "Since you don't believe Jesus' own words that he is the only way to the Father, I'm concerned for your salvation. I want to pray for you that you'll accept his words as true, and be saved."

A hot, fight-or-flight sensation flushed through me. Since my direct honesty had led me to feel stronger the week before, I decided to restrain my urge to run, and fight instead.

"I'm really feeling judged by you right now," I shot back, "and I don't appreciate being shoved into your box. You have no right to take your belief and push it on me!"

"It's not my belief," he countered. "Not even my words—but the words of Jesus. Either you believe them or you don't. And if, as you say, you don't, then you're not saved. That makes me worried about your ministry. If you don't have this basic starting point of faith, sooner or later you're going to go off into areas that will lead you and others away from God."

For awhile, we crossed verbal swords, as the other two men watched. I didn't leave, largely because I'd come to respect Carl through past times of debating together both personal and theological issues. When it became clear we'd reached an impasse, we fell silent. Determined not to waste the occasion, I prayed that God would somehow use all this upset for something good.

Since I had stood my ground with integrity, I felt covered—open and unafraid of the others' judgment. In the strength of that freedom, I decided to voice a question that had been in my mind since our marathon debate the week before: "OK, what is my real objection to that text, anyhow?" I mused out loud. "I mean, what would keep me from affirming that Jesus is the only true way to God?"

Taken aback by my humble forthrightness, the others sat quietly. I paused, asking God to help me reach the deepest truth. "What I'm really afraid of," I allowed, with a deliberate look at my inquisitors there, "is that **I've suffered enough from being judged and shamed myself, and I don't want to do that to others and hurt them like that**. I've heard that text used so often by self-righteous people in a way that only shames others and turns them off to Jesus."

I paused. "Also," I declared finally, "I guess I'm afraid that if I affirm that text, all my liberal-universalist friends will reject me."

ASK JESUS

With that, I turned matter-of-factly to Carl. "Actually, I already have a good enough relationship with Jesus that I suppose I could just go ahead and ask him if that text is true. But if you want to pray to heal my emotional wounds from being judged by others, that much would be fine," I offered. "We can see if that leads to anything else."

The three glanced uneasily at each other. Uncertain, they nevertheless agreed and laid hands on me, praying for my healing from wounds of judgment and shame. Soon, a gentle peace settled over me.

OK, Jesus, I prayed quietly at last: *Is it true or not? Are you the only way to the Father, or are there other ways besides you that are just as valid?*

At once, a cloudy darkness seemed to fill my mind and then, a wide shaft of light extending from top to bottom, like a channel of brightness bordered by the darkness. Suddenly, I saw Jesus, hovering above, blending in and out of the shaft as if He and the light were the same. Then I heard in my mind a voice, quiet and unhurried.

"It's true," the voice said matter-of-factly, with no hint of judgment. "I am the way. That's why I came, to be the way. The Father loves His children, and wants them to come to Him. He grieves to see his children go astray. Others have pointed to a path, and some of these come closer to the Father than others. **But all of them fall short and, sooner or later, lead into the darkness. That's why the Father sent me, so all His children would be able to come to Him and not be lost.**"

The others were silent, and in that moment, I realized that my earlier fear of being judged had disappeared entirely. In fact, I was completely at peace.

Deeply, restfully, I sighed. "It's true," I repeated aloud those simple words I had just heard Jesus speak—because I knew at last in my heart that it is indeed true. Thanking the other brothers for their prayer and concern, I told them what Jesus himself had said to me. I then stood up, shook their hands, thanked them for covering me in prayer, and left.

Later that night I set the cross between me and my seminary and ordained denomination, renounced and cast out of myself a demon of universalism, which both affirmed. In its place, I asked Father God to give me instead a spirit of faith, to embrace both His truth and His grace.

Unto today, I have no doubts that the voice I heard then was that of the Risen Christ, who promises to be present whenever two or three gather in His name. As *The Interpreter's Bible*—which I bought at Harvard—concludes its exposition on Jesus as the one who reveals the Father's love,

> For the way to know God is not merely to assemble correct thoughts and notions of Him in one's mind, which remain intellectual concepts: it is to live with Him; to have firsthand experience of Him; to put this whole matter to the proof, testing it for oneself; to let what we have been told about Him have its chance to do for us and in us what it can.[87]

For me, the question of whether the words in John 14:6 were in fact spoken 2000 years ago by Jesus is therefore moot. For I have heard him speak those words even now, even to me. And—doubting Thomas though I may be at times—now, I believe them.

WITHOUT JUDGMENT

That vision became so credible to me because it was the first time I had ever heard those words spoken in a way that I could accept, namely, without judgment. The voice I heard was not a vengeful judge, anxious to hide something wrong in himself by shaming those who disagree or disbelieve. Nor did I hear a slippery, all-tolerant guru quick to deny evil and smoothly accept all propositions without discernment.

Rather, this was a loving Father, confident in His purposes and power to fulfill them, anxious only to protect His children for those purposes. I saw thereby that, in fact, it's not Jesus, but rather, the other faiths that exclude people from the Father's wide arms of grace, by ultimately misleading them into the darkness.

Furthermore, my vision reflected precisely the same non-judgmental spirit as the scriptural account itself. The entire context for Jesus' words in John 14 is established in the first verse, when he says to the disciples, "Do not be worried and upset" (John 14:1). What follows flows from a spirit of compassion and reassurance, not judgment.

Webster's dictionary defines "universalism" as "the doctrine of universal salvation"—that is, without needing Jesus. This doctrine, I realized, is a spiritual deception which misleads people from fully connecting to Father God. That deception, therefore, is promoted and animated by the enemy of God.

Eventually, the question struck me: Why does this image of Father God as ultimately oriented toward His children's welfare, rather than as Cosmic Judge, seem so unfamiliar? Likely because many of us today as children experienced parental boundaries as shaming rather than protective, and we project that fear onto Father God.

The demon of universalism, in fact, finds its most enthusiastic recruits among those shamed by religion—even as sheep beaten by the shepherd flee to the wolf. The children of fundamentalists, in particular, grow up wounded by its grace-less religion, and become determined to renounce it along with the parents who subjected them to its judgment. With no more accurate, grace-full view of Jesus, they reject him along with Father God and welcome a spirituality based wholly on grace—albeit dangerously lacking in truth.

Too often, religious parents and church leaders exhort children to "obey God." But they do not demonstrate by example how to honor your heart and *trust* a God called Father. So their sons and daughters take refuge from religious shame and judgment in the deceptive promises of universalism, that is, in all-accepting ideology and all-embracing spirituality. Meanwhile, their longing for a father's love goes unrecognized and ultimately, unmet—until they let Jesus take them to Father God.

Interestingly, a similar phenomenon is growing among Jews. A news article "More US Jews identify as Jewish but not religious," quotes one woman who as a girl "loved lighting the braided candle and singing to mark the end of Shabbat," and even "relished studying the Talmud and weighing its ethical questions." As an adult, however, she eventually considered herself a "non-religious Jew":

But sitting in synagogue left her cold. "I was stuffed with religion," she said. "But I had no deep connection to it."[88]

And so the question remains: How can you communicate the simple but powerful truth of Jesus' unique role in a spirit of grace? Certainly not, as the Conservatives, by demanding it—which only communicates disrespect. But neither, as the Liberals, by avoiding it—which ultimately communicates abandonment.

My personal experience suggests that **the question is not, How do we communicate this truth to others? but rather, How do we bring others close enough to Jesus so that they can hear it from Him?** If so, judgment must be avoided, as few will be drawn close to Jesus if he's portrayed simply as waiting to condemn us for wrong belief.

I suspect, in fact, that those who "come to Christ" through fear of judgment will grasp after correct doctrine, and in doing so, will eventually find it difficult to rest in God's love and minister to others out of divine compassion. Even as I had often heard Evangelicals quote John 3:16, I rarely heard them add verse 17: "For God did not send his Son into the world to be its judge, but to be its savior."

As a plant grows toward the light, so persons are drawn toward Jesus precisely as they sense his grace-full acceptance and his unique and manifest power to rescue them from our human sin-nature. As the living Body of Christ, we in the Church today must reflect these attributes of Jesus to others in order to be credible witnesses.

TWO RESPONSES

For me, the truth that Jesus is the only way to fully connect with God beckons two responses.

First, I'm not to condemn or judge those who don't believe this, if only because to do so would clearly violate the Spirit who inspired it in the Bible, and by whom it was communicated directly to me.

When the Samaritans rejected Jesus, for example, the disciples immediately lashed back, "Lord, do you want us to call fire down from heaven to destroy them?" (Luke 9:54). But Jesus "turned and rebuked them" (9:55) for that suggestion. Other manuscripts add that Jesus explained, "You don't know what kind of Spirit you belong to; for the Son of Man did not come to destroy men's lives, but to save them."

But neither am I to remain silent. As in the ancient and ongoing biblical tradition, I'm responsible to tell the story of what God has done in my life—as I'm doing here—trusting that this will spread and water the seed of faith in others. **You can't argue with a testimony,** as others have noted.

After that, evangelism is a matter between the other person and Jesus.

My calling as a Christian, therefore, is not to convince people that Jesus is the Son of the Living God. That's Holy Spirit's job. "(N)o one can confess 'Jesus is Lord' unless he is guided by the Holy Spirit," as Paul declared (1 Corinth. 12:3).

Nevertheless, while the work of true in-depth conversion is God's alone, our job is far more difficult than either exhorting others to believe in Jesus, as the Conservatives, or rationalizing why you don't have to, as the Liberals.

Our job, daily, is to bring our own proud human selves to the cross to die to our sin-nature and allow God to continue saving us from it. Redeemed thereby for His purposes, we can share the boons of His victory in us by exercising His power in the world. We witness Jesus' identity to the world, that is, not simply with words, but with acts of healing, deliverance, reconciliation, and love so boldly and effectively that others recognize a super-human, super-natural power at work in us.

For those who are too proud to confess their need for God, the uniqueness of Jesus threatens our natural human power, our controlled worldview, our worldly sense of fairness and "tolerance of differences." But to those who are dying at the world's hands—from powers both without and within—it's the promise at last of true life. "For the message about Christ's death on the cross is nonsense to those who are being lost," as Paul declared, "but for us who are being saved it is God's power" (1 Corinth. 1:18).

Evangelical author Tony Campolo makes the point with a dramatic story:[89]

> It was one o'clock in the morning when I boarded the red-eye flight going from California to Philadelphia. I was looking

forward to getting some rest, but the guy next to me wanted to talk.

"What's your name?" he asked. I said, "Tony Campolo." And then he asked, "What do you do?"

Now when I want to talk, I say I'm a sociologist. And they say, "Oh, that's interesting." But if I really want to shut someone up, I say I'm a Baptist evangelist. Generally that does it.

"I'm a Baptist evangelist," I said.

"Do you know what I believe?" he asked.

I could hardly wait.

"I believe that going to heaven is like going to Philadelphia."

I certainly hope not, I thought.

"There are many ways to get to Philadelphia," he continued. "Some go by airplane. Some go by train. Some go by bus. Some drive by automobile. It doesn't make any difference how we go there. We all end up in the same place."

"Profound," I said, and went to sleep.

As we started descending into Philadelphia, the place was fogged in. The wind was blowing, the rain was beating on the plane, and everyone looked nervous and tight. As we were circling in the fog, I turned to the theological expert on my right. "I'm certainly glad the pilot doesn't agree with your theology," I said.

"What do you mean?" he asked.

"The people in the control booth are giving instructions to the pilot; 'Coming north by northwest, three degrees, you're on beam, you're on beam, don't deviate from beam.' I'm glad the pilot's not saying, 'There are many ways into the airport. There are many approaches we can take.' I'm glad he's saying, 'There's only one way we can land this plane, and I'm going to stay with it.'"

Campolo concludes, "There is no other name whereby we can be saved except the name of Jesus."

Like lane-marks on a highway, the airport controller is not trying to restrict, coerce, or otherwise exclude people from their destiny, but making deliberate efforts to protect them so they can get where they're going and fulfill it. In stating that Jesus is the only way, God is not playing favorites or trying to exclude others, but rather, graciously offering His saving power to those humble enough to confess they need it.

To celebrate Jesus and thereby entertain his Spirit, is to receive both the heart of God and divine power to carry out God's heartfelt desires in this world. Because powers in this fallen world oppose the plans of God, sooner or later you'll face a crossroads with non-believers—like my Solstice Cup encounter. At such times, we need wisdom not to let our fear and pride create human division, yet at the same time be prepared to affirm godly boundaries for our own and others' welfare.

Jesus' goal in life was not to destroy either Judaism or the Roman Empire, but rather, to initiate the rule of God among all humanity. Yet that was enough to threaten both Jews and Romans—even as us today. Faithfully moving in God's power and authority must eventually bring you to a dividing point, even competition, with other powers and authorities.

To negotiate that confrontation faithfully, it's helpful to remember that it's God's job to judge, not ours: "Do not judge others, so that God will not judge you," as Jesus declared (Matt. 7:1). Our job is to "love one another" as Jesus has loved us (John 13:34). If we're faithful about doing our job, we can trust God to do His—namely, to give us the truth and grace that allows Him to draw others to Himself through our witness.

> **Obedience is about what we do. Trust is about what God does.**

22

FROM OBEDIENCE TO TRUST

SLAVERY OR SONSHIP?

> *Those who are led by God's Spirit are God's sons. For the Spirit that God has given you does not make you a slave and cause you to be afraid; instead, the Spirit makes you God's children, and by the Spirit's power we cry out to God, "Father! My Father!"* (Romans 8:14)

SMILING, THE YOUNG MAN REACHED OUT enthusiastically after a conference to shake my hand—and then startled me. "Thank you," he said, "for your obedience in writing your books!"

I drew back, confused. Yes, I write books and Yes, it can be hard work. But I've never thought of my writing as an act of obedience.

"I appreciate your encouragement," I offered, "but actually, I don't write books because I'm obedient, but because I'm a writer. It's just who I am. It's tough work sometimes, but I enjoy it. When I do it, I feel like me—like this is what I was made to do."

That's true. It's not like the Father has commanded me to write, and so I do it out of duty or, indeed, fear of punishment. An idea somehow suggests itself, stirs an "Aha!" and takes hold in my mind. The more I think about it and offer myself to Father God as His scribe, other ideas come, and soon I have to write it down or I don't sleep well that night.

I'm increasingly dismayed by this elevation of "obedience" as a primary virtue among Christians.

When my son was 10 and fascinated by wolves, I took him on the Alaska Mt. Denali bus tour. There, we prayed to see a real wolf in the wild. When by the last hour we had seen no animals, I got into a prayer slugfest with the Father, begging Him to send a wolf for my son's sake—but none appeared. We were about to fall asleep, when the bus lurched to a stop as the driver pointed to a grey wolf standing nearby, majestic against a patch of white snow. It was a day my son and I will never forget (see "The Dad Who Cried Wolf" in *Do Pirates Wear Pajamas?*).

"Isn't it wonderful how God honored your obedience!" one Christian brother commented later when I shared this story.

"It's really not about my obedience," I urged, "but about my desperation—and the Father who hears my cry in behalf of my son!"

Again, I often tell stories about mistakes I've made or tough situations I've faced, and how the Father has overcome my shortcomings to bring something good out of it all. Inevitably, someone rises to say how much he appreciates my "obedience" in the midst of the crisis.

I don't get it. It's like I've built this marvelous house in my own strength, and at last it's burning down. I'm stranded on the rooftop, as on a stage, looking for recognition and applause. Below, Jesus stands with arms open, crying out, "Jump!"

But hey, my house is not destroyed yet, and it's still strong enough to support me. So I keep standing. When eventually the flames start biting my backside, finally I jump.

That doesn't seem like "obedience" to me. At least, not of any righteous variety that merits a Thank you.

OBEDIENCE AND DAD

True, God often commands obedience in the Old Testament, and later, Jesus exhorts His disciples to obey. What, then, is my problem with obedience? Is it just my sin-nature balking? Or could God's Word here be saying more than a Father's, "Do it because I said so—or else!"

For men, obedience to God is often confused by a boy's relationship with his father. Most boys learn to obey Dad because he punishes you if you don't. We rarely associate obedience with a loving father who directs in order to protect his child. As men, therefore, we can't hear Father God's heart urging, "Don't do that—please—it'll hurt you badly and sabotage your destiny!" Instead, when we're commanded to do something we either comply as wimps or refuse as rebels.

Under New Covenant grace, however, "the commandments become promises" as Argentine evangelist Juan Carlos Ortiz put it.[90] When the power of your Father's own Spirit is in you, that is, He no longer says, for example, "You shall not steal (or I'll kill you)," but rather, "Surrender to Me, give my Spirit room to work in you, and I promise—you shall not (i.e., won't) steal! You'll know how much your Father loves you and won't want to steal. You'll trust that He'll provide what you need in order not to, so His Spirit takes over and you don't steal.

The New Covenant in Jesus is not about obeying commands, but rather, about trusting your Father. It's born in surrender, which spawns a faith that He will do what you can't, in order for you to abide His protective boundaries.

For men abandoned as boys, this depth of trust can be terrifying.

"*I will* give you a new heart and a new mind," Father God therefore promised His people during the Old Covenant, to prepare them for this later new relationship with Him. "*I will take away* your stubborn heart of stone and give you an obedient heart. *I will put* my Spirit within you and *will see to it* that you follow my laws and keep all the commandments I have given you" (Ezek. 36:26ff., *italics mine*).

Under the New Covenant, as we do the surrendering, God's Spirit does the work. **He judges us not for our sinful nature—any** more than a cat for chasing a bird —but precisely for not calling on Him to overcome it.

"God gave the Law through Moses," as John declared, "but grace and truth He gave through Jesus Christ" (John 1:17). Most of us men as fathers are better at enforcing truth than imparting grace. Children, however, need both. Grace means blessing over and above forgiveness. It's the winsome avenue that allows truth to enter a boy's heart, so he can recognize its value and not resist it out of shame.

Without a father's grace, a boy's longing for approval from Dad misfocuses on obedience as the most clearly defined way to get it. Eventually, he idolizes surrogate authority figures, from gang leader to pastor, from cult guru to corporate boss.

CASH AND CARRY FAITH

In manhood, as this dynamic projects onto a God called Father, faith becomes a cash-and-carry deal: I'm in control. It's about what I do. If I obey the Father and "align with His principles," I get the goodies, in righteous esteem and prosperity. If I don't, that's my choice and I accept the punishment, in shame and misfortune.

Significantly, this charade is based on the absence of trusting relationship—which is precisely what the Father of us all sent Jesus to restore. Surrendered to Jesus, our sin-nature is covered by His blood, pre-empted by His Spirit. Knowing that your true Father wants not only to forgive, but even to bless, you can run broken into His throne room and cry out freely your deepest needs to the King of kings.

"For you did not receive a spirit that makes you a slave again to fear," as Paul declared, "but you received the spirit of sonship. And by him we cry, "*Abba*! Father!" (Rom. 8:15 NIV). An unfathered child lives in the spirit of slavery: "Obey your Father or He'll punish you!" Christians, however, live in the spirit of son/daughtership: "Save me, Daddy! I can't stop myself from doing what destroys me." As Paul noted to the Roman church, "I know that good does not live in me, that is, in my human nature. For even though the desire to do good is in me, I am not able to do it.... Who will rescue me from this body that is taking me to death?" (Rom. 7:18,24).

In the world, if you perform well you get the reward. In the Kingdom of God, it's understood that you can't perform well apart from the Father's blessing and power. Striving for "success" without first surrendering to receive God's direction and power thereby invites spirits of ambition, failure, and shame—and becomes a recipe for burnout.

Most of us are programmed from childhood by culture and family to focus on performance. We fear open, childlike relationship with the Living God, largely because we tried that as children and were wounded by adults we trusted. We don't know Father God's heart for us because we're afraid to trust Him long enough for Him to reveal it. We prefer the false comfort of our control to the genuine security of God's control.

Ultimately, those who never learned to trust as children are drawn to the righteous veneer of religion to cover our shame. As Christians, we seize upon Law and obedience as a way to deny our childlike dependence upon God and maintain the image of adult control.

We miss what Jesus died to give us, namely, the blessing and power of being a child of God.

In this fallen world, bad things happen. Father God's commandments tell you how to stay close to Him and fulfill your created purpose regardless of worldly circumstances that would sabotage it. To command behavior without providing the power to do it, however, would be cruel. The Father has thereby sent His son Jesus, that through him His Spirit might flow freely in and among us with just that power.

Our sin-nature, meanwhile, either doesn't want to avoid the bad things—many of which can feel pretty good for awhile—or fancies that our own natural strength is sufficient to resist them. And there's the rub.

Does God command us to obey Him? Absolutely.

Are we capable of obeying Him? Not according to Paul—nor to my own experience.

Are there consequences for not obeying God? Indeed, there are serious consequences—unto death itself. To disobey God is to disregard His safety regulations and expose yourself to destructive powers. "Be alert! Be on watch!" as Peter exhorted. "Your enemy the

devil roams around like a hungry lion, looking for someone to devour"
(1 Pet. 5:8).

If you're real, God can make you right. But if you're right, the
enemy will make you real. Lovingly, respectfully—if painfully—the
Father may allow the consequences of our pride to become painful and
destructive enough to bring us to our knees and cry out at last for His
healing and deliverance. "I will abandon my people until they have
suffered enough for their sins and come looking for me," as Hosea
proclaimed. "Perhaps in their suffering they will try to find me" (Hos.
5:15).

**Must we obey God? Certainly not. At least, no more than
you must obey the surgeon who tells you, "Your arteries are 99%
clogged—come in for surgery!"**

We're not holy robots. We're children of a wise and loving
Father who has given us free will to say either Yes or No to His heart.
Nevertheless, He's rooting for us to "choose life!" (Deut. 30:19).

REAL ENOUGH TO CONFESS

Father God wants us to obey Him because He loves us so much
He doesn't want us to get hurt. He knows our sin-nature will mislead
us to cast Him as a tyrant and thereby, to disobey Him.

Yet even if we're able to recognize God's heart for us and
deliberately choose to do what He has said is best for us, we're not
able in our natural strength and ability to do it. Is there any grace,
therefore, for those of us real enough to confess that we can't do what
God commands?

Indeed, there is. In fact, there's good company here with the
Apostle Paul, who concludes his thought to the Romans, "Who will
rescue me from this body taking me to death? Thanks be to God, who
does this through our Lord Jesus Christ!" (Rom. 7:24,25).

As a young man, obeying God seemed so hard. Born in 1944, I no
longer have energy today either to run from the truth or to accomplish
its goals. As aging strips from me all pretense of physical and moral
strength, my problem with obedience becomes clear:

Obedience is not hard.

It's impossible.

If we human beings were capable of obeying God, why did Jesus have to die on the cross? The threats of Moses would've been enough to keep us in line.

The Old Covenant system of law and punishment simply wasn't able to transfer the Father's protective boundaries from stone tablets into our hearts (see Jeremiah 31:31ff.). **Any atheist with a big enough whip can make someone obey. But only a parent's love can stir a child to trust. That's why Father God sent Jesus.**

Many Christians focus on obedience to help them avoid destructive behaviors. I respect that as a primary commitment. But even as the Old Covenant Temple had to fall, sooner or later we all burn out trying to save ourselves—until at last, we dare to experience the truth: only Jesus can save you from your sin-nature. What's more, only Holy Spirit can empower you to recognize what God created you to do and to do it. Not because you're obedient, but because it's who you are, as His son or daughter (see Mary Dalbey, *The REST of Your Life*).

We're a naturally disobedient species. In the Kingdom of God, however, the antidote to disobedience is not obedience—which also lies within the purview of law and performance instead of relationship—but rather, trust in the Father to give you the power to obey. The disobedience vs. obedience debate is hosted by the Tree of the Knowledge of Good and Evil; a lifestyle of trusting your Father is defined by the Tree of Life.

Here, then, is the essential distinction:

Obedience is about what you do; trust is about what your Father does.

Knowingly, God has commanded us to obedience even as He has made us incapable of it. Not because He's a sadistic tyrant who enjoys watching us suffer helplessly the consequences of turning away. Rather, it's because He's a loving Father who wants the best for His children—and knows that we can't accommodate that until we cry out desperately enough to appreciate it.

Jesus did not come to make slaves to the Law and its shame, but rather, sons and daughters of Father God by His grace. If you've struggled to obey Him—and with the shame of knowing you can't— it's time to renounce the spirit of slavery in you and in Jesus' name, cast it out. Ask the Father to replace it with His spirit of son/daughtership, which frees Him to do in and through you what you can't do for yourself.

It's called grace.

If my ministry has blessed you, therefore, don't thank me for my obedience. Instead, thank me for crying out to the Father for His saving power when I couldn't save myself.

That way, we can both thank Him together for hearing me.

ABOUT THE AUTHOR

Gordon Dalbey's widely acclaimed classic *Healing the Masculine Soul* helped pioneer the men's movement in 1988 and remains a bestseller today, with French and Italian translations. A popular speaker at conferences and retreats around the US and world, he has ministered in England, Hong Kong, Australia, New Zealand, Italy, France, Switzerland, Canada, and South Africa. A former news reporter (Charlotte NC), Peace Corps Volunteer (Nigeria), high school teacher (Chicago, San Jose CA) and pastor (Los Angeles), he holds an M.Div. from Harvard Divinity School, an M.A. in journalism from Stanford, and a B.A. from Duke.

The author of seven books, Gordon has appeared on many radio and TV programs such as *Focus on the Family*. His magazine publications include *Reader's Digest, The Los Angeles Times, Catholic Digest, Leadership Journal, Christian Century*, and *New Man*. He lives in Santa Barbara, CA, and may be reached at www.abbafather. com.

Other Gordon Dalbey Books at
www.abbafather.com

> Both refreshing and upending, Gordon Dalbey's books for men take us to depths of authentic manhood where we're humbled by its mystery and engaged by its call. Apart from either violence or lust, these books restore both courage and passion to manhood. Here's a masculinity you can trust—and the Father who makes it happen.

Healing the Masculine Soul

Today, politically correct voices cry out for men to be more sensitive, to tame our masculine nature. Meanwhile, the media bombards us with "macho" images of violence and lust. Is it any wonder men today are left bewildered about what manhood really is?

This pioneering, bestselling classic gives men hope for restoration by showing how Jesus enables us to get real with ourselves, with Him, and with other men. Its refreshing journey into the masculine soul dares men to break free from deceptive stereotypes and discover the power and blessing of authentic manhood.

Sons of the Father
Healing the Father-Wound in Men Today

"When you became a dad for the first time, did your own dad reach out to you with support, encouragement, or helpful advice?" Out of 350 Christian fathers, only 5 hands went up. "When you were 11 or 12, did your father talk to you about sex and relating to women?" I asked another gathering of 150 Christian men. Two hands.

Men today suffer a deep father-wound, which has left us unequipped for manhood. The father of Lies capitalizes on its shame and blackmails us into isolation, denial, and a host of bogus cover-ups—from money and guns to alcohol, sex, and performance religion.

The true Father of all men has come in Jesus to draw us back to Himself and to the man He created you to be. Here's the map to get you there.

Fight like a Man:
A New Manhood for a New Warfare

9/11 revealed the enemy of God and humanity as rooted in shame-based religion. The focus of warfare has now shifted dramatically from military battles to the hearts of men.

Fight like a Man focuses on the crippling byproduct of fatherlessness in men today, namely, shame—too often fostered by religion, always overcome by Jesus. It's not about how to be a man, but knowing the Father who rescues and restores men. It's not even about how to be a warrior, but surrendering to the Commander of the Lord's Army.

Here, you won't be exhorted to obey, but invited to trust. You won't be commanded to do it right, but freed to be real. You won't be warned to be strong, but promised your Father's strength as you experience the grace and dignity of being His son.

> Gordon Dalbey's books will stir you to a faith both passionate about its truth and compassionate in its grace. Here's freedom from universal tolerance on the one hand and narrow condemnation on the other—and Jesus at work today as God's vital Third Option to the world's self-defeating enmity.

Do Pirates Wear Pajamas?
And Other Mysteries
in the Adventure of Fathering

—"Daddy, it's not an adventure unless it's a little scary!"

—The lessons of fathering are the character of God.

—Watch for what God is doing in your child, and bless it.

In these impacting, real-life stories, you'll meet a bestselling Christian author who's a dad in on-the-job training—sometimes stumbling, sometimes celebrating, always learning. Experience teaches us the best lessons. But too often, we men miss the experience because we fear the shame of not knowing how to do it.

There's good news here for us dads: We're in this adventure together as men, and the Father of us all stands with us. You don't have to know how to do it. You just need to know Who does it—and trust Him to give you what you need to be the dad your child needs.

> The awful wounding of our times, from family breakups and sexual confusion to drugs and violence, has left us hungry for a faith that embraces reality as graphically as we're forced to in this increasingly lost and broken world.

No Small Snakes
A Journey into Spiritual Warfare

This is my upending personal story of meeting and learning to overcome the powers of evil as portrayed in the Bible.

The problem in confronting spiritual reality, I discovered, is not that our childish imagination gets hooked into foolish fears, but that something real is evil and we can't control it. This humbling truth stirs shame in our Western, control-oriented culture and we deny the reality of supernatural evil. But pretending there's no thief in your house doesn't protect you from being robbed; it only gives thieves free rein to steal whatever they want.

In Jesus, God has invited us to exchange the illusion of our control for the reality of His power. This book extends that invitation to you.

Broken by Religion, Healed by God

*Restoring the Evangelical, Sacramental,
Pentecostal, Social Justice Church*

This is my story of how I became born again among
Evangelicals, discovered the sacrament among Catholics, was
baptized with Holy Spirit with Pentecostals, and transformed
by social justice ministries among Oldline Reformers. But it's
also about the crippling brokenness in the Body of Christ today,
which that journey revealed—how the Church has divided
itself by these four very ways people meet Jesus, sabotaging its
credibility and mission.

The same spirit of shame and division which animated
the Pharisees and 9/11 terrorists has for centuries distracted
Christians from what Jesus is doing and kept us from seeing
each other as He does. Here's how to join Jesus as He battles
unto today to heal His broken Body—and through it, this
broken world.

NOTES

1   Morton T. Kelsey, *Afterlife: The Other Side of Dying* (New York: The Crossroads Publishing Company, 1979), p. 86. See also Raymond Moody, M.D., *Life after Life* and its sequel *Reflections on Life after Life* (Carmel: Guideposts, 1975, 1977), p. 175ff.

2   Ibid., p. 86.

3   Ibid., p. 87.

4   Elie Wiesel, *One Generation After* (New York: Pocket Books, 1970), pp. 28-29.

5   Elie Wiesel, *A Jew Today* (New York: Vintage Books, 1978), p. 11-12.

6   Cathleen Brooks, *The Secret Everybody Knows*, 1981.

7   Joseph L. Kellerman, *Alcoholism: A Marry-G-Round Named Denial* (Hazelden, 1970).

8   *Alcoholics Anonymous* (New York: Alcoholics Anonymous World Services, Inc, 1976), p. 569.

9   Tim McGrath, formerly of the Santa Monica Vineyard church, said this in a teaching.

10   "WBC Strips Boxer's Ranking," *Santa Barbara News Press*, 10/26/01, p. C2.

11   "Sheik Urges Death for Nonobservant," *Los Angeles Times*, 7/8/06, p. A4. The article notes that the sheik "confirmed his statement to Reuters after it ws broadcast on local media."

12   H.A.R. Gibb, *Mohammedanism* (New York: Oxford University Press, 1962), p. 9.

13   "Tale of an American Taliban," *Newsweek*, 12/10/01.

14   Ibid., p. 39-41.

15   Bill Johnson, *When Heaven Invades Earth* (Shippensberg, PA: Treasure House, 2003), p.41.

16   The late Rev. Jerry Fallwell of The Moral Majority made this statement and Pat Robertson of *The 700 Club* Christian TV show responded, "I totally concur." See http://www.actupny.org/YELL/falwell.html

17   "Michele Bachmann: 9/11, Benghazi Were God's 'Judgment,' So We Must Hold Day Of Prayer On Sept. 11," *Huff Post* 5/10/13.

18   All quotations are from Norman Grubb, *Rees Howells, Intercessor*, Christian Literature Crusade (Fort Washington, PA: 1980), pp. 246-262.

19   Wiesel, *A Jew Today,* p18.

20   Nando Parrado, *Miracle in the Andes* (New York: Crown Publishers, 2006), p. 110-112.

21   Ako Adjei, "Imperialism and Spiritual Freedom," *American Journal of Sociology*, quoted in Ram Desai, editor, *Christianity in Africa as Seen by Africans* (Denver, Allan Swallow: 1962), p.67.

22   E. A. Asamoa, "The Christian Church and African Heritage," in Ram Desai, *loc. cit*, p.37.

23   Laurens Van der Post, *The Dark Eye in Africa* (New York: Wm Morrow, 1955), p. 16.

24   Vincent Bevine, "Young may prove challenging for pope," *Los Angeles Times*, 7/24/13, p. A3.

25   Hempton, ibid.

26   Art Lindsley, *True Truth* (Downers Grove, IL, InterVarsity press, 2004), p. 31.

27   Alister McGrath, *Passion for Truth* (Dosner's Grove, IL: InterVarsity Press, 1996), p.219.

28   E.g, "Were You There?" in *The Hymnal for Worship & Celebration* (Waco, TC: 1986), p. 181.

29   Prince Nyabongo, "African Life and Ideals," in Ram Desai, loc. cit.

30   Mbono Ojike, "Religious Life in Africa," in Ram Desai, loc. cit.

31   In 2006, Gagarin's friend Colonel Valenitn Petrov attributed that statement rather to Premier Kruschev, who at the time was leading a propaganda campaign to discourage religious faith. "Yuri, just like very Russian, was baptized. He just could not say that." http://www.freerepublic.com/focus/f-news/1614581/posts

32   Jomo Kenyatta, *Facing Mt. Kenya*

33   Van der Post, p. 55.

34   Ibid., p. 60.

35   Ibid.

36   Van der Post, p. 7.

37   Harvey Cox, *Many Mansions* (Boston: Beacon Press, 1988), 8-9.

38   Wendy Griffith, "A Harvest Sown by Generations Past," CBN News, cbn.com http://www.cbn.com/spirituallife/ChurchAndMinistry/ChurchHistory/HarvestSown.aspx.

39   Ibid.

40   Van der Post, p. 41

41   Ibid., p. 52.

42   Ibid., p. 67.

43   Ibid., p. 77

44   A speaker at an Exodus International conference where I ministered made this statement. I have been unable to identify him.

45   Adapted from my article, "Gangs become surrogate fathers for boys," *Santa Barbara News Press*, 3/25/07.

46   Sue Horton, "Mothers, Sons, and Gangs," *Los Angeles Times Magazine*, 10/16/88, p. 8.

47   Blue Cross of California, *Newsweek*, 8/25/97, p. 52.

48   Rev. Margaret Crocker, *Journal of Pastoral Care*

49   Arthur Janov, *The Primal Scream*

50   *Los Angeles Times*, 3/23/78

51   Agnes Sanford, *The Healing Gifts of the Holy Spirit*

52   Dennis and Matthew Linn, *Healing Life's Hurts*

53   Crocker, *loc. cit.*

54   Sanford, *loc. cit.*

55   Elie Wiesel, *Souls on Fire* (New York: Random House, 1972), 73.

56   *Pretty Good Joke Book*, 5th Edition (Minneapolis, MN, Highbridge
Company, 2009), p. 264.

57   Richard J. Foster, *Celebration of Discipline* (San Francisco: Harper &
Row, 1978), 48.

58   *Family Circle* magazine, 9/24/85.

59   *Family Circle* magazine, 7/2/85.

60   Michael Moss, *Salt, Sugar, Fat: How the Food Giants Hooked Us*
(New York: Random House, 2013),

61   Huffpost Healthy Living, "Here's Why Your Favorite Foods
Are So Hard to Resist," http://www.huffingtonpost.com/2013/10/16/
junk-food_n_4043980.html?icid=maing-grid7%7Chtmlws-main-
bb%7Cdl17%7Csec1_lnk3%26pLid%3D392383, 10/17/13.

62   John Wilson, "The Masculine Mystique," *Christianity Today*, 4/26/93.

63   Michael Dye of Genesis Process Ministries, www.genesisprocess.org

64   Irene Moore, "Halloween: America's Gay Holiday," *Huffpost Gay
Voices*, http://www.huffingtonpost.com/irene-monroe/halloween-
americas-gay-holiday_b_1034013.html

65   "Man dies after botched hanging stunt," *Dallas Morning News*,
10/29/97.

66   "Don't Look to a Lottery if You Want Pennies From Heaven," *Los
Angeles Times*, Part II, 11/1/84, p 6.

67   *The American Heritage College Dictionary* (Boston: The Houghton
Mifflin Company, 2004), p. 838.

68   *Los Angeles Times*, 12/18/01 p. D1

69   *Uline Shipping Supply*, fall/winter 2013-14, p. 329.

70   "Soccer War," *Wikipedia*, http://en.wikipedia.org/wiki/Football_War

71   E.O. Wilson, "What's Your Tribe?" *Newsweek*, 4/9/12, p.42.

72   Roger Brown, ibid.

73   *Los Angeles Times*, C1,9/3/10.

74   *Time* Magazine, 3/13/83.

75 Asimov, ed., *Machines That Think.* (New York: Holt, Reinhart & Winston, 1983).

76 Asimov, *I, Robot* (New York: Doubleday, 1963).

77 *Time* Magazine, 1/9/84

78 Ibid.

79 "Deliver us from Evil," *L'Osservatore Romano*, quoted in F. MacNutt, *Healing* (New York: Bantam, 1977).

80 Christine Rosen, *Los Angeles Times*, 12/7/04, B13.

81 Josh Getlin, "Time Spent Watching Television Increases," *Los Angeles Times*, p. C3, 9/22/06.

82 Wm. Fore, "TV & Religion: The Shaping of Faith, Values & Culture," *Christian Century*, September 24, 1986, pp. 810-812.

83 H. Dennis Fisher, "Is Christ the Only Way to God?" *Evangelical Beacon*, 6/85, p. 9.

84 Michka Assayas, *Bono on Bono: In Conversation with Michka Assayas* (Riverhead Hardcover, 2005).

85 Bruce Vawter, C.M., "The Gospel According to John," *Jerome Biblical Commentary* (Englewood Cliffs, NJ: Prentice-Hall, Inc., 1968), v. II, p. 453.

86 Arthur John Gosspi, "The Gospel According to John: Exposition," *The Interpreter's Bible* (New York: Abingdon Press, 1952), v. VII, p. 702.

87 Loc. cit.

88 Emily Alpert, *Santa Barbara News Press*, 10/12/13, p. D6.

89 *World Vision*, Oct-Nov, 1988, cover.

90 Juan Carlos Ortiz, "Do Willingly and Joyfully His Will," teaching at Trinity Lutheran Church, San Pedro, CA, 3/24/87.